TWENTIETH CENTURY VIEWS

The aim of this series is to present the best in contemporary critical opinion on major authors, providing a twentieth century perspective on their changing status in an era of profound revaluation.

Maynard Mack, *Series Editor*
Yale University

ANDREW MARVELL

ANDREW MARVELL

A COLLECTION OF CRITICAL ESSAYS

Edited by

George deF. Lord

Prentice-Hall, Inc. *Englewood Cliffs, N. J.*

A SPECTRUM BOOK

Current printing (last number):
10 9 8 7 6 5 4 3 2 1

Contents

ANDREW MARVELL

Introduction

by George deF. Lord

I

The surge of interest in Andrew Marvell during the last half-century arose from the pioneering work of four great scholars and critics whose contributions to a new estimate of the poet were all very different from each other but all complemented each other. T. S. Eliot helped to commemorate the tercentenary of Marvell's birth in 1921 with an essay on his poetical sensibility which has had an influence out of all proportion to its brevity. It is fair to say that virtually all worthwhile critical work on Marvell is founded, whether explicitly or not, on Eliot. In the same year Sir Herbert J. C. Grierson published *Metaphysical Lyrics and Poems of the Seventeenth Century: Donne to Butler.*[1] This little anthology made available to the common reader ten of Marvell's best-known lyrics and supplied him with valuable historical and critical insights in the Introduction.

Meanwhile labor on a major edition of the poems by H. M. Margoliouth was proceeding apace after the long interruption of the war. The publication of *The Poems and Letters of Andrew Marvell* by Oxford in 1927 made all the lyric poems and some of the verse satires available for the first time in a critical edition with indispensable and learned annotations. A year later in France Pierre Legouis, a close friend of Margoliouth, published his copious and scholarly account of Marvell's life and works, *André Marvell, poète, puritain, patriote* (recently abridged, revised, and translated by the author), the prime factual source.[2] Thus, by a combination of luck and planning, the basic biographical, textual, and critical materials for the rediscovery of Marvell were made available in a short space of time after more than two centuries of neglect.

[1] Oxford: Clarendon Press, 1921.
[2] Paris: Henri Didier; London: Oxford University Press, 1928.

Between his death in 1678 and his literary resurrection after World War I, Marvell's reputation had been based on almost anything but the incomparable lyrics on which his present fame chiefly rests. In the intervening centuries he was celebrated as an incorruptible patriot or a scheming trimmer, a witty and outspoken defender of freedom or a writer of scurrilous libels, a strict puritan or an unprincipled eclectic, the fearless champion or the paramour of John Milton, the Whig hero invoked in 1776 against Lord North and George III or the bootlicking laureate of Cromwell, that Marvell—in short—in whom each kind of admirer or detractor could find almost any resemblance except that of the great lyric poet.

The reason for this astonishing exception is that from the time the lyric poems were first published in 1681 (by a fraudulent "Mary Marvell" posing as the poet's widow) they had long been outmoded in theme and style. Between their composition (mostly in the 1640's and 1650's) and their posthumous publication, a revolution in taste had intervened comparable to the political and religious upheavals that occurred between the outbreak of the Civil War and the restoration of Charles II in 1660. Today few copies of the slim folio of 1681 are to be found still containing the engraved frontispiece portrait of Marvell. Probably most buyers bought the book for the picture of the Whig hero and not for the outmoded and obscure verses. This explanation seems the more likely when one remembers that the poems which would probably have still held some appeal, the poems on Cromwell, had been cancelled from every known copy of the edition but one.

The seventeenth-century literary revolution entailed fundamental alterations in the subject matter and style of poetry. "The private world of the individual consciousness," in Mr. Toliver's phrase, which had provided Wyatt, Donne, George Herbert, and Marvell (among others) with their most fruitful material, ceased to command the interest of English poets for nearly a century and a half, until the advent of Blake and Wordsworth and Keats. It gave place to a public world of political, religious, philosophical, and literary issues exemplified in such manifestations as the emergence of political parties in the 1670's, the founding of the Royal Society, the revolt against religious "enthusiasm," and, accompanying the reaction against metaphysical poetry, the growing predominance of judgment over imagination in the partnership of "wit." Behind such widespread movements in the direction of order and reason and clarity lay deep-seated fears that individualism, especially when given political or religious expression, had caused the bloody disorders of the last two decades. The typical writer of the new age abjured or condemned the inward-looking ramifications of metaphysical wit as eccentric at best; at worst, mad or subversive.

The aim behind the new English classicism was to establish the unity of experience and to manifest it by a common language. His sensibility now normalized, the poet became increasingly a spokesman for some consensus or authority and decreasingly the searcher of his own inner experience. In a word, the social function of poetry came to predominate, as the major poems of Dryden and Pope clearly show.

Marvell is the only first-rate English poet whose work bridges the revolution and exemplifies it. Before 1655 he explored "the private world of the individual consciousness." Afterwards, he wrote only on public themes. This is not to suggest that the reasons for the change square exactly with the general change in taste, but the two groups of poems, as we shall see, shed a good deal of light on each other and on the general shift in sensibility as well.

In 1921 Eliot defined the critical task as squeezing "the drops of the essence of two or three poems." For most readers this was, in any event, an inevitable limitation until H. M. Margoliouth's fine edition of 1927 made all the lyric poems available. Despite the stringent limits Eliot proposed, he nevertheless managed to suggest much more about the nature of Marvell's poetry than the examination of a mere two or three poems could warrant; hence the pregnant definitions which have vitalized all subsequent criticism of Marvell: "the tough reasonableness beneath the slight lyric grace"; "the alliance of levity and seriousness"; the wit which "involves, probably, a recognition, implicit in the expression of every experience, of other kinds of experience which are possible."

These suggestive phrases were developed by Eliot's three principal critical legatees: the first by F. R. Leavis, whose chief contribution was to place Marvell in "the line of wit" descending from Jonson as well as from Donne;[3] the second by Cleanth Brooks in "Metaphor and the Tradition" and "Wit and High Seriousness" (1939);[4] and the third by William Empson in his famous essay on "The Garden" (in *Some Versions of Pastoral*, 1935),[5] a brilliant but sometimes misguided exploration of ambiguity.

---

[3] In *Revaluation,* New York: George W. Stewart, 1947.
[4] In *Modern Poetry and the Tradition,* Chapel Hill: University of North Carolina Press, 1939.
[5] Also entitled *English Pastoral Poetry,* New York: W. W. Norton & Company, Inc., 1938.

Perhaps "ambiguity" defines Marvell's sensibility better than any other term, if we take it to signify the constellation of meanings in a poem which augment, amplify, or qualify the literal meaning while seemingly contradicting it or each other. Though Marvell exemplifies all shades and types of ambiguity, he seems to have been most strongly attracted by paradox, above all in "A Dialogue between the Soul and Body" and "The Definition of Love." It is fair to say, however, that ambiguity for Marvell is not so much a feature of style as it is a way of feeling, thinking, and imagining embedded in his sensibility and in his view of the human condition. What Pope was to enunciate in the characteristic oppositions of Augustan dialectic—

> Caught in the isthmus of this middle state,
> A Being darkly wise and rudely great,

> *   *   *

> Prophet of Truth, in endless Error hurl'd,
> The Glory, Jest, and Riddle of this World

—Marvell embodied with subtler gradations of perception and feeling in his small but variegated collection of lyric poems. The poems and the sensibility behind them reflect an age almost as complex as our own, an age in which profound epistemological problems underlay sharp political, religious, and philosophical issues.

II

Perhaps the best way to see the complexity of the age and the complexity of Marvell's reactions to it is to look briefly at his life. He was born March 31, 1621, at Winestead-in-Holderness, Yorkshire, where his father was curate. Three years later the family, which included three older sisters, moved to Hull where the Reverend Andrew Marvell had been chosen lecturer in Holy Trinity Church. For most of his life the younger Marvell was to be closely identified with this important seaport borough. In 1633 he entered Trinity College, Cambridge, where the only tangible relics of his stay are two commendatory poems, one in Greek and one in Latin, published in a collection of undergraduate tributes to Charles I and Henrietta Maria. The Greek poem affects the frigid ingenuities sometimes found in the early work of bright undergraduates, but the Latin poem seems to have been sobered by the Horatian model it so closely imitates. In 1638, a year after these poems appeared, Marvell became a scholar of Trinity, where he continued until his father's death by drowning two years later. Little is known about the next eight years of the poet's life, except that four years were spent traveling as tutor on the continent. While in Rome, between 1645 and 1647, he composed a witty and heartless (and sometimes repulsive) invective against the threadbare poetaster Richard Flecknoe, whom Dryden was later to immortalize in *Mac Flecknoe*. Marvell's enemies were to charge him with cowardice for taking no part in the Civil War, but his abstention was possibly due to serious reservations about the war, as "An Horatian Ode" (1650) was to make clear. When he returned to England in 1648, however, he wrote commendatory verses on Lovelace's *Lucasta* and elegies on Lord Hastings and possibly on Lord Francis Villiers which show royalist sympathies.

The axe which struck off Charles I's head on January 30, 1649, struck real poetic fire from Marvell. Was he watching by the scaffold outside the banqueting hall when the Royal Actor "bow'd his comely head"

> While round the armed Bands
> Did clap their bloody hands?

Whether physically present or not Marvell realized the immediate and tragic reality of the event in "An Horatian Ode upon Cromwell's Return from Ireland" (1650), a poem crucial to our understanding of his life. The "Ode" is Shakespearean in its dramatic force and in the scrupulous fidelity with which it presents opposing regimes and leaders. It might profitably be compared to the Shakespearean tetralogy dealing with Bolingbroke's usurpation and its consequences, which seems to anticipate Marvell's tense, chiastic treatment of Cromwell and his martyred victim. Marvell's passionate love of England and sure grasp of political realities are like Shakespeare's.

To call Marvell's fidelity to contending realities Shakespearean is not to ignore the essential Horatian quality of the "Ode" which, as John S. Coolidge has shown, provides a salient clue to its otherwise perplexing treatment of Cromwell and the dead king. Horace's ode on the Roman victory over Cleopatra at Actium (I.37) is a paradigm for Marvell's poem. Marvell's praise of Cromwell "slides into a panegyric of the vanquished King" (to adopt Steele Commager's suggestive phrase) in much the same way that Horace's celebration of Octavius' victory "slides into a panegyric

of the vanquished Queen." An equally relevant Shakespearean analogue
would be the alternating Roman and Alexandrian perspectives on
Cleopatra, both of them true and therefore, apparently, incompatible.
Marvell's "Ode," like Shakespeare's *Antony and Cleopatra,* succeeds in
reconciling what reason and logic tell us are mutually exclusive opposites
and fusing them into truth of a higher order. One might even look back
to the Virgilian ambiguities surrounding the figure of Dido. As Eliot
said, "Marvell's best verse is the product of European, that is to say,
Latin, culture."

Until the very recent studies of Marvell and Horace by Leishman,
Commager, and Coolidge, critical disagreement about Marvell's attitude
toward Cromwell in the "Ode" suggested a misunderstanding of Marvell's
irony. If one distinguished critic could see the poem as covertly attacking
with irony the Cromwell it purported to praise while another equally
distinguished critic read it as an unqualified tribute, one must conclude
either that the critics were wrong or that Marvell's ambiguity in this
case has defeated itself and produced nothing but impotent equivoca-
tion. The latter conclusion (which seems implicit in the whole debate
between Cleanth Brooks and Douglas Bush)[6] might be a legacy from
Eliot's emphasis on Marvell's "recognition, implicit in the expression of
every experience, of other kinds of experience which are possible," or it
might be traced to the Empsonian assumption that the indiscriminate
proliferation of ambiguities is a poetic virtue. Professor Coolidge, together with Professor Commager[7] and the late J. B. Leishman,[8] has,
however, shown that Marvell's irony no more neutralizes the contending
attitudes of the poem than does Horace's. Marvell was not playing dialectical games with a national crisis. He was aware of the cost of Cromwell's
rise to power: the loss of ancient right, the killing of the King. He was
aware of the risks entailed in the usurper's assumption of power, but he
was also aware of the usurper's wisdom and restraint. The "Ode" makes
fine but crucial discriminations which, until the recent studies I have
mentioned, we were not wholly prepared to understand. The "Ode"
asserts the citizen's freedom in the face of threats posed by Cromwell's
usurpation and simultaneously poses a test of Cromwell's fitness to rule:

---

[6] Brooks' essay appeared in *English Institute Essays,* 1946 (New York: Columbia Uni-
versity Press, 1947), Bush's in *Sewanee Review,* LX (1952). Brooks replied in *Sewanee
Review,* LXI (1953). All three articles are reprinted in *Seventeenth-Century English
Poetry,* edited by William R. Keast (New York: Oxford University Press, 1962).

[7] Steele Commager, *The Odes of Horace,* New Haven: Yale University Press, 1963.

[8] J. B. Leishman, *Translating Horace,* Oxford: Cassirer, 1956.

If the ruler addressed falls off from the terms in which . . . the poet praises him, the praise will come to read, as Marvell's "Ode" does to readers who dislike Cromwell, as cruel, quiet irony.

(Coolidge, p. 98)

The "Horatian Ode" is an endorsement of Cromwell qualified by what Professor Coolidge calls "massive reservations."

If the royalist affinities of Marvell's poems on Lovelace, Hastings, and Villiers have helped to obscure his attitude toward Cromwell in the "Ode," written two years later, the appearance within five months of an intransigently royalist attack on the parliamentary leaders and their chronicler, Tom May, introduces contradictions which threaten to destroy any coherent picture of Marvell's behavior in these crucial years. As Legouis notes, it is inconceivable that Marvell would have written a poem attacking Fairfax at least by implication when he was in his employ or about to enter it. The incoherence mounts when we consider Marvell's flattering poem in Latin on one of the royalists' most hated enemies, Oliver St. John, written three months later.

"Tom May's Death" and two other poems that raise difficulties chiefly because of their poor quality, "Thyrsis and Dorinda" and "On the Victory obtained by Blake," were omitted from the authoritative text of Marvell's poems, the recently discovered Bodleian poetical MS. d.49.[9] Other spurious poems were fathered on Marvell after his death, and so there is nothing inherently unlikely in questioning the authenticity of these poems, although one wishes there were additional evidence. With "Tom May's Death" out of the canon, Marvell's acceptance of Cromwell and the Commonwealth, however reserved, begins in 1650 and continues (presumably with some implicit second thoughts about the invasion of Scotland) to grow until the death of the Lord Protector and the fall of the Commonwealth eight years later. The growing commitment to Cromwell may be charted in the poem on St. John (February 1651), the satirical "Character of Holland" (1653), the Latin poems on the embassy to Sweden (1654), "The First Anniversary of the Government under his Highness the Lord Protector" (1655), "Two Songs at the Marriage of the Lord Fauconberg and the Lady Mary Cromwell" (1657), and "A Poem upon the Death of his Late Highness the Lord Protector" (1658). Biographical facts support this view: Marvell abandons his York-

---

[9] The authenticity of these poems is discussed in the introduction to my edition of *Andrew Marvell: Complete Poetry,* New York: Random House, Inc., and Modern Library, 1968.

shire retirement early in 1653 and gets Milton to support his application for a position in the government. Although he does not receive the government position until four years later, Marvell accepts an interim post as tutor to Cromwell's ward and intended son-in-law, William Dutton, first at Eton, and then at Saumur. In 1657 he becomes Latin Secretary under Thurloe, and in 1658 is elected M.P. for Hull. Behind all this growing political commitment, furthermore, is the crucial decision worked out in retirement at Nun Appleton and explored in "Upon Appleton House," to enter public life, as I try to show in the essay reprinted herein. A corresponding transition in the realm of Marvell's political ideas occurs, as Professor John M. Wallace shows in his essay, when Marvell works out a characteristically eclectic and independent position which reconciles republican and monarchic principles.

It is fair to say that Marvell's evolution into a political activist did not entail the surrender of political independence. In his poetry and in his pamphlets he continued to discriminate between the members of political sects and of the parties which began to evolve in the 1670's. On the other hand, one must concede that his decision to take an active part in public affairs in 1653 involved probably an inevitable adaptation of thought and style to the pragmatic requirements of political writing. Whereas the idealism of the earlier poems was tempered with an unblinking recognition of pertinent realities, the ugly realities of political life under Charles II found full and bitter expression in the satires, although they did not entirely stifle Marvell's passionate idealism. Unquestionably the life of political action and political satire brought a coarsening of sensibility and a simplifying of issues, yet in the most shameful year in England's history Marvell could still appeal both to the corrupt partisans of Court and Country and to the true independents in Parliament:

> A gross of English gentry, nobly born,
> Of clear estates, and to no faction sworn;
> Dear lovers of their King, and death to meet,
> For country's cause, that glorious think and sweet;
> To speak not forward, but in action brave,
> In giving gen'rous, but in counsel grave;
> Candidly credulous for once, nay twice,
> But sure the Devil cannot cheat them thrice.
>
> ("Last Instructions," 287–94)

In a most rancorous and corrupt age Marvell generally managed to avoid the comforting and destructive simplicities of the "party-colour'd mind," while boldly standing up for freedom and the welfare of his country.

If ambiguity, as I suggested earlier, is a clue to Marvell's sensibility in the lyric poems, its counterpart in his satires and pamphlets and in his political career is a correspondingly independent judgment of issues. His life and work suggest alike the inadequacy of categories like royalist or republican, Puritan or Anglican, Whig or Tory. Perhaps the most important aspect of his nature was his simultaneous fidelity to the ideal and to the realities of ordinary life. In hundreds of letters to the Mayor and Aldermen of Hull he shows a grasp of practical affairs that would have shamed most of his fellow M.P.'s. It is this practical, undoctrinaire bent that gives real strength to his idealism and to his irony.

All this would be nothing without courage. After the Restoration, when old Cavaliers began to hunt down their enemies, Marvell intervened at great personal risk to prevent Milton from being excluded from the general amnesty. At other times he appeared to be quick-tempered and bellicose, as brawls in the House and on a diplomatic mission to Russia testify. In the early 1670's, when it became apparent that Charles II was conniving with Louis XIV against the political and religious liberties of his subjects, Marvell, in an unlikely association with desperadoes, took part in a Holland-based fifth column aimed at revolutionizing English foreign policy. Through covert dissemination of pamphlets exposing the plot, he helped to arouse strong parliamentary opposition against the French alliance against the Dutch and compelled Charles to make peace in 1674. The story has been recently unearthed from English and Dutch archives by K. H. D. Haley in *William of Orange and the English Opposition, 1672–74.*[10]

If Marvell's political activity entailed serious personal risks—and one should remember that John Ayloffe, a fellow fifth-columnist and satirist, was banished, outlawed, and eventually hanged, drawn, and quartered —there is no evidence that Marvell was deterred by them.[11] The 1670's also saw his witty and incisive prose attacks on political and ecclesiastical tyranny. *The Rehearsal Transpros'd* (1672), a defense of freedom of conscience, won the admiration of Charles II himself. There Marvell attacks ecclesiastical tyranny in the form of Samuel Parker, a former puritan and friend of Milton, but now the Archdeacon of Canterbury

---

[10] Oxford: Clarendon Press, 1953.

[11] Marvell's relation to Ayloffe is described in my essay "Satire and Sedition: The Life and Work of John Ayloffe," *Huntington Library Quarterly,* XXIX (June, 1966), 207–24.

and an eager proponent of religious persecution to compel uniformity. To write against such a man in support of religious toleration in 1672 was a risky matter, and the risk was greatly increased when Marvell, accused of hiding himself in anonymity, boldly printed his name to the Second Part with the following legend on the title page:

> Occasioned by Two Letters: The first
> Printed, by a nameless Author,
> Intituled, *A Reproof, &c.*
> The Second Letter left for me at a
> Friends House, Dated Nov. 3,
> 1673. Subscribed J.G. and
> concluding with these words; *If*
> *thou darest to Print or Publish*
> *any Lie or Libel against Doctor*
> Parker, *by the Eternal God I*
> *will cut thy Throat.*

Marvell's witty strategies, which exemplify the workings of a highly intelligent and independent mind, were to win from Jonathan Swift outspoken admiration as well as the flattery of imitation in *A Tale of a Tub.*

Marvell's title was a covert slap at John Dryden, who had been attacked earlier as the eccentric dramatist Bayes in the Duke of Buckingham's enormously successful satirical play, *The Rehearsal.* In his remarkable commendatory poem for the second edition of *Paradise Lost* (1674) praising the freedom of Milton's blank verse as against the trivializing rhymes of Dryden's operatic version, Marvell gave another twist to the knife:

> Well mightst thou scorn thy Readers to allure
> With tinkling Rhime, of thy own Sense secure;
> While the *Town-Bayes* writes all the while and spells,
> And like a Pack-Horse tires without his Bells.
>   ("On Mr. Milton's *Paradise Lost*")

In the preface to "Religio Laici" (1682) Dryden replied by calling Marvell "the Martin Marprelate of our times, the first Presbyterian scribbler who sanctified libels and scurrility to the use of the good old cause."

These brief encounters between two leading poets of the age indicate profound and far-ranging differences in almost every area. Marvell and Dryden were opposites in religion, politics, literature, and sensibility, and many of the crucial issues of the age are to be found in what we know or what we can intuit of these oppositions. Since it was an age where religious and political issues were inseparable and where these issues in turn influenced profoundly the content and even the style of letters, the differences can be seen most succinctly by comparing, say, Marvell's "Last Instructions to a Painter" with Dryden's "Annus Mirabilis" (written in 1667 and 1666, respectively), or *The Rehearsal Transpros'd* (1672, Part II, 1673) with "Religio Laici" (1682). Although Dryden, like Marvell, had served Cromwell and written an elegy upon him, he also, unlike Marvell, had composed a panegyric for Charles II on his restoration which some readers find indecently abject. Although Dryden's career resembles Marvell's in his adherence to a succession of different political and religious positions, the underlying motives were radically different from Marvell's. Against Marvell's independence and passionate commitment to freedom, Dryden's inherent and cautious conservatism stands out. Yet Dryden's conservatism is not like the conservative elements in Marvell's makeup—a deep attachment to ancient right—but rather an instinct to preserve the status quo, whatever the status quo may be. For Dryden "innovation is the blow of fate," and he constantly sought, through all the shifts and turns of his religious and political career, for institutional authority in church and state and for a conservative consensus to uphold the status quo. Dryden led the reaction against individualistic literature, political liberalism, and personal religion exemplified at its best in Marvell and at its worst in the rabid political and religious sects and in the metaphysical eccentricities which plagued English life and letters from the time of the Civil War. In letters, at least, Dryden won the battle by establishing a conservative, traditionally-oriented consensus as the norm of the new poetry. Social man became the hero of Restoration poetry and drama. Marvell's solitary contemplative gave way to Dryden's honored kinsman surrounded by political suitors at his weekend country house and later to Pope in his grot thronged with "chiefs, out of war, and statesmen, out of place." Nothing approaching the scrupulous inwardness of Marvell's lyrics was to appear until the Romantic Revival, although Pope and Collins succeeded in molding a social idiom into the illusion of inwardness.

"Annus Mirabilis" and "The Last Instructions to a Painter" are narrative poems dealing respectively with 1666 and 1667, perhaps the two worst years in the history of England. Both poems have clear political objectives: Dryden's heroic poem is an apologia for the regime of Charles II and attempts to present war, plague, and fire as a kind of testing of

God's chosen Englishmen after their apostasy; Marvell's mock-heroic poem attempts to expose the greed and incompetence in government, navy, and army which Dryden's splendid tropes and analogues conceal. Dryden cloaks a decadent and cynical regime with euphemistic Virgilian analogies. The conservative imagination cannot function without such myths and analogues, and Dryden's technique throughout his career was inveterately analogical: to make Charles II into Aeneas and later into David; to make Shadwell into a debased Augustus. Behind the analogical approach there lies, of course, a cyclical view of history which, when carried to a certain point, permits the conservative poet to avoid uncomfortable facts about the present time. "Annus Mirabilis" is an attempt to improve the royal image by substituting a softly-focused Virgilian myth. The soft focus extends to the simplicity with which issues of war and peace are represented: the Dutch, for instance, can only fight when drunk.

Marvell's technique is just the opposite. He sets out to "demythify" recent events by exposing us to a relentless succession of sharply delineated images, and by making effective use of the painter convention in the process. Some of the facts are distorted, no doubt, but "Last Instructions" has, nevertheless, enough truth in it to be a prime source for the parliamentary history of the time. In his satires, as in his lyric poems, Marvell generally subjects aspirations and pretensions to the test of fact. He does not employ myth in Dryden's fashion, as an overarching, unifying fable, but inserts fragments of myth in his narrative which often shock us into a sharper sense of reality by their incongruity, as in the following conclusion to the portrait of the King's insatiable mistress, Lady Castlemaine:

> Ah, Painter, now could Alexander live
> And this Campaspe thee Apelles give!

It must be emphasized, however, that this comparison of poems in two different genres is not entirely fair to Dryden, whose inspiration arose, after all, from a desire to give aid to a nation which had suffered profoundly from war, plague, fire, and civil dissension. Dryden prescribed balms and lenitives for the health of the troubled nation; Marvell, corrosives and abstersives. When, fifteen years later, the nation's peace was threatened by the Popish Plot and the ambitions of Shaftesbury and Monmouth, Dryden showed in "Absalom and Achitophel" that he had achieved the subtlest and wittiest satirical style yet seen in England. The introductory lines on David amount to an effective tacit rejoinder to muckraking satire like Marvell's in combining a loyal regard for the king with a witty and tactful acknowledgment of his faults. Later in the poem when Dryden's David finally indicts his enemies and his renegade son we find again Marvell's theme:

> Though Justice against Fate complain,
> And plead the antient Rights in vain:
> But those do hold or break
> As Men are strong or weak.
> (An Horatian Ode, 37–40)

When we compare two examples of polemical prose, Dryden's preface to "Religio Laici" and Marvell's *Rehearsal Transpros'd,* we find corresponding distinctions. Dryden's pose is that of a spokesman; Marvell's that of an independent-minded individual. Dryden speaks for a consensus of likeminded, level-headed, witty gentlemen. Marvell, in exercising his own judgment and feelings freely, exemplifies the sturdy individual sticking up for his rights. Dryden, like many conservatives before and since, fears and despises the individualistic tendencies of religious nonconformity:

> While we were Papists, our Holy Father rid us, by pretending authority out of the Scriptures to depose princes; when we shook off his authority, the Sectaries furnish'd themselves with the same weapons; and out of the same magazine, the Bible: so that the Scriptures, which are in themselves the greatest security of governors, as commanding express obedience to them, are now turn'd to their destruction; and never since the Reformation has there wanted a text of their interpreting to authorize a rebel. And 't is to be noted by the way that the doctrines of king-killing and deposing, which have been taken up only by the worst party of the Papists, the most frontless flatterers of the Pope's authority, have been espous'd, defended, and are still maintain'd by the whole body of Nonconformists and Republicans.

An extraordinary indictment (by implication, of course) of all those who were apprehensive about a Catholic successor to the throne and the arbitrary tendencies of Charles II and his brother! As Marvell had written of another Mr. Bayes, "the Church of England is much oblig'd to Mr. *Bayes* for having proved that Nonconformity is the sin against the Holy Ghost."

Marvell held a higher opinion of what Miss Bradbrook and Miss Lloyd Thomas call "the English capacity to evolve a suitable form of government as if by an instinctive process of self-adjustment":

In all things that are insensible there is nevertheless a natural force always operating to expel and reject whatsoever is contrary to their sub-
sistence. . . . The common People in all places partake so much of Sense
and Nature, that, could they be imagined and contrived to be irrational,
yet they would ferment and tumultuate at last for their own preservation.
Yet neither do they want the use of Reason, and perhaps their aggregated
Judgment discerns most truly the Errours of Government, forasmuch as
they are the first, to be sure, that smart under them. In this only they come
to be short sighted; that though they know the Diseases, they understand
not the Remedies; and though good Patients, they are ill Physicians. The
Magistrate onely is authorized, qualified and capable to make a just and
effectual Reformation, and especially among the Ecclesiasticks.

(The Rehearsal Transpros'd) [12]

Marvell did not share Dryden's aristocratic contempt for the average
Englishman, nor did he share Dryden's perhaps exaggerated respect for
authority in political and religious matters. There was no question,
however, as to his stand on the rightful authority of the secular power:

The Power of the Magistrate does most certainly issue from the Divine
Authority. The Obedience due to that Power is by Divine Command; and
Subjects are bound both as Men and as Christians to obey the Magistrate
Actively in all things where their Duty to God intercedes not. . . .[13]

In conclusion, one might say that while Marvell and Dryden in their
writings on public issues (and even a layman's faith was a public issue
then) shared a deep concern for the welfare of church and state, while
both took positions near the center on these issues—between the ex-
tremists of right and left, and while both usually tried to advance
moderate positions through conciliatory strategies, they were tempera-
mental, philosophical, and spiritual opposites. Stylistically, the distinction between them is elusive, and yet I feel in Dryden's social tone the
voice of a cultivated, witty man of the world advancing arguments
which we, who *ipso facto* are equally cultivated, gentlemanly, and witty,
must inevitably accept. Against this wonderful insinuating style Marvell
tends to sound more like an individual speaking to another individual,
an effect unquestionably due in part to the individualistic emphasis of
the puritan tradition as against the greater Anglican emphasis on the
catholic and the communal. Dryden's style is normative, Marvell's more

---

[12] M. C. Bradbrook and M. G. Lloyd Thomas, *Andrew Marvell* (Cambridge University Press, 1961), p. 102; also in *The Complete Works of Andrew Marvell*, ed. A. B.
Grosart (London, 1872–1875), Vol. III, p. 382.

[13] *Works,* ed. Grosart, p. 370.

idiosyncratic; Dryden's humor directed at aberrations from what society or certain institutions regard as good; Marvell's at the crushing weight of institutions misemployed to oppress the individuals they are meant to serve. Marvell's style is a witty demonstration of the operations of the free mind:

> In the flexibility of his attack, Marvell produced what might roughly be taken as the prose version of the "metaphysical" style. There is the same synchronization of the important with the trivial, the same free combination of colloquialism and learning, the same variety in the points of view.[14]

"The free combination of colloquialism and learning" is certainly present, though perhaps to a lesser extent, in Dryden, but it is usually in the service of authority.

When freedom was jeopardized by a more formidable enemy than Mr. Bayes in Charles II's suspension of parliamentary sessions between 1675 and 1677, Marvell's style became less variable and more sombre, as in his last known work, *An Account of the Growth of Popery and Arbitrary Government in England* (1677). He died the following year, having rejected, according to unauthenticated rumor, an opulent offer from the King. He died so suddenly that there were dark hints of political murder, but he seems to have been a victim only of medical incompetence.

III

My sketch of Marvell's life has neglected most of his best poetry, because most of the lyrics can be dated only by conjecture. Like everything else we know of Marvell, the lyrics are characterized by extraordinary variety. As the late J. B. Leishman observed, "There is something in almost every one of them that recalls some other seventeenth-century poet, and yet perhaps no single one of them is really like a poem by anyone else." [15] Leishman concludes:

> Nevertheless, although Marvell cannot equal any of the poets I have mentioned (Donne, George Herbert, Vaughan, Crashaw) in their special intensities, he can surpass each and all of them in variety and breadth. This is partly because he is, in comparison with them, singularly uncommitted. His poetry is, so to speak, the poetry of a temperament rather than of any

[14] Bradbrook and Thomas, *op. cit.*, p. 109.
[15] "Some Themes and Variations in the Poetry of Andrew Marvell," *Proceedings of the British Academy*, XLVII (1961), 223.

urgent personal experience, but of a temperament in which nearly all the most attractive virtues of the earlier seventeenth century seem to be combined.[16]

I would only add that if Marvell seems uncommitted, it is because of a deep commitment to the truth of extremely complex states of mind and feeling. His profound aversion to partisan or doctrinaire politics has its counterpart in an aversion to misleadingly simple attitudes in the poetry. Unlike Donne he does not eclipse the world with a wink or make his mistress's bedchamber an everywhere. The meanings of his best poems are achieved through a dialectical contest of all pertinent attitudes, both personal and social. Sometimes the contest ends in a draw, as in "A Dialogue between the Soul and the Body," where fidelity to conflicting aspects of human nature requires a decision not to decide between the contestants, a state of mind close to Keats' "Negative Capability." Sometimes the conflict is resolved through paradox, as in "A Definition of Love" and "To His Coy Mistress," poems where Marvell achieves something like the romantic irony of "Ode on a Grecian Urn" but with an unblinkingly realistic emphasis instead of romantic pathos. The realism is another aspect of Marvell's Horatianism, as Eliot implies by quoting "Pallida Mors aequa pulsat pede pauperum tabernas Regumque turris" [17] in discussing "To His Coy Mistress." In other poems irony converts one feeling or attitude into its opposite, as in the *tours de force* which conclude "Daphnis and Chloe" and "Mourning." Yet despite Marvell's doublemindedness (most clearly seen, perhaps, in the intricate self-analysis of "The Coronet")—perhaps even because of it— he could convey with great force the singlemindedness of the puritan faithful in the paradise of "Bermudas."

In conclusion one might say that there is an experimental, independent attitude in Marvell's life and work and that he characteristically tests the claims of the ideal by the realities of what is possible. The *dégagé* ending of "Upon Appleton House," the poem in which I believe he worked out the most important decision of his life, shows an antididactic conviction that poetry is not everything, that the individual poem is, like Appleton House, only "an *Inn* to entertain / Its *Lord* a while, but not remain." Paradoxically, this attitude accounts for much of the strength and charm of his poetry. Although Dryden was to write finer satires than any of Marvell's, his idea of himself as a professional poet and spokesman worked against this kind of freedom.

---

[16] *Ibid.*, p. 224.
[17] "Pale Death strikes impartially the hovels of the poor and the towers of kings."

In the essays collected here I have sought to represent both Marvell's variety and the variety of critical responses to it. Except for Eliot's, all the essays constitute a second generation of views on Marvell, having absorbed or modified the pioneering insights of Eliot himself and Empson, Leavis, and Brooks. The first four items identify and define central aspects of Marvell's poetry. Eliot, as I have suggested, performs the indispensable critical task of placing Marvell's lyrics in the tradition of English and European poetry. John Hollander illuminates in a highly original way the musical images which occur throughout Marvell's poetry. Joseph Summers investigates the rich complexities of "nature" in Marvell's lyrics. My essay relates the political poems to the lyrics and to what we know of Marvell's public career.

The seven other essays deal more specifically with individual works and exemplify a variety of approaches. Harold Toliver's scintillating explication of "A Definition of Love" also provides a compact analysis of Marvell's irony, while John Coolidge's sensitive investigation of the "Horatian Ode" lays to rest contending misconceptions of the nature of Marvell's ambiguity. Geoffrey Hartman marshals an elaborate but relevant epistemology to penetrate "The Garden," while Michael O'Loughlin relates the elusive (and allusive) subtleties of "Upon Appleton House" to a series of poems going back to the *Odyssey*, *The Song of Songs*, and the *Georgics*. Through a detailed examination of seventeenth-century political theory John M. Wallace reveals the true significance of "The First Anniversary" in the development of Marvell's political thought and provides thereby a bridge to the last twenty-five years of Marvell's career. Finally, Earl Miner points the way to a better understanding of Marvell's satirical technique in his study of the iconic imagery of "The Last Instructions to a Painter."

Marvell has been well served by his twentieth-century critics, whose wide range of interests and techniques is only sampled in this collection. Strict limitations of space have forced me reluctantly to exclude many worthy candidates, of which quite a few, fortunately, are available in other collections of essays.

Andrew Marvell

by T. S. Eliot

The tercentenary of the former member for Hull deserves not only
the celebration proposed by that favored borough, but a little serious
reflection upon his writing. That is an act of piety, which is very different from the resurrection of a deceased reputation. Marvell has stood
high for some years; his best poems are not very many, and not only
must be well known, from the *Golden Treasury* and the *Oxford Book of
English Verse,* but must also have been enjoyed by numerous readers.
His grave needs neither rose nor rue nor laurel; there is no imaginary
justice to be done; we may think about him, if there be need for thinking, for our own benefit, not his. To bring the poet back to life—the
great, the perennial, task of criticism—is in this case to squeeze the drops
of the essence of two or three poems; even confining ourselves to these,
we may find some precious liquor unknown to the present age. Not to
determine rank, but to isolate this quality, is the critical labor. The fact
that of all Marvell's verse, which is itself not a great quantity, the really
valuable part consists of a very few poems indicates that the unknown
quality of which we speak is probably a literary rather than a personal
quality; or, more truly, that it is a quality of a civilization, of a traditional
habit of life. A poet like Donne, or like Baudelaire or Laforgue, may
almost be considered the inventor of an attitude, a system of feeling or
of morals. Donne is difficult to analyse: what appears at one time a
curious personal point of view may at another time appear rather the
precise concentration of a kind of feeling diffused in the air about him.
Donne and his shroud, the shroud and his motive for wearing it, are
inseparable, but they are not the same thing. The seventeenth century
sometimes seems for more than a moment to gather up and to digest into
its art all the experience of the human mind which (from the same

point of view) the later centuries seem to have been partly engaged in repudiating. But Donne would have been an individual at any time and place; Marvell's best verse is the product of European, that is to say Latin, culture.

Out of that high style developed from Marlowe through Jonson (for Shakespeare does not lend himself to these genealogies) the seventeenth century separated two qualities: wit and magniloquence. Neither is as simple or as apprehensible as its name seems to imply, and the two are not in practice antithetical; both are conscious and cultivated, and the mind which cultivates one may cultivate the other. The actual poetry, of Marvell, of Cowley, of Milton, and of others, is a blend in varying proportions. And we must be on guard not to employ the terms with too wide a comprehension; for like the other fluid terms with which literary criticism deals, the meaning alters with the age, and for precision we must rely to some degree upon the literacy and good taste of the reader. The wit of the Caroline poets is not the wit of Shakespeare, and it is not the wit of Dryden, the great master of contempt, or of Pope, the great master of hatred, or of Swift, the great master of disgust. What is meant is some quality which is common to the songs in *Comus* and Cowley's Anacreontics and Marvell's Horatian Ode. It is more than a technical accomplishment, or the vocabulary and syntax of an epoch; it is, what we have designated tentatively as wit, a tough reasonableness beneath the slight lyric grace. You cannot find it in Shelley or Keats or Wordsworth; you cannot find more than an echo of it in Landor; still less in Tennyson or Browning; and among contemporaries Mr. Yeats is an Irishman and Mr. Hardy is a modern Englishman—that is to say, Mr. Hardy is without it and Mr. Yeats is outside of the tradition altogether. On the other hand, as it certainly exists in Lafontaine, there is a large part of it in Gautier. And of the magniloquence, the deliberate exploitation of the possibilities of magnificence in language which Milton used and abused, there is also use and even abuse in the poetry of Baudelaire.

Wit is not a quality that we are accustomed to associate with "Puritan" literature, with Milton or with Marvell. But if so, we are at fault partly in our conception of wit and partly in our generalizations about the Puritans. And if the wit of Dryden or of Pope is not the only kind of wit in the language, the rest is not merely a little merriment or a little levity or a little impropriety or a little epigram. And, on the other hand, the sense in which a man like Marvell is a "Puritan" is restricted. The persons who opposed Charles I and the persons who supported the

Commonwealth were not all of the flock of Zeal-of-the-land Busy or the United Grand Junction Ebenezer Temperance Association. Many of them were gentlemen of the time who merely believed, with considerable show of reason, that government by a Parliament of gentlemen was better than government by a Stuart; though they were, to that extent, Liberal Practitioners, they could hardly foresee the tea-meeting and the Dissidence of Dissent. Being men of education and culture, even of travel, some of them were exposed to that spirit of the age which was coming to be the French spirit of the age. This spirit, curiously enough, was quite opposed to the tendencies latent or the forces active in Puritanism; the contest does great damage to the poetry of Milton; Marvell, an active servant of the public, but a lukewarm partisan, and a poet on a smaller scale, is far less injured by it. His line on the statue of Charles II, "It is such a King as no chisel can mend," may be set off against his criticism of the Great Rebellion: "Men . . . ought and might have trusted the King." Marvell, therefore, more a man of the century than a Puritan, speaks more clearly and unequivocally with the voice of his literary age than does Milton.

This voice speaks out uncommonly strong in the *Coy Mistress.* The theme is one of the great traditional commonplaces of European literature. It is the theme of *O mistress mine,* of *Gather ye rosebuds,* of *Go, lovely rose;* it is in the savage austerity of Lucretius and the intense levity of Catullus. Where the wit of Marvell renews the theme is in the variety and order of the images. In the first of the three paragraphs Marvell plays with a fancy which begins by pleasing and leads to astonishment.

> *Had we but world enough and time,*
> *This coyness, lady, were no crime,*
> *. . I would*
> *Love you ten years before the Flood,*
> *And you should, if you please, refuse*
> *Till the conversion of the Jews;*
> *My vegetable love should grow*
> *Vaster than empires and more slow. . . .*

We notice the high speed, the succession of concentrated images, each magnifying the original fancy. When this process has been carried to the end and summed up, the poem turns suddenly with that surprise which has been one of the most important means of poetic effect since Homer:

> *But at my back I always hear*
> *Time's wingèd chariot hurrying near,*
> *And yonder all before us lie*
> *Deserts of vast eternity.*

A whole civilization resides in these lines:

> *Pallida Mors aequo pulsat pede pauperum tabernas,*
> *Regumque turris. . . .*

And not only Horace but Catullus himself:

> *Nobis, cum semel occidit brevis lux,*
> *Nox est perpetua una dormienda.*

The verse of Marvell has not the grand reverberation of Catullus's Latin; but the image of Marvell is certainly more comprehensive and penetrates greater depths than Horace's.

A modern poet, had he reached the height, would very likely have closed on this moral reflection. But the three strophes of Marvell's poem have something like a syllogistic relation to each other. After a close approach to the mood of Donne,

> *then worms shall try*
> *That long-preserved virginity . . .*
> *The grave's a fine and private place,*
> *But none, I think, do there embrace,*

the conclusion,

> *Let us roll all our strength and all*
> *Our sweetness up into one ball,*
> *And tear our pleasures with rough strife,*
> *Thorough the iron gates of life.*

It will hardly be denied that this poem contains wit, but it may not be evident that this wit forms the crescendo and diminuendo of a scale of great imaginative power. The wit is not only combined with, but fused into, the imagination. We can easily recognize a witty fancy in the successive images ("my *vegetable* love," "till the conversion of the Jews"), but this fancy is not indulged, as it sometimes is by Cowley or Cleveland, for its own sake. It is structural decoration of a serious idea. In this it is superior to the fancy of *L'Allegro, Il Penseroso,* or the lighter and less successful poems of Keats. In fact, this alliance of levity and seriousness (by which the seriousness is intensified) is a characteristic of the sort of wit we are trying to identify. It is found in

> *Le squelette était invisible*
> *Au temps heureux de l'art païen!*

of Gautier, and in the *dandysme* of Baudelaire and Laforgue. It is in the poem of Catullus which has been quoted, and in the variation by Ben Jonson:

> *Cannot we deceive the eyes*
> *Of a few poor household spies?*
> *'Tis no sin love's fruits to steal,*
> *But that sweet sin to reveal,*
> *To be taken, to be seen,*
> *These have sins accounted been.*

It is in Propertius and Ovid. It is a quality of a sophisticated literature; a quality which expands in English literature just at the moment before the English mind altered; it is not a quality which we should expect Puritanism to encourage. When we come to Gray and Collins, the sophistication remains only in the language, and has disappeared from the feeling. Gray and Collins were masters, but they had lost that hold on human values, that firm grasp of human experience, which is a formidable achievement of the Elizabethan and Jacobean poets. This wisdom, cynical perhaps but untired (in Shakespeare, a terrifying clairvoyance), leads toward, and is only completed by, the religious comprehension; it leads to the point of the *Ainsi tout leur a craqué dans la main* of Bouvard and Pécuchet.

The difference between imagination and fancy, in view of this poetry of wit, is a very narrow one. Obviously, an image which is immediately and unintentionally ridiculous is merely a fancy. In the poem *Upon Appleton House,* Marvell falls in with one of these undesirable images, describing the attitude of the house toward its master:

> *Yet thus the laden house does sweat,*
> *And scarce endures the master great;*
> *But, where he comes, the swelling hall*
> *Stirs, and the square grows spherical;*

which, whatever its intention, is more absurd than it was intended to be. Marvell also falls into the even commoner error of images which are over-developed or distracting; which support nothing but their own misshapen bodies:

> *And now the salmon-fishers moist*
> *Their leathern boats begin to hoist;*
> *And, like Antipodes in shoes,*
> *Have shod their heads in their canoes.*

Of this sort of image a choice collection may be found in Johnson's *Life of Cowley*. But the images in the *Coy Mistress* are not only witty, but satisfy the elucidation of Imagination given by Coleridge:

> This power . . . reveals itself in the balance or reconcilement of opposite or discordant qualities: of sameness, with difference; of the general, with the concrete; the idea with the image; the individual with the representative; the sense of novelty and freshness with old and familiar objects; a more than usual state of emotion with more than usual order; judgment ever awake and steady self-possession with enthusiasm and feeling profound or vehement. . . .

Coleridge's statement applies also to the following verses, which are selected because of their similarity, and because they illustrate the marked caesura which Marvell often introduces in a short line:

> *The tawny mowers enter next,*
> *Who seem like Israelites to be*
> *Walking on foot through a green sea . . .*
>
> *And now the meadows fresher dyed,*
> *Whose grass, with moister colour dashed,*
> *Seems as green silks but newly washed . . .*
>
> *He hangs in shades the orange bright,*
> *Like golden lamps in a green night . . .*
>
> *Annihilating all that's made*
> *To a green thought in a green shade . . .*
>
> *Had it lived long, it would have been*
> *Lilies without, roses within.*

The whole poem, from which the last of these quotations is drawn (*The Nymph and the Fawn*), is built upon a very slight foundation, and we can imagine what some of our modern practitioners of slight themes would have made of it. But we need not descend to an invidious contemporaneity to point the difference. Here are six lines from *The Nymph and the Fawn:*

> *I have a garden of my own,*
> *But so with roses overgrown*

> *And lilies, that you would it guess*
> *To be a little wilderness;*
> *And all the spring-time of the year*
> *It only lovèd to be there.*

And here are five lines from *The Nymph's Song to Hylas* in the *Life and Death of Jason,* by William Morris:

> *I know a little garden close*
> *Set thick with lily and red rose,*
> *Where I would wander if I might*
> *From dewy dawn to dewy night,*
> *And have one with me wandering.*

So far the resemblance is more striking than the difference, although we might just notice the vagueness of allusion in the last line to some indefinite person, form, or phantom, compared with the more explicit reference of emotion to object which we should expect from Marvell. But in the latter part of the poem Morris divaricates widely:

> *Yet tottering as I am, and weak,*
> *Still have I left a little breath*
> *To seek within the jaws of death*
> *An entrance to that happy place;*
> *To seek the unforgotten face*
> *Once seen, once kissed, once reft from me*
> *Anigh the murmuring of the sea.*

Here the resemblance, if there is any, is to the latter part of *The Coy Mistress.* As for the difference, it could not be more pronounced. The effect of Morris's charming poem depends upon the mistiness of the feeling and the vagueness of its object; the effect of Marvell's upon its bright, hard precision. And this precision is not due to the fact that Marvell is concerned with cruder or simpler or more carnal emotions. The emotion of Morris is not more refined or more spiritual; it is merely more vague: if any one doubts whether the more refined or spiritual emotion can be precise, he should study the treatment of the varieties of discarnate emotion in the *Paradiso.* A curious result of the comparison of Morris's poem with Marvell's is that the former, though it appears to be more serious, is found to be the slighter; and Marvell's *Nymph and the Fawn,* appearing more slight, is the more serious.

> *So weeps the wounded balsam; so*
> *The holy frankincense doth flow;*

> The brotherless Heliades
> Melt in such amber tears as these.

These verses have the suggestiveness of true poetry; and the verses of Morris, which are nothing if not an attempt to suggest, really suggest nothing; and we are inclined to infer that the suggestiveness is the aura around a bright clear center, that you cannot have the aura alone. The day-dreamy feeling of Morris is essentially a slight thing; Marvell takes a slight affair, the feeling of a girl for her pet, and gives it a connection with that inexhaustible and terrible nebula of emotion which surrounds all our exact and practical passions and mingles with them. Again, Marvell does this in a poem which, because of its formal pastoral machinery, may appear a trifling object:

> Clorinda. *Near this, a fountain's liquid bell*
> *Tinkles within the concave shell.*
> Damon. *Might a soul bathe there and be clean,*
> *Or slake its drought?*

where we find that a metaphor has suddenly rapt us to the image of spiritual purgation. There is here the element of *surprise,* as when Villon says:

> *Necessité faict gens mesprendre*
> *Et faim saillir le loup des boys,*

the surprise which Poe considered of the highest importance, and also the restraint and quietness of tone which make the surprise possible. And in the verses of Marvell which have been quoted there is the making the familiar strange, and the strange familiar, which Coleridge attributed to good poetry.

The effort to construct a dream-world, which alters English poetry so greatly in the nineteenth century, a dream-world utterly different from the visionary realties of the *Vita Nuova* or of the poetry of Dante's contemporaries, is a problem of which various explanations may no doubt be found; in any case, the result makes a poet of the nineteenth century, of the same size as Marvell, a more trivial and less serious figure. Marvell is no greater personality than William Morris, but he had something much more solid behind him: he had the vast and penetrating influence of Ben Jonson. Jonson never wrote anything purer than Marvell's *Horatian Ode;* this ode has that same quality of wit which was diffused over the whole Elizabethan product and concentrated in the work of Jonson. And, as was said before, this wit which pervades the poetry of Marvell is more Latin, more refined, than anything that succeeded it. The great danger, as well as the great interest and excitement, of English prose and verse, compared with French, is that it permits and justifies an exaggeration of particular qualities to the exclusion of others. Dryden was great in wit, as Milton in magniloquence; but the former, by isolating this quality and making it by itself into great poetry, and the latter, by coming to dispense with it altogether, may perhaps have injured the language. In Dryden wit becomes almost fun, and thereby loses some contact with reality; becomes pure fun, which French wit almost never is.

> *The midwife placed her hand on his thick skull,*
> *With this prophetic blessing: Be thou dull . . .*

> *A numerous host of dreaming saints succeed,*
> *Of the true old enthusiastic breed.*

This is audacious and splendid; it belongs to satire besides which Marvell's Satires are random babbling, but it is perhaps as exaggerated as:

> *Oft he seems to hide his face,*
> *But unexpectedly returns,*
> *And to his faithful champion hath in place*
> *Bore witness gloriously; whence Gaza mourns*
> *And all that band them to resist*
> *His uncontrollable intent.*

How oddly the sharp Dantesque phrase "whence Gaza mourns" springs out from the brilliant contortions of Milton's sentence!

> *Who from his private gardens, where*
> *He lived reservèd and austere,*
> *(As if his highest plot*
> *To plant the bergamot)*

> *Could by industrious valour climb*
> *To ruin the great work of Time,*
> *And cast the kingdoms old*
> *Into another mold;*

> *   *   *

> *The Pict no shelter now shall find*
> *Within his parti-coloured mind,*
> *But, from this valour sad,*
> *Shrink underneath the plaid:*

There is here an equipoise, a balance and proportion of tones, which, while it cannot raise Marvell to the level of Dryden or Milton, extorts an approval which these poets do not receive from us, and bestows a pleasure at least different in kind from any they can often give. It is what makes Marvell a classic; or classic in a sense in which Gray and Collins are not; for the latter, with all their accredited purity, are comparatively poor in shades of feeling to contrast and unite.

We are baffled in the attempt to translate the quality indicated by the dim and antiquated term wit into the equally unsatisfactory nomenclature of our own time. Even Cowley is only able to define it by negatives:

> *Comely in thousand shapes appears;*
> *Yonder we saw it plain; and here 'tis now,*
> *Like spirits in a place, we know not how.*

It has passed out of our critical coinage altogether, and no new term has been struck to replace it; the quality seldom exists, and is never recognized.

> *In a true piece of Wit all things must be*
> *Yet all things there agree;*
> *As in the Ark, join'd without force or strife,*
> *All creatures dwelt, all creatures that had life.*
> *Or as the primitive forms of all*
> *(If we compare great things with small)*
> *Which, without discord or confusion, lie*
> *In that strange mirror of the Deity.*

So far Cowley has spoken well. But if we are to attempt even no more than Cowley, we, placed in a retrospective attitude, must risk much more than anxious generalizations. With our eye still on Marvell, we can say that wit is not erudition; it is sometimes stifled by erudition, as in much of Milton. It is not cynicism, though it has a kind of toughness which may be confused with cynicism by the tender-minded. It is confused with erudition because it belongs to an educated mind, rich in generations of experience; and it is confused with cynicism because it implies a constant inspection and criticism of experience. It involves, probably, a recognition, implicit in the expression of every experience, of other kinds of experience which are possible, which we find as clearly in the greatest as in poets like Marvell. Such a general statement may seem to take us a long way from *The Nymph and the Fawn,* or even from the *Horatian Ode;* but it is perhaps justified by the desire to account for that precise taste of Marvell's which finds for him the proper degree of seriousness for every subject which he treats. His errors of taste, when he trespasses, are not sins against this virtue; they are conceits, distended metaphors and similes, but they never consist in taking a subject too seriously or too lightly. This virtue of wit is not a peculiar quality of minor poets, or of the minor poets of one age or of one school; it is an intellectual quality which perhaps only becomes noticeable by itself, in the work of lesser poets. Furthermore, it is absent from the work of Wordsworth, Shelley, and Keats, on whose poetry nineteenth-century criticism has unconsciously been based. To the best of their poetry wit is irrelevant:

> *Art thou pale for weariness*
> *Of climbing heaven and gazing on the earth,*
> *Wandering companionless*
> *Among the stars that have a different birth,*
> *And ever changing, like a joyless eye,*
> *That finds no object worth its constancy?*

We should find it difficult to draw any useful comparison between these lines of Shelley and anything by Marvell. But later poets, who would have been the better for Marvell's quality, were without it; even Browning seems oddly immature, in some way, beside Marvell. And nowadays we find occasionally good irony, or satire, which lack wit's internal equilibrium, because their voices are essentially protests against some outside sentimentality or stupidity; or we find serious poets who are afraid of acquiring wit, lest they lose intensity. The quality which Marvell had, this modest and certainly impersonal virtue—whether we call it wit or reason, or even urbanity—we have patently failed to define. By whatever name we call it, and however we define that name, it is something precious and needed and apparently extinct; it is what should preserve the reputation of Marvell. *C'était une belle âme, comme on ne fait plus à Londres.*

Marvell's Commonwealth
and "The Empire of the Ear"

by John Hollander

Occurrences of *musica speculativa* in the poetry of Andrew Marvell are relatively sparse. With the exception of *"Musicks Empire,"* Marvell's musical references are confined to conventional uses that have been observed heretofore. In two of the satires, for example, musical allusions are employed in the ridicule of particular faults and aspirations of the respective victims. In "Clarindon's House-Warming," popular objections to the costly town house of Charles II's Lord Chancellor are used as an occasion for a general vilification of Clarendon. After condemning the barrenness of Clarendon's daughter, wife of the future James II, Marvell harps on the "vanity and folly" which Clarendon himself admitted had characterized his own assumption of the prodigious construction costs.

> And wish'd that his Daughter had had as much grace
> To erect him a pyramid out of her Quarry.
>
> But then recollection how the harper *Amphyon*
> Made *Thebes* dance aloft while he fidled and sung.
>
> He thought (as an Instrument he was most free on)
> To build with the Jews-trump of his own tongue.[1]
> (ll. 15–20)

"Jews-trump" or, more commonly, "jew's harp," was the relatively simple twanging instrument still known to children and rustics. In contrast to Amphion, builder of cities, Clarendon is depicted as having played on a rather opprobrious substitute. But the real point here is

[1] Andrew Marvell, *Poems and Letters*, ed. H. M. Margoliouth (Oxford, 1927), I, 137. Hereafter referred to as "Margoliouth."

that, as Dr. Percy Scholes has pointed out,[2] the jew's harp was employed
during the later seventeenth century as a cheap gimcrack commodity for
barter with the American Indian. The "Jews-trump of his own tongue,"
then, would refer to Clarendon's carelessness about costs and to an
implication that his money or his credit was unsound.[3] In these lines, a
musical reference is simply part of an invidious mythological comparison,
extremely common in all satire, complicated by a further topical joke
that refers back to the original basis of the comparison as between two
builders.

A rather more simple piece of wit, but involving musical lore to a
greater degree, occurs in the satire "Fleckno, or an English Priest of
Rome." The poet, after having been bored to distraction by his subject's
monstrous verses, is subjected to his music-making, when

> . . . the Tyrant, weary to persecute,
> Left off, and try'd t'allure me with his Lute.
>   Now as Instruments, to the same key
> Being tun'd by Art, if the one touched be
> The other opposite as soon replies,
> Mov'd by the Air and hidden Sympathies;
> So while he with his gouty Fingers crawles
> Over the Lute, his murmuring Belly calls,
> Whose hungry Guts to the same streightness twin'd
> In Echo to the trembling Strings repin'd.
>   I, that perceiv'd now what his Musick meant,
> Asked civilly if he had eat this Lent . . .[4]

(ll. 35–46)

As the gut strings vibrate across the belly of the lute, so rumble the en-
trails, in sympathetic vibration, of the unfortunate cleric who, for Dryden, "In Prose and Verse was own'd, without dispute / Through all
the realms of Non-sense, absolute."

While Marvell may have been prompted by certain musical and / or
gastric habits of his target to pinion him in this fashion, the passage is
fairly typical of the tradition of Juvenalian, or what Joseph Hall called
"biting," satires. In its use of a musical image to represent the feigning
or aspirations of one whose actuality is most unmusical, it is suggestive of
Donne's lines in his fourth "Satyre," ll. 77–78. The fawning sycophant

[2] Percy Scholes, *The Puritans and Music* (London, 1934), pp. 23–24; see also pp. 381–384.
[3] Cf. Margoliouth's note on this line, I, 264.
[4] Margoliouth, I, 84. Cf. Donne, "Satyre 1," ll. 77–78.

under attack answers the Poet's doubts as to the heuristic value of supposed courtly virtues as "He, like to a high stretcht lute string squeaked, O Sir, / 'Tis sweet to talk of Kings."

If these musical references are little more than accepted satiric devices, a few examples of cosmological hyperbole show rather nicely the course of this musical figure during the later seventeenth century. In his pastoral poems, Marvell conventionally employs the heavenly music as an image of perfection. In "A Dialogue Between Thyrsis and Dorinda," a pastoral seduction is conducted as an *"Invitation au Voyage."* The promised "Elizium" where *"tout n'est qu'ordre et beauté"* stands to the Arcadian meadow upon which the dialogue occurs as that meadow stands to the world:

> *Thyrsis.* Oh, ther's neither hope nor fear
> Ther's no Wolf, no Fox, nor Bear.
> No need of Dog to fetch our stray,
> Our Lightfoot we may give away;
> No Oat-pipe's needfull, there thine Ears
> May feast with Musick of the Spheres.[5]
>
> (ll. 21–26)

This "Elizium" resounds to no rustic piping, and the rejection of the syrinx is a little like Polybius' angry denial of the pastoral myths that even in his own time had grown up about his native Arcadia. (It was an ethical realm, he insisted, echoing to no Panic flutes, but where "The children learn to cipher and to sing" in well-regulated academies.) In another poem, "Clorinda and Damon," the wild pastoral piping is itself transformed directly into the *harmonia mundi:*

Chorus

> *Of Pan the flowring Pastures sing,*
> *Caves eccho, and the Fountains ring.*
> *Sing then while he doth us inspire;*
> *For all the World is our* Pan's *Quire.*[6]

But traditional lore, wrenched from its banal use by a conceit, soon approaches mere overstatement. Thus, Marvell treats the appeal of the Sisters of Nun Appleton to the future Lady Isabel Fairfax so as to employ this sort of figure, although in the context of the poem he

---

[5] *Ibid.*, I, 19.
[6] *Ibid.*, I, 18. Cf. E. K.'s gloss on the May eclogue of *The Shepheardes Calender:* "*Great Pan* is Christ, the very God of all shepheards, which calleth himself the greate and good shepheard . . ."

probably intends it as a sweet but wanton wile, if not as a blasphemous one:

> Your voice, the sweetest of the Quire
> Shall draw Heav'n nearer, raise us higher.[7]
> ("Upon Appleton House," ll. 161–162)

A more elaborate version of such literally high-flown compliment occurs in "The Fair Singer":

> To make a final conquest of all me,
> Love did compose so sweet an Enemy,
> In whom both Beauties to my death agree,
> Joyning themselves in fatal Harmony;
> That while she with her Eyes my Heart doth bind,
> She with her voice might captivate my Mind.
>
> I could have fled from One but singly fair:
> My dis-intangled Soul it self might save,
> Breaking the curled trammels of her hair.
> But how should I avoid to be her Slave,
> Whose subtile Art invisibly can wreath
> My Fetters of the very Air I breath?
>
> It had been easie fighting in some plain,
> Where Victory might hand in equal choice,
> But all resistance against her is vain,
> Who has th'advantage both of Eyes and Voice,
> And all my Forces needs must be undone,
> She having gained both the Wind and Sun.[8]

This is very like a Cavalier lyric; we might call it a Metaphysical poem on an Augustan subject. The distinctions between eyes, physical beauty, and the sun, on the one hand, and the voice, intellectual beauty, and the wind, on the other, elegantly support the compliment which raises the lady to the order of the elements themselves. Without the consistent fabric of wit, the elevation would be an unsteady one.

Marvell's most elaborate use of a figure from traditional *musica speculativa* occurs toward the beginning of "The First Anniversary of the Government under O.C." This long musical conceit starts out with the observation that inadequate rulers "No more contribute to the state of

[7] Margoliouth, I, 64.
[8] *Ibid.*, I, 31.

Things, / Then wooden Heads unto the Viols strings," an image even more precise than the modern cliché of the figurehead upon the ship of state. Following this, a rather direct cosmological hyperbole leads into an elaborate comparison of Cromwell to Amphion, and a brilliant version of the old notion of the state as a musical concord:

> While indefatigable *Cromwell* hyes,
> And cuts his way still nearer to the Skyes,
> Learning a Musique in the Region clear,
> To tune this lower to that higher sphere.
> So when *Amphion* did the Lute command.
> Which the God gave him, with his gentle hand,
> The rougher Stones, unto his Measures hew'd,
> Dans'd up in order from the Quarreys rude;
> This took a Lower, that an Higher place,
> As he the Treble alter'd, or the Base:
> No Note he struck, but a new Story lay'd,
> And the great Work ascended while he play'd.
> The listning Structures he with Wonder ey'd,
> And still new Stopps to various Time apply'd:
> Now through the Strings a Martial rage he throws,
> And joyning streight the *Theban* Tow'r arose;
> Then as he strokes them with a Touch more sweet,
> The flocking Marbles in a Palace meet;
> But, for he most the graver Notes did try,
> Therefore the Temples rear'd their Columns high:
> Thus, ere he ceas'd, his sacred Lute creates
> Th'harmonious City of the seven Gates.
> Such was that wondrous Order and Consent,
> When *Cromwell* tun'd the ruling Instrument;
> While tedious Statesmen many years did hack,
> Framing a Liberty that still went back;
> Whose num'rous Gorge could swallow in an hour
> That Island, which the Sea cannot devour:
> Then our *Amphion* issues out and sings,
> And once he struck, and twice, the pow'rful Strings.[9]
>
>   (ll. 45–74)

The "ruling Instrument" is the Instrument of Government of 1653 by means of which Cromwell established the Protectorate. Significantly, Marvell has clearly distinguished between the Instrument, or means,

[9] *Ibid.,* I, 104–105.

and the harmony of the state itself, or end. The heavenly figure in lines 47–48 is supported argumentatively by the reference, in the following couplet, to the traditional imitation of cosmic harmony in practical music. The actual creation of the state is allegorized in the story of Amphion's legendary founding of the city of Thebes in a marvellous way. The changes of pitch sounded upon the governing instrument control the corresponding architectural positions of the dancing masonry, and, by extension, create corresponding degrees in the order of nature. But following this (ll. 57–66), the already ordered structures again arrange themselves, this time with respect to differences of kind and use. These final arrangements, however, are effected not by the varying pitches of the music, but by the respective modes employed. As we have already seen, garbled notions of Greek modality, traditionally handed down, had become by the seventeenth century purely literary, esthetic concepts. Although no particular modes are mentioned by name in this passage, it is quite clear that Marvell's readers might have recognized in "a Martial rage" the Phrygian, in "a touch more sweet" the Hypolydian, and in "the graver Notes," the Dorian mode, their conventional affections being rousing, voluptuous, and stately, respectively. In running through various modes on his instrument, Cromwell-Amphion effects certain changes in the state of the world; I think that another myth can be seen to intrude itself here. Cromwell is being covertly invoked as Timotheus, the fictional musician of the court of Alexander the Great. A famous anecdote about him, retold by John Case in *The Praise of Music* and later employed by Dryden, tells how the fabulous performer, playing Phrygian and Dorian melodies in succession, first urges his monarch to the brink of war and then rapidly calms him again.

The stated comparison throughout this passage, however, treats Cromwell as Amphion, and all the precise elaboration can be seen as the kind of writing that would ordinarily be expected of Marvell, an intricate conceit employing knowledge, lore, and doctrine with the same immediacy as if they were the data of direct sensuous experience. And while the musical ideas here employed are of a completely conventional variety, Marvell's particular use of them in praise of Cromwell raises an interesting problem.

What looked to be a far-reaching critical controversy arose in the recent past over the nature of Marvell's political attitude toward Cromwell as expressed in the "Horatian Ode upon Cromwell's Return from Ireland." Cleanth Brooks, arguing from an ironic reading of the beginning phrase, "The forward Youth," and of

So restless *Cromwell* could not cease
In the inglorious Arts of Peace,
But through adventurous War
Urged his Active Star,[10]

(ll. 9–12)

maintained that the received view that Marvell was unambiguously praising Cromwell would simply not do.[11] He went on to insist that these and other ironies demanded a reading which would account for what he calls the "tension" in the poem's language by referring, in some way, to attitudes. Douglas Bush replied [12] that he could see no irony at all in the poem, that the praise intended was direct and bold. In describing Marvell as a "17th century liberal," [13] Professor Bush seemed to imply that the poet's strong Republican feelings, as evidenced by his loyal and undissenting political service, could easily encompass the actions of a revolutionary leader whom an orthodox royalist would indict with the crime of Brutus. It might be added that while Marvell was willing to imply such a comparison himself ("And *Caesar's* head at last / Did through his Laurels blast"), his use of it in connection with a description of praiseworthy audacity might bespeak an interpretation vastly different from that of a royalist.

It was perhaps unfortunate that the whole controversy died out[14] before any enlightening discussion had occurred of two central problems: namely, the question of how indeed Marvell's attitude toward Cromwell might be determined from his poetry, and the more general question of the relationship of intentions to both poetic and ordinary languages of praise and blame.[15] As far as we are concerned, however, Marvell's treatment of Cromwell need present no crucial problem. We may perceive Marvell's fairly general literary program of describing the Commonwealth in orthodox cosmological and pastoral images, and of invoking its leader as a kind of emperor. And we may, as a consequence, deal with any particular rhetorical difficulty as an irony engendered by

[10] *Ibid.*, I, 87.
[11] Cleanth Brooks, "Literary Criticism," in *English Institute Essays, 1946* (New York, 1947), pp. 127–158.
[12] Douglas Bush, "Marvell's 'Horatian Ode,'" *Sewanee Review,* LX (1952), pp. 363–376.
[13] *Ibid.*, p. 376.
[14] Brooks retorted in *Sewanee Review,* LXI (1953), pp. 129–135.
[15] Indeed, the discussion soon drifted into one of critical theory, and the role of historicism as against that of the "ontological criticism" practiced by Brooks. It ended up as little more than a defense of each position; no fruitful conclusions were reached about the "Horatian Ode."

two conventionally antithetical modes of discourse, rather than as an irony in the more usual sense, resulting from a conflict of attitude and formal expression. Marvell's pastoral name for England is *Eliza,* and it was the cosmology, at the center of which that earlier reign considered itself, that provided the raw material for so many of his metaphors. If Cromwell's regicide could prove a mortal sin to a royalist, a parliamentarian could retort that

> 'Tis madness to resist or blame
> The force of angry Heavens flame.[16]
> ("Horatian Ode," ll. 25-26)

In Marvell's poetic universe, Cromwell's triumph vaulted over those of his actions that in an earlier Tudor "Elizium" might have been branded as infamies. Cromwell killed a king who "nothing common did or mean" at the scene of his death, and served as the leader of a state who, unlike the king he had replaced, could not perpetuate his leadership through natural inheritance. Similarly, Man, in "The Mower Against Gardens," develops the arts of horticulture and formal gardening and "in the Cherry" does "Nature vex, / To procreate without a sex," at once adulterating and giving order to the "wild and fragrant Innocence" of a pastoral scene. In both cases, however, the ordering by an Intelligence of what was once free and unruly is observed in passing to be *contra naturam.* But our observation must move, along with Marvell's, one step further past these ironies. For Man, the gardener, and Cromwell, the ruler, both govern model universes in which, if innocence is no longer possible, knowledge and the ordering power of imagination are in some sense necessary.

The point is simply that to understand Marvell's political ideology we must try to disentangle such quasi-paradoxes as arise in nearly all the poems (save perhaps for the later satires) by treating them as knots in the thread of the argument in which each occurs, rather than as clusters of conflicting attitudes. And we must realize that the kind of responsibility that Marvell maintained toward his government and toward his constituency in Hull shared his sincerity and even, perhaps, his belief with his commitments to his style. I have raised this point not only in connection with the musical passage in the "First Anniversary" poem, but because of its relevance to the earlier "Musicks Empire." The possible invocation of Cromwell in the final stanza of this apparently simple piece of *laus musicae* might otherwise easily be misinterpreted on the

---

[16] *Ibid.,* I, 88.

grounds that the poem's subject provides an uncongenial environment for such an allusion.[17] The entire poem had best be quoted:

MUSICKS EMPIRE

I.

First was the World as one great Cymbal made,
Where Jarring Windes to infant Nature plaid.
All Musick was a solitary sound,
To hollow rocks and murm'ring Fountains bound.

II.

Jubal first made the wilder notes agree;
And *Jubal* tuned Musicks *Jubilee*:
He call'd the *Ecchoes* from their sullen Cell,
And built the Organs City where they dwell.

III.

Each sought a consort in that lovely place;
And Virgin Trebles wed the manly Base.
From whence the progeny of numbers new
Into harmonious Colonies withdrew.

IV.

Some to the Lute, some to the Viol went,
And others chose the Cornet eloquent.
These practicing the Wind, and those the Wire,
To sing Mens Triumphs, or in Heavens quire.

V.

Then Musick, the *Mosaique* of the Air,
Did of all these a solemn noise prepare:
With which She gain'd the Empire of the Ear,
Including all between the Earth and Sphear.

[17] It has been traditional to read "a gentler Conqueror" as Marvell's patron, Fairfax; see Margoliouth's note, I, 226, for example. M. C. Bradbrook and M. G. Lloyd Thomas in *Andrew Marvell* (Cambridge, 1940), pp. 76–77, 81, also make this identification, assigning the poem to the years 1651–1653, when Marvell was at Nunappleton. Also see *ibid.*, pp. 2–3. Percy Scholes, *op. cit.*, p. 153, suggests Cromwell, probably basing his judgment on his own researches into the latter's personal love of music (see Scholes, pp. 137–149). It will be clear that I agree with him for different reasons. As long as the provenance and precise date of the poem remain uncertain, the identifications seem equiprobable on the basis of outside evidence; on the basis of my reading below, Fairfax might still form a *figura* with Cromwell as a type of the secular political leader celebrated as music in the poem.

VI.

Victorious sounds! yet here your Homage do
Unto a gentler Conqueror than you;
Who though He flies the Musick of his praise,
Would with you Heavens Hallclujahs raise.[18]

The subject here is hardly a traditional praise of music through allusion
to *harmonia mundi;* in the first place, music is dealt with throughout
as having undergone a kind of historical evolution, parallelling the social history of mankind. In the second place, *musica instrumentalis* is
considered historically prior to the celestial harmony, and the normal
notion of practical music as the macrocosmic model of the universal
music is certainly rearranged, if not actually reversed. Most important
of all, however, is that the musical conceit is combined with a political
one in a way vastly different from the more traditional treatment in
"The First Anniversary of the Government Under O.C." for example,
where conventional musical metaphors and myths are revitalized only
in the wit.

"Musicks Empire" commences with the random sounds of nature. A
physical world "as one great Cymbal made" is the sounding instrument
struck by its own disordering elements. The winds themselves are qualified with a standard epithet of discord ("jarring"), but there is no in-
dication that the untamed babble, the "solitary sound" which exhausts
the domain of the audible, is in any metaphysical sense inharmonious.
"Infant" nature's wildness gives promise of a growth into orderly ma-
turity.

At this point, we are still in possession of an argumentative schema
admitting of various interpretive developments; from what we have come
to see of the treatment of both practical and speculative music in the
writing of the period we might expect the poem to take any one of a
number of courses. An elaborate description of harmony as an ordering
principle might follow, personified in Orpheus or Amphion, for example, or perhaps some moralized recounting of the fabled Pythagorean
"invention" of the intervals. But in the second stanza, Marvell introduces Jubal, "the father of all those who handle the harp and organ," [19]
as his heroic initiator of practical music. It is with Jubal that the meta-
phorical growth of empire begins. The echoes of the original natural
music ("natural" as is the sound of the wind in native forests as com-

pared to the sounds played upon the wood of those same hewn trees, fashioned into lutes—an old figure) are treated, here as throughout the poem, as men. "Sullen" means merely "solitary" here, and we have the sense of two images working at once: men are called from their poor, lonely caves (we are tempted to continue the paraphrase with "solitary, poor, nasty, brutish and short," for this stage of the growth of empire is the very birth of society itself). On the other hand, there is the distinct implication, in "Cell," of a monastic isolation, and music is here figured as breaking down the walls of monasteries by summoning forth the inhabitants into a world of cities, into the realities of Protestantism and political economy. The organ is almost completely a secular instrument here.

In the "Organs City" the population of musical sounds is fruitful and multiplies. Starting with the pun on "consort" as sexual mate and instrumental ensemble, the images of stanzas ii–iv depict the gradual overproduction of sounds in the city of towering pipes, resulting in a varied and overflowing music, filling the whole world in search of *Lebensraum*. The "Progeny of numbers new" is undoubtedly all the musical compositions ever invented, here related through a quasi-genetic descent to the primal natural noises. "Harmonious" names both the populations and the political condition of these colonies.

What looks to be a rather conventional catalogue of the instruments in the fourth stanza is turned upside down by the fact that it is the music that seeks out the several instruments. We may see how, in the contest between Welsh and English musicians in Drayton's *Poly-Olbion*, various dispositions of different men were satisfied by their choice of instruments when they

> Strooke up at once and sung each to the Instrument;
> (Of sundry sorts that were, as the Musician likes)
> On which the practic'd hand with perfect'st fingring strikes,
> Whereby their height of skill might liveliest be exprest.
> The trembling Lute some touch, some straine the Violl best . . .[20]
> (*Poly-Olbion*, Song iv, ll. 352–356)

But in "Musicks Empire" the composed sounds themselves choose the instruments by means of which they will applaud the triumphs, the successful advancing marches of human enterprise. The allusion to "Heavens quire" seems almost like a gratuitous tag here, so completely does the idea of mundane expansion dominate the poem.

[20] Michael Drayton, *Works*, ed. J. W. Hebel (Oxford, 1933), iv, 78.

In the penultimate stanza, the rigor of the conceit appears to relax somewhat. Music, now generally personified, is described as "the Mosaique of the Air." In this remarkable image, however, the multiplicity of the "harmonious Colonies" is recalled by reference to the variegated tesserae of a mosaic which can merge, from any distant viewpoint, into an overwhelming unified figure. It is with a concerted effort of all its diversities in a "solemn" (i.e. religious) noise, corresponding to the assembled mosaic figure, that Music accomplishes her final triumph, gaining "the Empire of the Ear, / Including all between the Earth and Sphear." In the sense of the earlier metaphors, music's heaven is the ultimate civil and territorial acquisition. But in another sense the general personification of Music in this stanza has rendered it as more abstract, and the "Empire of the Ear" is its empirically proper dwelling-place, a heaven of pure audibility.

The word "Mosaique" resonates even further, however. Marvell may or may not have been aware of the common etymological origin of "music" and "mosaic" in the Greek *mousa* ("muse"); perhaps the juxtaposition of the two words in the line was for him the same kind of mock-etymological punning that he had effected earlier in the poem between "Jubal" and "Jubilee." The concealed allusion to Moses he had also employed elsewhere. In the woods about Appleton House, the Poet, "easie Philosopher," divines in the birds and the vegetation all the works of Man:

> Out of these scatter'd *Sibyl's* leaves
> Strange *Prophecies* my Phancy weaves:
> And in one History consumes,
> Like *Mexique Paintings,* all the *Plumes.*
> What *Rome, Greece, Palestine,* ere said
> I in this light *Mosaick* read.
> Thrice happy he who, not mistook,
> Hath read in Natures mystick Book.[21]
> ("Upon Appleton House," ll. 577–584)

Both the ascription of prophecy to fancy and the Hebraic notion of the historical role of *torah,* the Mosaic Law, point to a pun here involving the reading of "light *Mosaick*" as both an adjective-noun and noun-adjective qualification. The notion of music as "the *Mosaique* of the Air," then, might reverberate in a moral and religious dimension as well; it is as a Biblical moral leader that music finally gains the higher reaches of the universe.

In the final stanza, the metaphoric ground again shifts a little as laudatory music attendant upon triumphal processions is recalled. The "Victorious" sounds are at once the flourishes of victory and the actual conquerors of the foregoing parts of the poem. But even they must bend the knee before "a gentler Conqueror," a nobler leader, perhaps the Lord Protector himself. So closely does the growth of music's empire hew to a condensation of human history that it is tempting to suggest that Marvell may have in some way felt the gap between stanzas iv and v to have covered the period 1649–1653, at the end of which time the Protectorate was established. In any case, Cromwell may be said to have brought to "Elizium" the Mosaic leadership historically necessary, a Puritan would undoubtedly have argued, for heaven's consent.

The superimposition of musical lore on a persuasively designed historical frame results, in "Musicks Empire," in a reversal of the usual mythological treatments of *laus musicae*. Earth is filled with sound before Heaven is; the music of the spheres, only obliquely invoked, appears first as a kind of cosmic, triumphal applause. The two conceits on music and human political development interweave so closely that the first five stanzas might be said to address themselves to the subject of "Empire's Music," rather than the other way around. Marvell's historical construction of speculative music is in many ways unique. What Cowley cast into pedantic footnotes appended to a handful of lines of the *Davideis,* Marvell took as the *données* of a compact pseudo-narrative. "Musicks Empire" is, after all, modelled on treatments of the praise of music that we have already considered, but only in the sense that Elizabethan lyrics are, by and large, modelled on *songs,* that Metaphysical lyrics are modelled on *arguments.* The last stanza is an *envoi* to Cromwell, replacing a salute to the Muse; its place there, given the historical narrative that has led to it, is inevitable.

Marvell's "Nature"

by Joseph H. Summers

The similarities between the verse of Marvell and that of many modern poets are seductive. A number of Marvell's poems have been cited as evidence to support the critical assumption, based largely on modern poetic practice, that the most mature and rich works of literature are necessarily ironical. One can disagree with the assumption and still recognize that irony, not of a paralyzing variety, is central to most of Marvell's poems. Marvell's surfaces, moreover, are close to one modern ideal. The tones of the typical modern *personae* echo the sensuous richness of Marvell more often than the logical violence of Donne—that poet who wrote "To Mr. Samuel Brooke," boastfully yet accurately, "I sing not Siren like to tempt; for I / Am harsh." The "speakers" of Marvell's poems are farther removed from immediate embroilment in action than are Donne's. They approach their situations from some distance, with a wider and a clearer view. Their speech is closer to that of meditation or of a quiet colloquy in a garden than to the raised voice, the immediate and passionate argument. And the verse which they speak shows a concern for euphony, a delicate manipulation of sound patterns suggesting Campion's songs—or much of the verse of Eliot and MacLeish and many younger poets.

The differences between Marvell and the moderns, however, are equally noteworthy, and failure to perceive them has resulted in strange readings of a number of Marvell's poems. To prevent misreadings, to define any specific poem, we need to achieve some sense of the body of Marvell's work. And here is the difficulty, for our sense of that work is likely to be an impression of dazzling fragments, each brilliant and disparate. The reader may feel that the sixth stanza of "The Gallery," the poem in which the poet invites Chlora to view her portraits in his soul as " an inhumane

"Marvell's 'Nature'" by Joseph H. Summers. From *ELH*, XX (1953), 121–35. Copyright 1953 by The Johns Hopkins Press. Reprinted by permission of The Johns Hopkins Press.

murtheress," Aurora, "an enchantress," Venus, and "a tender shepherd-ess," applies more justly to the poet than to Chlora:

> These Pictures and a thousand more.
> Of Thee, my Gallery do store;
> In all the Forms thou can'st invent
> Either to please me, or torment.

Yet the poem assures us that Chlora is one, however numerous her pictures; and the poet who could take various and even contradictory positions on the claims of the active and contemplative lives, of the body and the soul, of the time-honored plea to "seize the day," of gardens ("These Pictures and a thousand more") is equally one poet. The attempts to bring intellectual order out of the apparent confusion by means of a hypothetical biographical development of the poet have been unconvincing. The development or rather break in his poetic practice after 1660 is clear. Before that time, the single poem "Upon Appleton House" indicates that Marvell was an extraordinarily sophisticated poet, capable of employing numerous traditions and multiple attitudes as occasions or moments demanded. Among the few attitudes which I have been unable to discover in Marvell's poetry, however, are those expressed in two of the modern poems which owe most to Marvell. Archibald MacLeish's "You, Andrew Marvell" concludes with the lines,

> And here face downward in the sun
> To feel how swift how secretly
> The shadow of the night comes on . . .

Robert Penn Warren's "Bearded Oaks" includes the following stanza:

> Upon the floor of light, and time,
> Unmurmuring, of polyp made,
> We rest; we are, as light withdraws,
> Twin atolls on a shelf of shade.

In Marvell's verse man is neither an atoll nor an island, and if night is anticipated, so is light.

An examination of Marvell's uses of "Nature," the world of the flowers and fruits and the green grass, provides a sketch not only of the virtuosity and multiple intellectual and moral stances within the poems, but also of the central vision which occurs most frequently in the most successful poems. Occasionally Marvell used nature as an image of classical order, an artfully contrived realization of the mean which man is to imitate —or, more properly, which a specific man has imitated. Jonson had shown

in his ode "To the Memory of Sir Lucius Cary and Sir Henry Morison"
that nature conceived as an ordered mean was a most effective source of
hyperbolical compliment. In "Upon the Hill and Grove at Bill-borow,"
Fairfax too is at one with nature. After his active life (in which he had
"thunder'd" "Through Groves of Pikes," "And Mountains rais'd of dying
Men"), Fairfax has returned to the retirement of the hill and grove; the
humanized landscape is both his ward and his image:

> See how the arched Earth does here
> Rise in a perfect Hemisphere!
> The stiffest Compass could not strike
> A Line more circular and like;
> Nor softest Pensel draw a Brow
> So equal as this Hill does bow.
> It seems as for a Model laid,
> And that the World by it was made.   (st. i)

*   *   *

> See what a soft access and wide
> Lyes open to its grassy side;
> Nor with the rugged path deterrs
> The feet of breathless Travellers.
> See then how courteous it ascends,
> And all the way it rises bends;
> Nor for it self the height does gain,
> But only strives to raise the Plain.   (st. iii)

After this delightfully artificial description of landscape as Republican
gentleman, we are not surprised that these Roman oaks should speak
oracles of praise for Fairfax. In the opening lines of "Upon Appleton
House," an ordered and properly proportioned nature is again the symbol for Fairfax and his dwelling, particularly in contrast to the "unpro-
portion'd dwellings" which the ambitious have constructed with the aid
of "Forrain" architects: "But all things are composed here, / Like Nature,
orderly and near." Nature is also near and extraordinarily "orderly"
when a natural object, "A Drop of Dew" for example, is examined as an
emblem. Here we are close to Herbert, but in Marvell we are chiefly compelled by the ingenuity with which the natural is made to reflect the
conceptual.

More often nature is nearer if not so orderly when it is conceived as the
lost garden, whether Eden or the Hesperides or England:

> O Thou, that dear and happy Isle
> The Garden of the World ere while,
> Thou *Paradise* of four Seas,
> Which *Heaven* planted us to please,
> But, to exclude the World, did guard
> With watry if not flaming Sword;
> What luckless Apple did we tast,
> To make us Mortal, and The Wast?
>
> ("Upon Appleton House," st. xli)

The lost garden represents not measure but perfect fulfillment; its memory is an occasion for ecstasy:

> And Ivy, with familiar trails,
> Me licks, and clasps, and curles, and hales.
> Under this *antick Cope* I move
> Like some great *Prelate of the Grove,*
>
> Then, Languishing with ease, I toss
> On Pallets swoln of Velvet Moss.
>
> ("Upon Appleton House," st. lxxiv-lxxv)

> What wond'rous Life in this I lead!
> Ripe Apples drop about my head;
> The Luscious Clusters of the Vine
> Upon my Mouth do crush their Wine;
> The Nectaren, and curious Peach,
> Into my hands themselves do reach;
> Stumbling on Melons, as I pass,
> Insnar'd with Flow'rs, I fall on Grass.
>
> ("The Garden," st. v)

It is in this vein that Marvell occasionally gives a sensuous particularity to his descriptions of natural objects which may remind us of Vaughan's "those faint beams in which this hill is drest, / After the Sun's remove" ("They are all gone into the world of light!"), and which has led some readers to consider him a romantic born too early. And yet the "gelid *Strawberryes*" and "The hatching *Thrastles* shining Eye" of "Upon Appleton House" contribute to a complicated vision of nature which is finally unlike the nineteenth-century's; the *"Hewel's* wonders" (the activities of the woodpecker) teach the *"easie Philosopher"* who "Hath read in *Natures mystick Book"* the just relationships between sin and death:

Who could have thought the *tallest Oak*
Should fall by such a *feeble Strok'*!

Nor would it, had the Tree not fed
A *Traitor-worm,* within it bred.
(As first our *Flesh* corrupt within
Tempts impotent and bashful *Sin.*)
And yet that *Worm* triumphs not long,
But serves to feed the *Hewels young.*
While the Oake seems to fall content,
Viewing the Treason's Punishment.

("Upon Appleton House," st. lxix-lxx)

In "The Garden," too, identification with nature is neither complete nor simple. The famous fifth stanza which I have quoted above, expertly "imitates" the bodily ecstasy, and the following stanzas systematically portray the higher ecstasies of the mind and the soul; all, moreover, are framed with witty and civilized reversals of the ordinary civilized values, of classic myth, of the biblical account of the creation of woman, and of the idea that sexual relations are "natural." To read "The Garden" and "The Mower Against Gardens" in succession is to realize that in Marvell's poetry the man-made garden and the "natural" meadows are significant not intrinsically but instrumentally. Both poems are ultimately concerned with lost perfection. "The Garden" presents a fictional and momentary attempt to recapture what has been lost. In "The Mower against Gardens," the garden itself is an image of the sophisticated corruption responsible for the loss of "A wild and fragrant Innocence." Marvell's image of the lost garden is as much an occasion for the recognition of man's alienation from nature as it is for remembered ecstasy.

The degree to which Marvell both followed and modified conventional practice can be seen most clearly in the "pastoral" poems in which he substituted the mower for the traditional shepherd. The life of the shepherds had imaged the pre-agricultural golden age, the paradisiacal simplicity ideally if not actually associated with the simple country life, away from cities and civilizations, wars and corruptions. When love was concerned, the passion was usually direct, uncontaminated by worldly considerations, and not much affected by age, even if the lover was unhappy or the mistress proved untrue. The good shepherd and his sheep could imply the ideal political relation between the ruler and the ruled, and the Christian poets explored the rich possibilities of the Good Shepherd and his flock and the large pastoral inheritance of the Psalms. Milton, who retained the shepherd image in "Lycidas," kept the humanist emphasis on higher man (the poet, the pastor) as the guide of less perceptive humanity through the labyrinth of nature to an ultimate goal. The shepherd followed Christ, and he also led his own sheep into the true fold. Marvell used some of this material in a direct if not very distinguished fashion in "Clorinda and Damon," and although the participants are oarsmen rather than shepherds, the spirit of the tradition is present in "Bermudas." He gave up most of these associations, however, when he chose the figure of the mower as his central image. That figure, of course, had its own traditions. As "Damon the Mower" mentions, the mower's craft had long served to picture man's greatest mystery and fear:

> Only for him no Cure is found,
> Whom *Julianas* Eyes do wound.
> 'Tis death alone that this must do:
> For Death thou art a Mower too.

The mower who cut down the living grass was a natural symbol for death. Because of the seasonal nature of his activities, he was also a symbol for time. Marvell's mower does not lead; he destroys. However simple his character or sincere his love, he cuts down for human ends what nature has produced. He symbolizes man's alienation from nature:

> With whistling Sithe, and Elbow strong,
> These Massacre the Grass along:
> While one, unknowing, carves the *Rail*,
> Whose yet unfeather'd Quils her fail.
> The Edge all bloody from its Breast
> He draws, and does his stroke detest;
> Fearing the Flesh untimely mow'd
> To him a Fate as black forebode.
>
> ("The Appleton House," st. 1)

"The Mower's Song" is a playful and elaborately artificial lament of a lover, but it is more than that. The refrain insists that the mower-lover's relation to nature exactly parallels his cruel mistress's relation to him:

> For *Juliana* comes, and She
> What I do to the Grass, does to my Thoughts and Me.

Greenness in this poem, as so often in Marvell's verse, represents hope and vitality and virility, the fertile promise of life which man desires and destroys. The mower, angry that there is no true sympathy between man and nature, "fictionally" determines to destroy nature to make the symbolism more complete:

Unthankful Medows, could you so
A fellowship so true forego,
And in your gawdy May-games meet,
While I lay trodden under feet?
When *Juliana* came, and She
What I do to the Grass, does to my Thoughts and Me.

But what you in Compassion ought,
Shall now by my Revenge be wrought:
And Flow'rs, and Grass, and I and all,
Will in one common Ruine fall.
For *Juliana* comes, and She
What I do to the Grass, does to my Thoughts and Me.

The Mower poems conveniently define the crucial terms of Marvell's
most frequent poetic use of nature. Marvell did not discover an impulse
from the vernal wood which spoke unambiguously to the human heart
and which offered a possibility for man's at-oneness with all. Nor did he,
like George Herbert, usually see in nature patterns of a distinguishable
and logical divine will, the *paysage moralisé* which offered a way to the
understanding and imitation of God. Human moral criteria do not apply
to most of Marvell's landscapes. In his poems nature apart from man is
usually "green," vital, fecund, and triumphant. Since it affirms life it is, as
part of the divine plan, "good," but its goodness is neither available nor
quite comprehensible to man. Man is barred from long or continuous
spiritual communion, and his intellect cannot comprehend the natural
language. Since his alienation with the departure from Eden, man can
only live in nature either as its observer or its destroyer; since he partially
partakes of nature, he is, if he acts at all, also his own destroyer. His
capacity for self-destruction is clearly implied by the contrast between
nature's fecundity and man's harassed and frustrated attempts at love.
Faced with unrequited love, man the mower only sharpens his scythe
for the destruction of the grass and sharpens the "Woes" which destroy
himself:

How happy might I still have mow'd,
Had not Love here his Thistles sow'd!
But now I all the day complain,
Joyning my Labour to my Pain;
And with my Sythe cut down the Grass,
Yet still my Grief is where it was:
But, when the Iron blunter grows,
Sighing I whet my Sythe and Woes.

("Damon the Mower")

But man destroys the natural and dies not only because he is inferior but also because, suspended between the natural and divine, he is superior to the green world. In "A Dialogue between the Soul and the Body" each of the protagonists charges wittily and convincingly that the other is the source of human misery; of the first 40 lines, each speaks 20, and points are made and capped so expertly as to produce a forensic stalemate. But the Body wins and ironically resolves the argument with its final additional four lines:

> What but a Soul could have the wit
> To build me up for Sin so fit?
> So Architects do square and hew
> Green Trees that in the Forest grew.

Without the soul the body would be truly a part of nature and could not sin. Yet architecture, whether external or internal, is the product and desire of a higher part of man, even though many "Green trees" may be destroyed for it. Whether the building is used for good or ill, man's capacities for reason, for structure, for creation outside the carnal, are not natural but Godlike. Man's distinctive gifts are as destructive within the post-Eden garden as are his weaknesses and his corruption.

It is, moreover, exactly man's superiority to the vegetative world which allows him to recognize his alienation. Nature does not possess the capacity for man's choices between the active and contemplative lives: it can only vegetate. The rival claims of those two chief modes of man's life are ever present in Marvell's poetry, and they are closely related to his themes of nature and time. Man must act and he must contemplate, and he must do each in accordance with the demands of time. Yet the contemplative life is usually the more desirable way—at least for the poet. The poet surpasses most men in the degree and consistency of his recognition of man's alienation, for he is chiefly concerned with the contemplation of the condition of man. In Marvell's poetry, significantly, natural beauty is usually described and appreciated as if it were an imitation of the works of man. The fort and artillery of the garden in "Upon Appleton House" are not simply factual or fanciful. In "The Mower to the Glo-Worms" nature is the gracious and kindly courtier to man, so lost in love "That I shall never find my home." In one of the most memorable descriptions in "Bermudas" God Himself is the manlike decorator:

> He hangs in shades the Orange bright,
> Like golden Lamps in a green Night.
> And does in the Pomgranates close,
> Jewels more rich than *Ormus* show's.

It is the artifacts, the "golden Lamps" and the "Jewels more rich than *Ormus* show's," which contribute most of the sensuous richness to the passage. In relation to the garden man is the judge and the measure as well as the accused.

Whatever the immediate resolutions, man is usually suspended between the greenness and God at the conclusions as well as at the beginnings of Marvell's poems. Within "A Dialogue between The Resolved Soul, and Created Pleasure," the Soul deftly propounds the orthodox thesis that the sensuous and worldly pleasures are only appearances, that the soul possesses the quintessence of all pleasures in his resolution. Yet the tensions are still felt, and the soul's conclusions, while "true," are also partial. At the moment of death "The rest" (both the ease and the remainder of all the pleasures) *does* "lie beyond the Pole, / And is thine everlasting Store." But before that moment, Marvell and most of his contemporaries believed that no man enjoyed fully and continuously either the flesh or the spirit, that the battle was constantly renewed so long as a living spirit inhabited a living body. This did not imply that the battle lacked interest nor that decisions and momentary achievements were impossible. Such decisions and such achievements were, in fact, the poet's subjects, not only in "A Dialogue" but also "To his Coy Mistress." The speaker of the latter poem seems to resolve clearly for sensuality: *Carpe diem* appears to be all. The image of the "birds of prey," however, makes us realize the costs of a resolution to "devour" time, to choose destructive brevity of life since eternity cannot be sensually chosen.

The reader's awareness of Marvell's complex use of nature should cast light on almost any one of the poems. Within such light, the presentation of Cromwell in "An Horatian Ode" as a force of nature seems not perplexing but inevitable. "Upon Appleton House" is Marvell's most ambitious and in many respects his most interesting poem. A full consideration of it would require another essay, and I only wish to suggest here that it is a mistake to read it as an artificial "public" poem interesting chiefly for a few "personal" passages. Similarly, "The Picture of little T. C. in a Prospect of Flowers" is not a graceful trifle which somehow goes wrong. It is a fine poem, and it elucidates Marvell's central vision of man and nature:

i

> See with what simplicity
> This Nimph begins her golden daies!
> In the green Grass she loves to lie,
> And there with her fair Aspect tames

The Wilder flow'rs, and gives them names:
But only with the Roses playes;
And them does tell
What Colour best becomes them, and what Smell.

ii

Who can foretel for what high cause
This Darling of the Gods was born!
Yet this is She whose chaster Laws
The wanton Love shall one day fear,
And, under her command severe,
See his Bow broke and Ensigns torn.
Happy, who can
Appease this virtuous Enemy of Man!

iii

O then let me in time compound,
And parly with those conquering Eyes;
Ere they have try'd their force to wound,
Ere, with their glancing wheels, they drive
In Triumph over Hearts that strive,
And them that yield but more despise.
Let me be laid,
Where I may see thy Glories from some shade.

iv

Mean time, whilst every verdant thing
It self does at thy Beauty charm,
Reform the errours of the Spring;
Make that the Tulips may have share
Of sweetness, seeing they are fair;
And Roses of their thorns disarm:
But most procure
That Violets may a longer Age endure.

v

But O young beauty of the Woods,
Whom Nature courts with fruits and flow'rs,
Gather the Flow'rs, but spare the Buds;
Lest *Flora* angry at thy crime,
To kill her Infants in their prime,
Do quickly make th' Example Yours;
And, ere we see,
Nip in the blossome all our hopes and Thee.

The opening stanza of the poem tells us of the child's alienation from and superiority to nature, as well as of her delight in it. Her apparently successful imposition of her own order and value on nature raises in-

evitably the question of the prospect of time, and we see prophetically
in the second stanza her future triumph over "wanton Love"—and over
man. Not a combatant, the speaker of the poem resolves to observe the
dazzling scene from the shade which allows vision, for the god-like glories
cannot be viewed immediately by profane man. If he is to admire her
triumph, it must be from a distance where there is no fear of its destructiveness. With the "Mean time" of the fourth stanza we are back at the
present prospect, and the observer from his advantageous point of view
advises the present T. C. At the golden moment when "every verdant
thing" charms itself at her beauty, she is instructed to prepare for her
future career by reforming the "errours of the Spring." At first it seems,
or perhaps would seem to a child, an almost possible command. With the
talismanic power of her "fair Aspect" she already "tames / The Wilder
flow'rs, and gives them names," and she tells the roses "What Colour best
becomes them, and what Smell." At least within the circle of her immediate view she may, perhaps, by a judicious bouquet arrangement cause the
tulips to share in sweetness, and it is possible to disarm roses of their
thorns with assiduous labor. But the thing which should be "most" procured is impossible for the human orderer even within his small area. And
all of it is, of course, impossible if all the "errours of the Spring" are in
question. For, in comparison either with the triumph of T. C. or the
vision of Eden, Spring is full of errors; the decorative details suggest
exactly how far nature fails to sustain human visions of propriety, delight, and immortality. T. C. and the idealizing aspect of man wish
delight and beauty and goodness to be single, but they cannot find such
singleness within the promising verdancy of nature; if they desire it they
must impose it on nature or must seek it in an "unnatural" or supernatural world. The tulips show how improperly the delights of the senses
are separated in this world; the roses with their thorns traditionally indicate the conjunction of pain and pleasure, the hidden hurts lying under
the delights of the senses; and the transience of the violets is a perpetual
reminder of the mortality of life and innocence and beauty. The description of the preceding triumph is placed in a doubtful light. If T. C.'s
reformation of floral errors is so doomed, how much real hope or fear
can there be of her reformation of the errors of that higher order, man?
Is the former description a fantasy, ideal yet frightening, of what might
happen if the superhuman power as well as the superhuman virtue
were granted, a fantasy proceeding from the observer's sharing for one
moment the simplicity of the nymph?

In the exclamatory warning of the final stanza the observer and the
reader see the picture of little T. C. in the full prospect of time which the

flowers have furnished. At the present moment "Nature courts" her "with fruits and flow'rs" as a superior being; she represents the promise of an order higher than we have known. But she is also the "young beauty of the Woods," and she is a "Bud." The child of nature as well as its potential orderer, she shares the mortality as well as the beauty of the flowers; her own being, in the light of the absolute, is as "improper" as are the tulips or the roses. The former vision of her triumph implied full recognition of only one half of her relationship to the fruits and flowers. The introduction of Flora reminds us more sharply than anything else in the poem of the entire relationship. However lacking in the ideal, Flora has her own laws which man violates at the peril of self-destruction. Flora decrees that life shall continue: the infants shall not be killed "in their prime"—either in their moment of ideal promise or in their first moment of conception. The sexual concerns which have been suggested throughout the poem are made explicit in the final stanza. The picture in the central stanzas of the complete triumph of T. C., the absolute rule of human notions of propriety, has inevitably meant that "wanton Love's" bow will be broken, his ensigns torn: there will be no more marriages. With a recognition of mortality and of the power of Flora, we recognize also the doom of such a triumph, for both the ideal and the reality will soon die, and there is no prospect of renewal in future "T. C.'s." The conclusion, however, is neither a Renaissance nor a modern "naturalism." Because perfect fulfillment is impossible, man is not therefore to abandon his attempts at perfection. T. C. is allowed and even commanded to "Gather the Flow'rs," to expend her present and her future energies in ordering the natural nearer to the ideal pattern—so long as she spares the buds. The qualification is all important. Man must beware of attempting to anticipate heaven by imposing the ideal absolutely on earth. The killing of the infants in their prime is not only a crime against Flora but against all the gods, for man is never free to commit either murder or suicide in the pursuit of the abstract ideal. The human triumph must function within and wait upon the fulness of time. It must recognize the real and individual as well as the ideal and the general or it becomes a horror. The ending of the poem revalues everything which has gone before. "Ere we see" may mean something equivalent to "in the twinkling of an eye"; it certainly means, "Before we see what will become of you and the vision of a new and higher order." What will be nipped "in the blossom," in the first full flowering, unless the warning is heeded will be not only "all our hopes" (our hopes of the idealized child and of a possible new order, our hopes of love and of a new generation), but also "Thee," the living child.

"The Picture of little T. C. in a Prospect of Flowers" is characteristic of Marvell's poetry both in its complexity and in its subtle use of superficially "romantic" or decorative detail. It may remind us of modern poetry, but ultimately Marvell is both more complex and more assured of his meanings than are most of the moderns. Marvell does not present a *persona* simply and finally torn between this world and the next, distracted by the sensuous while attempting to achieve a spiritual vision. For Marvell, as for most Renaissance poets, the perception of a dilemma was not considered a sufficient occasion for a poem. Marvell made precise the differences between the values of time and of eternity. He recognized that man exists and discovers his values largely within time; he also believed that those values could be ultimately fulfilled only outside time. The recognition and the belief did not constitute a paralyzing dilemma. Each of his early poems implies the realization that any action or decision costs something; yet each presents a precise stance, an unique position and a decision taken at one moment with a full consciousness of all the costs. The costs are counted, but not mourned; the position is taken, the poem is written, with gaiety.

When we have understood what the "prospect of flowers" implies, "The Coronet" does not seem a churchly recantation of all that Marvell valued, but an artful recognition of the ultimate issues. Here the decision is taken in the full light of eternity, and, as in George Herbert's "A Wreath" (which Marvell probably remembered), the intricate and lovely form of the poem provides an index to the joy. The speaker of the poem describes his attempt to create a coronet for Christ. He dismantles "all the fragrant Towers / That once adorn'd my Shepherdesses head" to gather the necessary flowers, but he discovers that the Serpent has entwined himself into the proposed offering, "With wreaths of Fame and Interest." The poet prays that Christ would untie the Serpent's "slipp'ry knots,"

> Or shatter too with him my curious frame
> And let these wither, so that he may die,
> Though set with Skill and chosen out with Care.
> That they, while Thou on both their Spoils dost tread,
> May crown thy Feet, that could not crown thy Head.

The poem is moving as well as orthodox in its expression of willingness to sacrifice man's sensuous and aesthetic structures to a divine necessity. But Marvell's most Miltonic line, "Though set with Skill and chosen out with Care," ruefully insists that, whatever his vision of ultimate value, the living poet also values the structures of time.

From Contemplation to Action: Marvell's Poetical Career

by George deF. Lord

> We make out of the quarrel with others, rhetoric, but of the quarrel with ourselves, poetry.
>
> —W. B. Yeats

I

Andrew Marvell's poetical career seems perfectly to exemplify the dissociated sensibility which Eliot has deplored as a feature of the literary revolution in post-Restoration England. Marvell's lyrics, in their subtle articulation of sense, intellect, and imagination, are triumphs of an integrated sensibility which could organize vast varieties of experience, while the political poems, in sacrificing wholeness and complexity to a predominantly analytical concern with public affairs, are the products of a dissociated or excessively limited sensibility. Some such distinction may be regarded as indicating other major literary developments of the later seventeenth century: the shift from fancy to judgment as senior partner in the term "wit"; the growing interest in man as a social being rather than as an individual; the newly established priority of consensus over personal apprehension as the basis of value judgments. While we may well find these and other major shifts exemplified in the poems which Marvell wrote in the quarter-century which spans his poetical career from about 1650 to 1675, they are subordinate to the main concern of this essay which is to trace the process by which he developed from a Metaphysical lyricist to an Augustan satirist.

We should begin by making some distinctions between the lyrical and the political modes. In one way or another most of Marvell's lyrics are concerned with withdrawal from business, war, politics, or society in quest of some higher good.

In the typical Marvell lyric personal value triumphs over the temptations or encroachments of the world. Disengagement from the secular dimensions takes a number of forms. In *Bermudas* physical isolation through shipwreck allows a body of pilgrims to celebrate with one voice (almost as if they were a single person) the divine providence that has bestowed upon them an Eden-like refuge:

> Thus sung they, in the *English* boat
> An holy and a cheerful Note,
> And all the way, to guide their Chime,
> With falling Oars they kept the time.

Escape from the alien world, here represented by "the Storms, and Prelat's rage," is the precondition to their achieving harmony with each other, with God, and with nature. In the pastoral dialogues the selectivity of the pastoral setting filters out, as it usually does, most of what we call the world, while the two partners in dialogue manage to arrive at a corresponding harmony with each other and with their environment. Clorinda and Damon conclude their duet in a chorus celebrating the perfect rapport between themselves and the pastoral world:

> Sing then while he doth us inspire;
> For all the world is our Pan's quire.

The Coronet and *On a Drop of Dew,* exploring attitudes that are specifically Christian, reject the irrelevances of the world in favor of a longed-for consummation with "the glories of th'Almighty Sun." In *To his Coy Mistress* the lover wittily exploits the threatening spectre of world and time to induce a moment of exalted passion by which momentarily to annihilate them, while his counterpart in *The Definition of Love* exposes in the same forces a jealousy which, in preventing the consummation of his passion, ensures its continuing perfection. Yet another variation on the theme (and a favorite of Donne's) finds in the love relationship a superior substitute for the world and the essence of all value:

> So we alone the happy rest,
>   Whilst all the world is poor,
> And here within ourselves possess
>   All Love's and Nature's store.

When "the world" does collide with the lyric world of innocence, it can appear as the mindless brutality of "the wanton troopers riding by" who slay the nymph's fawn. Or it invades the green meadows of Damon in the guise of Juliana, who induces tormenting self-division in the formerly contented mower. In another guise it may induce a hybridized self-division in Nature herself:

> The Pink then grew as double as his mind;
> The Nutriment did change the Kind.

The most emphatic rejection of the world and the most imaginative celebration of the values of retirement occur, of course, in *The Garden*. Turning scornfully from the "uncessant labors" of ambitious worldlings, the poem goes on to enact the experience of contemplative retirement in a way that unites the sensuous and the spiritual. When admirers of Marvell lament his later dedication to political subjects, they think of *The Garden* as the embodiment of the values and talents which they feel he abandoned.

Certainly the political poems, in both matter and manner, seem to present a stark contrast to what *The Garden* epitomizes, whether one considers the increasingly partisan celebrations of Oliver Cromwell or the later satires on the régime of Charles II. This may help to explain why so many readers of the first of these poems, *An Horatian Ode*, refuse to accept its explicit praise of Cromwell's remorseless power and Machiavellian strategy as anything but ironic. Coming from the subtle balance and meditative detachment of the lyrics one finds the commitment to political action a real shock.[1] It is hard to believe, for example, that the man who so scrupulously and beautifully explores his own tangled motives in *The Coronet* could afterwards write in total disregard of such complexities. It is perhaps even harder to believe that a lyric poet of unexcelled grace and sensitivity could have produced such a poem as *Last Instructions to a Painter*, a poem that is often derisive, tendentious, cynical, and ugly. The Cromwell poems, as recent studies by Mazzeo and Wallace show, are closely-knit, unified compositions, but

---

[1] What Steele Commager says of the great odes of Horace also characterizes Marvell's *Horatian Ode* perfectly: "And if they offer the best parallel in Latin poetry to the *Aeneid*, it is by virtue of their massive reservations and ambiguities no less than by their commitment to Augustus and to the Roman state" (*The Odes of Horace* [New Haven and London: Yale University Press, 1962], p. 33). John S. Coolidge, in "Marvell and Horace" [reprinted in this collection, pp. 85–100] also cites Commager and works out in detail and with great sensitivity the implications of Marvell's Horatianism.

a satire like *Last Instructions* seems to lack any principle of organization.[2] Much of it, indeed, appears to fall below *any* serious conception of poetry:

> When grievance urg'd, he swells like squatted toad,
> Frisks like a frog to croak a tax's load;
> His patient piss he could hold longer than
> An urinal and sit like any hen;
> At table jolly as a country host
> And soaks his sack with Norfolk like a toast;
> At night than Chanticleer more brisk and hot,
> And Sergeant's wife serves him for Pertelotte.

> (877–884)

Marvell's satire seems to be embedded in a discrete, alien world that is banished from the lyrics, a world, as the following ugly parody of *Paradise Lost* shows, in which experience is subject to an unceasing process of devaluation:

> Her, of a female harpy, in dog days,
> Black Birch, of all the earth-born race most hot
> And most rapacious, like himself, begot;
> And of his brat enamour'd, as't increas'd,
> Bugger'd in incest with the mongrel beast.

II

Towards the end of our discussion we shall return to the careworn and distraught "drunkards, pimps, and fools" who people Marvell's satires. Our immediate aim now is to trace the process by which the poet of rural retirement and contemplation became the poet of political involvement and action.

An Horatian Ode upon Cromwell's Return from Ireland has usually escaped the hostility or indifference which students of Marvell have often felt for his other poems on political subjects. In fact, the *Ode* has recently become the focal point of many critical appraisals which have been as unanimous in their high esteem as they have been diverse in

---

[2] Joseph A. Mazzeo, "Cromwell as Davidic King," *Renaissance and Seventeenth-Century Studies* (New York: Columbia University Press, 1964), pp. 183–208. John M. Wallace, "Andrew Marvell and Cromwell's Kingship: 'The First Anniversary,'" *ELH*, XXX (1963), 209–235 [reprinted below, pp. 143–164].

their explications of Marvell's attitude toward his subject. Much of the *Ode*'s astounding popularity may be attributed to critical attitudes which set a high value on tension, ambivalence, and dialectical subtlety. Some is perhaps also due to a natural scholarly penchant for solving riddles. In this case the riddle is a major one, for its solution would shed new light on Marvell's entire development as a poet. The problem which the *Ode* poses for most critics is the apparent incompatibility of two sets of values which it presents. These two sets of values are precisely the ones with which this paper is concerned—the dualities of retirement and involvement, of contemplation and action. In one way or another the critical problem of the *Ode* amounts to this: is the praise of Cromwell as a remorselessly active political force compatible with the profound regret which the poem expresses for the King and the ancient rights which Cromwell destroyed in his rise to power? This is primarily a question of tone. An ancillary question which involves the philosophical beliefs expressed in the *Ode* and also in Marvell's other poems, is whether the celebration of a usurper totally involved in war and statecraft is compatible with the deep feeling for the retired, contemplative life expressed in the lyric poems and in this ode as well.

One can readily see that the problems posed by the *Horatian Ode* are versions of those posed by Marvell's whole development as a poet, for when we put the political poems side by side with the lyrics the same apparent incompatibilities appear.

The Garden, for example, illuminates the *Horatian Ode* and vice versa. To some extent the two poems are corollaries, one withdrawing from a life of fruitless ambition into a life of contemplative fulfillment, the other abandoning the austere and secluded garden for the arena of political and military activity. From the perspective of the garden, ambitious and successful men seem misguided and foolish; from the perspective of Cromwell's strenuous achievements, the "muses dear" and "numbers languishing" of the retired life seem equally unseasonable and absurd. Thus the dominant mode in either poem exposes its opposite as alien, irrelevant, and *demodé,* although the *Ode* qualifies its criticism with the elegiac tribute to Charles I and nostalgic allusions to "ancient right." One should also remember that the circumstances assumed in either poem are fundamentally different, for while *The Garden* assumes an ideal, speculative viewpoint, the *Ode* emphasizes the insistent pressure of a crucial historical moment which does not permit a purely philosophical choice. The contrast between the contemplative freedom of *The*

Garden and the necessitarian rigor of the *Ode* is also expressed in the relaxed, expansive tone and rhythm of one poem as against the relentless and insistent tone and rhythm of the other.

III

In the dialectical structure of *Upon Appleton House* the dualities of retirement and involvement, of contemplation and action are more fully presented than in any other of Marvell's poems. The circumstances surrounding this poem allow the protagonist to assume a succession of viewpoints which extends from one extreme to the other. The retirement of Lord Fairfax as commander-in-chief of the army in 1650 provides a broader point of view on the issues that appear in *The Garden* and the *Horatian Ode*. This broader point of view is supported, furthermore, by the protagonist, who is simultaneously an admirer of Fairfax, a solitary contemplative (as in *The Garden*), and a patriot concerned for the welfare of his country in a time of crisis. While this historical crisis is present in the poem, and the protagonist is therefore compelled to make a choice, the historical pressures are sufficiently remote to permit him the fullest exercise of his judgment and imagination.

Upon Appleton House employs a succession of altering perspectives to evaluate the dualities we have mentioned. Its action is a dialectical movement through modulations of these dualities to a conclusion that is equally appropriate to political and personal ideals and to the complex demands of the immediate historical moment. The poem may be divided into seven sections: (1) lines 1–80 celebrating Appleton House and its master as models of the good life in the *beatus ille* tradition; (2) lines 81–280 narrating the triumph of Fairfax's ancestors over the sequestrating nuns, who represent a perversion of the good life; (3) lines 281–368 describing the garden Fairfax made "in the just figure of a Fort"; (4) lines 369–480 narrating the protagonist's descent into the meadow; (5) lines 481–623 narrating the protagonist's retirement into the wood and his meditative experience there; (6) lines 624–648 narrating his return to the meadow; and (7) lines 649–776 presenting the advent of the tutelary deity of Nunappleton and the scion of the Fairfax dynasty, Maria.

The occasion of *Upon Appleton House,* though nowhere explicitly stated, is implied throughout. In June 1650 Fairfax resigned as Lord General of the army because he disapproved on moral grounds of Cromwell's projected invasion of Scotland. Later in the same year Marvell joined Fairfax on his Yorkshire estate as tutor to young Mary, the only child. Fairfax employed his time in managing his estate, in gardening, and in writing poems in praise of the retired life. Although Marvell did not approve unequivocally of Fairfax's withdrawal from public affairs, "Upon Appleton House" would have been an entirely appropriate tribute.

In the succession of radically altering perspectives mentioned earlier, Marvell presents a series of retirements that correspond to the seven sections of the poem we have outlined. First, in the tradition of Horace, Virgil, and Ben Jonson, he praises his master's moral and spiritual attributes exemplified in Appleton House as the foundation of the good society. Next, he contrasts with this virtuous and benevolent life of rural retirement the perverted seclusion of the nuns who once came close to thwarting the dynasty that was to serve England so well. The poem then moves to a description of the garden Fairfax has laid out, where an uneasy alliance of art and nature has produced fort-like flower beds with sentinel bees and regimented tulips. Although this section pays tribute to the hero's self-command, the rather incongruous garden setting seems more appropriate to the post-war recreations of Uncle Shandy and Corporal Trim than to the retirement of a sage and hero like Fairfax. The tone changes toward the end of the section, however, where an elegiac tribute is paid to England as an erstwhile "garden of the world." The tribute is informed with much the same love and lyric intensity that one finds in John of Gaunt's dying speech on "this other Eden, demi-paradise" in *Richard II*:

> Oh Thou, that dear and happy Isle
> The Garden of the World ere while,
> Thou *Paradise* of four Seas,
> Which Heaven planted us to please,
> But, to exclude the World, did guard
> With watry if not flaming Sword;
> What luckless Apple did we taste
> To make us Mortal, and Thee Waste?
>
> (321–328)

While the section ends with unstinting praise for Fairfax's personal virtues—"For he did with his utmost skill / Ambition weed, but Conscience till"—it also expresses regret that Fairfax should have elected to confine himself to a private life and abandon the power which might have helped to make England a paradise once more:

> And yet there walks one on the Sod
> Who, had it pleasèd him and *God,*
> Might once have made our Gardens spring
> Fresh as his own and flourishing.
> But he preferr'd to the Cinque Ports
> These five imaginary Forts:
> And, in those half-dry Trenches, spann'd
> Pow'r which the Ocean might command.
>
> (345–352)

Surely this tribute is qualified by regret for a power unnecessarily curtailed and misapplied, especially in "five imaginary Forts" and "half-dry Trenches." The passage marks a major step in Marvell's resolution of the dualities. There are times—and this is one of them, he implies—when, subject to a qualifying Providence, men like Fairfax must leave the retired life they rightly prize and enter the lists of war and politics in defence of that life. The sanctions for Fairfax's return to public affairs at this juncture are far stronger than they were for "the forward youth who would appear" of the *Horatian Ode.* Fairfax alone combines the wisdom, virtue, and power that might restore England as "the Garden of the World." It is not surprising, then, that Fairfax's puttering among make-believe forts and flowery bastions at Nunappleton seems a little silly in the context of such an exalted opportunity.

This is as far as Marvell's argument relates specifically to Lord Fairfax, but lines near the end of the poem enunciate most vigorously the national obligations of the Fairfax dynasty as represented by Maria:

> Hence She with Graces more divine
> Supplies beyond her *Sex* the *Line;*
> And, like a sprig of *Mistleto,*
> On the *Fairfacian Oak* does grow;
> Whence, for some universal good,
> The *Priest* shall cut the sacred Bud;
> While her *glad Parents* most rejoice,
> And make their *Destiny* their *Choice.*
>
> (737–744)

The "universal good" for which Maria must some day abandon the family tree is clearly one that takes precedence over the personal values of life at Nunappleton. Life at Nunappleton,

> In a *Domestick Heaven* nurst
> Under the *Discipline* severe
> Of Fairfax, and the starry *Vere,*

has nevertheless been an essential preparation for a career devoted to the preservation of the values which it represents. Under certain circumstances, then, the devotee of the garden must leave it in order to be faithful to the values which it embodies; must even act in defense of the life of contemplation. Even the *Horatian Ode* seems to regard Cromwell as peculiarly fitted for political and military leadership *because of* the "private Gardens, where / He liv'd reservèd and austere."

Our discussion of *Upon Appleton House* has limited itself thus far to the relatively clear-cut treatment of the theme of retirement in the first three sections of the poem. As we descend with the protagonist into the abyss "Of that unfathomable Grass" at line 369, we begin to participate in the experience of meditative retirement itself. At this point the primarily social perspective of the first three sections gives way to a more inward vision of the values which the meadows and woods of Nunappleton foster. These meadows and woods and the protagonist's experiences there approximate in all essentials the experience of *The Garden*, as Fairfax's ceremonial tour of inspection among his regimented tulips does not. The sea of grass undergoes a bewildering succession of metamorphoses in the protagonist's imagination which corresponds to *The Garden's* image of the mind as an "Ocean where each kind / Does streight its own resemblance find." The constantly changing meadow collaborates with the contemplative imagination of the protagonist to recreate, as Maren-Sofie Røstvig has so brilliantly shown, the universal history of man.[3] Although the meadow is like the "ocean of the mind" in *The Garden*, however, we must recognize one crucial difference between *The Garden's* vegetable innocence and the bloody simulacrum of war in the mowing scene. If the "massacring" of the grass seems a little fanciful, the slaughter of the rails who nest "below the Grasses root" and show that "Lowness is unsafe as Hight" introduces a grim allusion to political realities that is absent from *The Garden*. Retirement and humility cannot, at this moment in history, provide the security which they were traditionally thought to ensure. The implicit lesson for a Fairfax is obvious.

In the fifth section the protagonist withdraws even further from the world to take sanctuary in the wood, a "yet green yet growing Ark." Here he becomes in Miss Røstvig's terms a "hortulan saint" whose meditations on the *res creatae* culminate in the deepest spiritual insights:

> Out of these scatter'd *Sibyls* Leaves
> Strange *Prophecies* my Phancy weaves:

[3] *The Happy Man*, I (2nd ed., Oxford: Basil Blackwell, 1962), pp. 172–190.

And in one History consumes,
Like *Mexique Paintings,* all the *Plumes.*
What *Rome, Greece, Palestine,* ere said
I in this light *Mosaick* read.
Thrice happy he who, not mistook,
Hath read in *Natures mystick Book.*

(577–584)

Immured among the ancient trees and armed with this accumulated wisdom, the protagonist celebrates his immunity to the temptations and distractions of the world:

How safe, methinks, and strong, behind
These Trees have I incamp'd my Mind;
Where Beauty, aiming at the Heart,
Bends in some tree its useless Dart;
And where the World no certain Shot
Can make, or me it toucheth not.

(601–606)

Miss Røstvig sees the culminating stage of the meditation as a symbolic imitation of "the crucial moment in the universal history of man—the crucifixion." She is unquestionably right in seeing these allusions, especially in lines 615–16,

Do you, *O Brambles,* chain me too,
And courteous *Briars* nail me through,

but the meaning of this section of the poem depends heavily, as it often does in Marvell, on the tone. In my opinion the tone has grown increasingly bizarre the nearer we approach the meditative climax. The protagonist's attention is increasingly obsessed by his own activities in a way that verges on narcissistic buffoonery:

Or turn me but, and you shall see
I was but an inverted Tree.

The Oak-Leaves me embroyder all,
Between which Caterpillars crawl:
And Ivy, with familiar trails,
Me licks, and clasps, and curles, and hales.
Under this *antick Cope* I move,
Like some great *Prelate of the Grove.*

Much more could be cited to indicate the unhealthy self-concern of these alleged readings in "Natures mystick Book." And where, finally, does the meditative vision culminate? Certainly not in self-discovery or self-forgetfulness, aspects of true visions, but in the angler's furtive and shamefaced retreat before the *"young Maria,"* who seems to embody the true wisdom he lacks:

> Hide trifling Youth thy Pleasures slight.
> 'Twere shame that such judicious Eyes
> Should with such Toyes a Man surprize;
> *She* that already is the *Law*
> Of all her Sex, her *Ages Aw.*

Here again poetic intentions cross, and the real hero of this supposed poem of "rural solitude" turns out to be a young girl destined to emerge from retirement and devote herself to some "universal good." Her studious hours at Nunappleton have been a period of preparation "Till Fate her worthily translates, / And find a *Fairfax* for our *Thwaites.*" As the model of Maria's future husband Marvell has significantly chosen, not her father, to whom he dedicated the poem, but that ancient Fairfax "Whose offspring fierce / Shall fight through all the Universe." Through the figure of Maria the poem has reconciled the hitherto incompatible demands of private virtue and public service. In the anguished complexities of the year 1650 Marvell realized that the garden required an angel with a flaming sword to guard it.

IV

Two main conclusions are to be drawn from Marvell's development up to this point: first, that under certain conditions one must enter public affairs in order to defend or preserve the values which the garden represents; secondly that only a man imbued with the virtue and wisdom which the garden represents is fitted for such public service. Marvell's own career in politics and in the poems which followed *Upon Appleton House* must be seen in terms of these conclusions.

If the *Horatian Ode* deals with the disintegration of a régime that had ancient right but no power to enforce it, *The First Anniversary* addresses itself to the problem of building a commonwealth that can exert its claims in the name of both might and right. As he appears in this poem Cromwell combines the astounding force which characterizes him in the *Horatian Ode* with the creative skill that can engage all political forces in the construction of a new constitution. Furthermore, as John M. Wallace shows, *The First Anniversary* is a plea for Cromwell to re-establish monarchy with himself as king. In this way Marvell would secure the future stability of the constitution through the hereditary features of monarchy. Taking the *Ode* unironically, we nonetheless find Cromwell lacking some necessary qualifications as ruler. Though nurtured in the stoic virtues of the garden, though modest and wise in the exercise of power, Cromwell as a usurper yet lacks the legitimacy that could sanction his rule. Without such a sanction Marvell saw him as doomed to the ceaseless exercise of force and political arts to maintain his position. Under the circumstances Marvell could only urge this son of Fortune to "march indefatigably on."

Cromwell's brush with death in a coaching accident, which plays a prominent part in *The First Anniversary,* only makes explicit what is implied in the *Ode*: that sooner or later Cromwell's death is bound to bring political chaos back to England unless something is done to legitimize his situation and consequently to ensure the succession. Even in his derisive comments on the ineffective projects of "heavy monarchs," Marvell recognizes one indispensable advantage in the hereditary feature of kingship:

> Well may they strive to leave them to their Son
> For one Thing never was by one King don.

In one respect, however, Cromwell's position as ruler has improved significantly in *The First Anniversary,* for his political authority no longer depends entirely on the ceaseless assertion of his power. Through the Ruling Instrument he has now created a balanced political constitution that engages the energies and interests (and even the hostilities) of all his subjects. The constitution which, Amphion-like, he has created is the classical mixed state upon which much seventeenth-century political theory, both royalist and republican, was based.[4] The essential principle of the mixed state was that political harmony depended on the proper interrelation between discordant interests. This theory of a political *concordia discors* is nowhere presented more imaginatively than here:

> None to be sunk in the Foundation bends,
> Each in the House the highest Place contends,
> And each the Hand that lays him will direct,
> And some fall back upon the Architect;
> Yet all compos'd by his attractive Song,

[4] Z. S. Fink, *The Classical Republicans* (2nd ed., Evanston: Northwestern University Press, 1962).

>   Into the Animated City throng.
>   The Common-wealth does through their Centers all
>   Draw the Circumf'rence of the publique Wall;
>   The crossest Spirits here do take their part,
>   Fast'ning the Contignation which they thwart;
>   And they, whose Nature leads them to divide,
>   Uphold, this one, and that the other Side;
>   But the most Equal still sustein the Height,
>   And they as Pillars keep the Work upright;
>   While the resistance of opposed Minds,
>   The Fabrick as with Arches stronger binds,
>   Which on the basis of a Senate free,
>   Knit by the Roofs Protecting weight agree.
>
> (81–98)

All that is needed to preserve this harmonious political structure through the years is to ensure the continuance of "the Roofs Protecting weight" by reintroducing hereditary monarchy. Under the circumstances, then, Cromwell's continued refusal of the crown exposes the state to the threat of renewed chaos:

>   Thou with the same strength, and an Heart as plain,
>   Didst (like thine Olive) still refuse to Reign;
>   Though why should others all thy Labor spoil,
>   And brambles be anointed with thine Oyl,
>   Whose climbing Flame, without a timely stop,
>   Had quickly Levell'd every Cedar's top.
>
> (257–262)

The refusal of the olive to reign seems to be related to Cromwell's deep but, under the circumstances, misguided attachment to the virtues of retirement:

>   For all delight of life thou then didst lose
>   When to Command thou didst thy self Depose;
>   Resigning up thy Privacy so dear,
>   To turn the headstrong Peoples Charioteer.
>
> (221–224)

As in *Upon Appleton House,* a "universal good" sometimes requires one fit for public service to sacrifice his strongest personal inclinations, to "depose himself."

Marvell's treatment of this theme reaches its conclusion in *Upon the*

Death of O.C., which hails Richard as the hereditary successor of Oliver.
At last the dynasty has been established and the state stabilized:

> We find already what these Omens mean,
> Earth ne'er more glad, nor Heaven more serene.
> Cease now our griefs. calme peace succeeds a war,
> Rainbows to storms, Richard to Oliver.
>
> (319–322)

Richard also embodies, as we might expect, those virtues essential to a
true political leader which can only be bred in retirement:

> He, as his father, long was kept from sight
> In private, to be view'd by better light;
> But open'd once, what splendour does he throw?
> A Cromwell in an houre a prince will grow.
>
> (309–312)

V

The fall of Richard Cromwell and the ensuing political chaos which
culminated in the restoration of the Stuart monarchy thwarted Marvell's
hopes of a providential dynastic protectorate for England. The glorious
conjunction of the times and the man envisioned in *The First Anniversary* faded in the mundane light of the Restoration. While still deeply
involved in state affairs Marvell found less and less to celebrate in Charles
II's England. For the first five years of the new epoch his political activity
was limited to relatively uncontroversial parliamentary tasks and an
embassy to Russia, and he apparently wrote no poetry. The humiliating
miscarriages of the Second Dutch War, however, drove him at last to
break silence with a number of satires directed principally against the
Lord Chancellor Clarendon, whom he rightly or wrongly regarded as a
monster of selfish ambition and the chief architect of England's shame.
In the lampoons and mock-heroic poems of the 1660's Clarendon serves
as the antitype of the self-sacrificing and spiritual figure of Cromwell in
the poems of the preceding decade. If Cromwell had been the Amphion
who would create the just new state and harmonize conflicting private
interests, Clarendon was the pseudo-Amphion whose ostentatious palace,
built with the stones of old St. Paul's and funds diverted from the public
service, symbolizes the wrecking of the social fabric under the guise of
creation. Marvell underscores the manner in which the Lord Chancellor

travesties the achievements of the Lord Protector by adapting the Amphion myth to satirical purposes:

1

When Clarendon had discern'd beforehand
(As the cause eas'ly foretell the effect)
At once three deluges threat'ning our land,
   'Twas the season, he thought, to turn architect.

4

He had read of Rhodopis, a lady of Thrace,
   That was digg'd up so often ere she did marry,
And wish'd that his daughter had had as much grace
   To erect him a pyramid out of her quarry.

5

But then recollecting how harper Amphion
   Made Thebes dance aloft while he fiddled and sung,
He thought (as an instrument he was most free on)
   To build with the jews' trump of his own tongue.

11

The Scotch forts and Dunkirk, but that they were sold,
   He would have demolish'd to raise up his walls,
Nay, even from Tangier sent back for the mold,
   But that he had nearer the stones of St. Paul's.[5]

The series of narrative poems mocking Waller's grandiose *Instructions to a Painter* is a much more ambitious and comprehensive treatment of the crucial issues and events of 1665–67. *The Second Advice to a Painter, The Third Advice to a Painter,* and *The Last Instructions to a Painter* comprise a detailed mock-heroic account of state affairs during the Second Dutch War that is comparable in scope and depth with the heroic poems of the Cromwellian era: *An Horation Ode, The First Anniversary,* and *A Poem upon the Death of O.C.*[6] The bombastic misrepresentation of history in Waller's *Instructions* provided a perfect opportunity for a satirical adaptation of the genre in which the corruption of England's leaders and the grandeur of the form mock each other. In these poems the mood ranges from cynical to tragic and the style from mock-heroic

---

[5] *Clarendon's Housewarming*, 1–4, 13–24. This and all subsequent passages quoted are from *Poems on Affairs of State: Augustan Satirical Verse, 1660–1714*, I (New Haven: Yale University Press, 1963).

[6] Marvell's authorship of *The Second Advice to a Painter* and *The Third Advice to a Painter* is still a matter of dispute. See my articles and those of Ephim G. Fogle in *Evidence for Authorship*, ed. David Erdman and Ephim G. Fogle (Ithaca: Cornell University Press, 1966).

and burlesque to true heroic. Some of the best passages combine several
moods and styles in a rather complex way which leaves one midway between laughter, indignation, and tears;

> Then, Painter, draw cerulean Coventry,
> Keeper, or rather chanc'llor, of the sea;
> Of whom the captain buys his leave to die,
> And barters or for wounds or infamy;
> And more exactly to express his hue,
> Ultramarine must do 't, the richest blue.
> To pay him fees, one's silver trumpet spends;
> The boatswain's whistle on his place depends.
> Pilots in vain repeat the compass o'er,
> Until of him they learn that one point more:
> The constant magnet to the pole does hold,
> Steel to the magnet, Coventry to gold.
>
> *(Second Advice*, 25–36)

Underlying all three poems, however, is the norm of the self-sacrificing
patriot, the Lawson or the Marlborough or the Jordan or the Douglas
who is the counterpart of Fairfax or Charles I or Cromwell. When these
figures appear, usually in elegiac passages, the tone alters radically, an
alteration especially notable in the long tribute to "brave Douglas" in
Last Instructions, which should be quoted at length:

> Like a glad lover the fierce flames he meets
> And tries his first embraces in their sheets.
> His shape exact, which the bright flames enfold,
> Like the sun's statue stands of burnish'd gold.
> Round the transparent fire about him glows,
> As the clear amber on the bee does close,
> And as on angels' heads their glories shine,
> His burning locks adorn his face divine.
> But when in his immortal mind he felt
> His alt'ring form and solder'd limbs to melt,
> Down on the deck he laid himself and di'd,
> With his dear sword reposing by his side
> And on the flaming plank so rests his head
> As one that's warm'd himself and gone to bed.
> His ship burns down and with his relics sinks,
> And the sad stream beneath his ashes drinks.
> Fortunate boy! If either pencil's fame,
> Or if my verse can propagate thy name,

> When Œta and Alcides are forgot,
> Our English youth shall sing the valiant Scot.
>
> (677–696)

This is not only an elegy on Douglas but an elegy on the old-fashioned and heroic virtues which he embodies, as the ornate, archaic Elizabethan symbolism and rhetoric of the passage suggest. Heroes like Douglas cannot comprehend or be comprehended by the alien, cynical world of Charles II's court. In another instance, where Marvell pays tribute to a handful of disinterested patriots in the Commons, the style modulates into a simpler gravity:

> Nor could all these the field have long maintain'd
> But for th' unknown reserve that still remain'd,
> A gross of English gentry, nobly born,
> Of clear estates, and to no faction sworn;
> Dear lovers of their King, and death to meet,
> For country's cause, that glorious think and sweet;
> To speak not forward, but in action brave,
> In giving gen'rous, but in counsel grave;
> Candidly credulous for once, nay twice,
> But sure the Devil cannot cheat them thrice.
>
> (285–294)

A sober heroic past is further evoked here by the echo of Horace's famous ode on endurance and fidelity ("dulce et decorum est pro patria mori").

Such elegiac glimpses of an older and nobler order appear but rarely amid the predominantly sombre indictments of the Restoration world, yet the indictments do not arise from the piqued frustration of a doctrinaire idealist. In his most exalted vision of a political order, *The First Anniversary*, Marvell, like Denham in *Cooper's Hill*, recognized selfishness and ambition as inevitable forces in any society. One mark, for him, of the great creating statesman was the art of engaging the energies of the disaffected in the dynamic *concordia discors* of the state ("Fastening the contignation which they thwart"). But what hope can there be when all the nation's chief statesmen are devoted to no end beyond their own aggrandizement? Or when that "state-Daedalus" Clarendon, the master builder, immures the King in a labyrinth of political intrigue? [7]

The only hope that animates Marvell's painter poems of the 1660's is that the King will reassume his power and responsibility and rid himself of the "swarms of insects" who "devour our land and intercept our sun"

---

[7] *The Second Advice to a Painter*, 353 ff.

(*Second Advice*, 350). Each of the three poems ends, accordingly, with an envoy invoking Charles to reign in the name of traditional and heroic royal sanctions:

> Shake but like Jove thy locks divine and frown—
> Thy sceptre will suffice to guard thy crown.
> Hark to Cassandra's song ere Fate destroy,
> By thy own navy's wooden horse, thy Troy.
>
> (*Third Advice*, 445-448)

The sun image of *Second Advice* provides the point of departure for the concluding adjurations of *Last Instructions* in which Marvell also gives the rationale for his deeply patriotic satire:

> To the King
> So his bold tube man to the sun appli'd
> And spots unknown to the bright star descri'd,
> Show'd they obscure him while too near they prease,
> And seem his courtiers, are but his disease.
> Through optic trunk the planet seem'd to hear,
> And hurls them off e'er since in his career.
>   And you, great Sir, that with him empire share,
> Sun of our world, as he the Charles is there,
> Blame not the Muse that brought those spots to sight,
> Which in your splendor hid, corrode your light:
> Kings in the country oft have gone astray
> Nor of a peasant scorn'd to learn the way.
> Would she the unattended throne reduce,
> Banishing love, trust, ornament, and use,
> Better it were to live in cloister's lock,
> Or in fair fields to rule the easy flock.
> She blames them only who the Court restrain
> And, where all England serves, themselves would reign.
>
> (949-966)

The wistful glance at the appeals of the retired life (sentimentally reduced to the dimensions of the Petit Trianon) here recall the many earlier instances where the impulse to withdraw has tugged against the claims of affairs of state. For Marvell the poet and Marvell the politician alike, the only ultimately valid reason for involvement in public life was the "universal good" exemplified in *communitas*—more specifically exemplified in the classical mixed state under a hereditary ruler responsible to God and responsive to the rights of his subjects. It was the "universal good" which led him from the lyric and contemplative world of Nunappleton to share the brief glories of the Protectorate and the even briefer hopes of the restored Stuart dynasty. As these hopes dimmed with the growing cynicism of Charles' reign, Marvell turned to satire in their defense. The painter poems are didactic injunctions to corrective action which nevertheless embody, though intermittently and sometimes crudely, the lyric, elegiac, and heroic themes of the earlier poems.

When Marvell realized in the 1670's that his King would not or could not profit from gazing into such a mirror for magistrates, he abandoned serious political satire. The Dutch War of 1672–74 revealed to the astute and disillusioned M.P. for Hull that Charles' policies were fundamentally opposed to the political and religious liberties of his subjects. At this stage of affairs Marvell involved himself even more deeply in the life of action by taking a key part in the pro-Dutch pro-Protestant fifth column that helped to reorient Parliamentary policy and forced the King to sue for peace.[8] After the Treaty of Westminster (1674) Marvell made his wry adieux to imaginative literature in lampoons on "the mimic so legally seiz'd of Whitehall" cast in lurching doggerel, fitting tributes to the King who had killed Poetry.

[8] See K. H. D. Haley, *William of Orange and the English Opposition, 1672–4*, Oxford University Press, 1953; also my "Satire and Sedition: the Life and Work of John Ayloffe," *Huntington Library Quarterly*, XXIX (1966), 255–273.

Marvell's "Definition of Love" and Poetry of Self-Exploration

by Harold E. Toliver

To an extent beyond the medieval lyric, Wyatt, Donne, Marvell, and other poets of the sixteenth and seventeenth centuries deal with the private world of the individual consciousness; and as a result the structure and style of the lyric come to depend less upon established rhetorical figures and standard meditative patterns and more upon the movement of the poet's thought and feeling under particular circumstances. This is obvious enough in Donne, but it counts in Marvell, too, especially in "The Definition of Love." The tangled experience of the self demands a sophisticated poetic and leads to the eccentricities and startling analogies which characterize Marvell at his best, which he unquestionably is in "The Definition." Behind his lyric fluency Marvell is often in dialectical combat against himself and against situations which the old rituals and rhetorical patterns no longer handle quite satisfactorily.

In poems whose contention and "trial by what is contrary" are more explicit than in "The Definition," Marvell pursues the "negative way" of chastity and rejection to the discovery of the minimal essentials of the self and only then reaffirms confidence in the soul's strength. In "Clorinda and Damon," for example, Damon rejects nature; he then sings lustily about it—and about Great Pan—in duet with his temptress; the middle stanzas of "The Garden" explore the mind's creative power in the green shade only after red and white passions and social commitments have been sloughed off; and "A Dialogue between the Resolved Soul and Created Pleasure" reveals the Soul to be "that thing divine" only after an extensive combat against Pleasure. The thing which per-

"Marvell's 'Definition of Love' and Poetry of Self-Exploration" by Harold E. Toliver. From *Bucknell Review*, X (May, 1962), 263–74. The essay also appears in *Marvell's Ironic Vision* by Harold E. Toliver (New Haven: Yale University Press, 1965). Copyright © 1964 by Yale University Press. Reprinted by permission of the author, *Bucknell Review*, and The Yale University Press.

haps impresses us most about these poems, especially the latter, is that sustenance and self-knowledge are drawn out of the conflict itself: the Resolved Soul knows the workings of Pleasure from the inside, but through irony and dialectical skill avoids committing itself to pleasure principles. It makes use of Pleasure's own metaphors, but strips them of their veil of sensuous "art," and, hurling them back, turns the exercise into proof of its own "resolved Heart." We would not be entirely correct in calling such displays of ironic fencing the products of a Protestant sensibility, though we can see that Crawshaw and Southwell belong in another category, no less introspective but less self-critical and witty than Marvell's;[1] rather, these displays comprise a structural principle and a style available to all poets in which the Protestant sensibility seemed especially at home, whether equipped with Miltonic resonance and argumentative capacity or with Marvellian irony and inclusive awareness.

In "The Definition of Love" this habit of subjecting everything to dialectical scrutiny is reinforced by a tradition of love-definitions stemming from Plato and characterized more by critical analysis than by unquestioning reverence. Socratic irony lies at the heart of the poem. Rather than speculate about these historical currents directly, however, I should like to explore the poem itself and notice its background only in passing. Like Rochester's satire "Upon Nothing," "The Definition" demonstrates a triumph of reason even while it undermines the capacity of the mind to have its way among recalcitrant circumstances. A disciplined and intense intellectual energy underlies the flat declaration of love's strangeness and elevation and the cryptic account of its begetting, which involves union in one sense but irrevocable disunion in another:

I

My Love is of a birth as rare
As 'tis for object strange and high:

---

[1] Cf. Louis L. Martz's chapter "Self-Analysis in the Works of Southwell" in *The Poetry of Meditation* (New Haven, 1954), pp. 203–210. Southwell's poems "only describe the need for self-analysis: they do not present, with quivering intensity, the very act of analysis, as the poems of Donne and Herbert do. Southwell, we must concede, never shows in his poetry the introspective power that he reveals in his Latin prose remains" (p. 207). Professor Martz cautions that to regard the fierce inward scrutiny of Puritanism as something calling for "more intelligence and more concentration than any of the Catholic techniques" would be a "misapprehension." So far as self-examination is concerned, he continues, "the fact is that both Catholic and Puritan, while accusing each other bitterly of neglecting the inner life, were pursuing the art of self-knowledge by methods equally intense and effective—methods that had, on both hands, developed a subtlety of self-awareness that went far beyond the popular achievements of the Middle Ages" (pp. 121–122).

It was begotten by despair
Upon Impossibility.

II

Magnanimous Despair alone
Could show me so divine a thing,
Where feeble Hope could ne'er have flown
But vainly flapt its Tinsel Wing.

Despite the apparent clarity, the "bright, hard precision" serves only to make vaguely felt the contours of an inexpressible, or at least of an unexpressed, emotion. Is the "rarity" of this kind of love, for example, a reflection upon a world which too seldom sees true love, or a special blessing? The basic paradox, of course, is clear enough: the very impossibility of achieving union has "begotten" love, the sexual metaphor reflecting ironically upon that impossibility. But we might expect despair to be more despairing. As a productive, even "magnanimous," creature (including the Latin sense of *magnus animus* or "great-souled"), Despair is more than a mere adjunct of love—it alone could reveal "so divine a thing" as the "strange and high" object, the implication being that unless there were a refractory "opposition of the stars" this kind of love could not exist. The impossibility is despairing then, but Despair itself is magnanimous, and charitable to boot, because it prevents "feeble Hope" from arousing itself fruitlessly.

Despite the tautness of the dilemma, the discrepancy between what one desires and what the world gives is not treated solemnly. So portentous an event as Despair mating Impossibility and bringing forth Love, expressed in such bare and laconic terms, recoils upon itself. The poem gets into metaphysical speculations rapidly rather than exploiting the conventions of ordinary love poems, but it also reflects upon the exaggerations common to those conventions. "Strange" and "object" at first glance seem merely curious; looking back at them from the end of the stanza, we grow apprehensive. Our momentary assumption that the object might be a Petrarchan mistress of some sort falls short of exhausting the possibilities but is never proved wrong. Whatever the object, lack of a name for it is scarcely an accident and not likely a trick. The word "Impossibility" also has curious effects. Filling nearly a line, it calls attention to itself as a word; it is part of a self-conscious "definition," [2] an

---

[2] Frank Kermode believes that Marvell is "not at all concerned to express '*la substance* . . . *et le naturel fond*' of love considered in abstract," but rather the "rarity, the unusual qualities, of his particular love." This seems to me a curious opinion, whether or not Marvell's poem belongs to the genre of abstract definitions cited by

exercise in choosing the right words which dissolves suddenly into irony and yet refuses to dissolve completely. We cannot tell at this point whether to expect gaiety or seriousness; as we learn, either expectation by itself would be deficient.

The paradox and the irony are sharpened in the second stanza, which continues to reverse normal expectations, that is, expectations from run-of-the-mill poems on love: not only has Despair become great-souled and Hope a poor, tinsel bird, but satiric thrusts are made at love itself, or at least the kind practiced by ordinary hopeless lovers, those who feed their despair and starve their hope. In addition, there is a more than casual penetration into the common human dilemma in which a brief glimpse of Beatrice is nourished into divine aspiration, while love runs out of affairs which, not being star-crossed, are 'fixed' by permanent union. But these satiric and ironic voices are muffled behind masks; the main statement continues to be perfectly straightforward and elusive. The focus upon personal despair and impossibility is broadened to a consideration of "Fate" as the force behind disjunction:

III
And yet I quickly might arrive
Where my extended Soul is fixt,
But Fate does Iron wedges drive,
And alwaies crouds it self betwixt.
IV
For Fate with jealous Eye does see
Two perfect Loves; nor lets them close:
Their union would her ruine be,
And her Tyrannick pow'r depose.

Only now are we approaching something tangible in the way of definition. The union of "two perfect Loves" would be the ruin of Fate because Fate operates in the realm of becoming. When the soul is "fixt" where it is extended, it has in a sense achieved Being, having no desire for the unattainable, no mutability, hence no debt to Fate. But "extended" means 'stretched out *to*,' as well as 'united *with*,' the object and both senses are involved. Fate can afford to be officious against love in its

---

Miss Tuve and Mr. Davison; it would appear to be based on the assumption that essentials and particulars are incompatible. See "Definitions of Love," *RES*, 7 (1956), 183–185; cf. Dennis Davison, "Marvell's 'The Definition of Love,'" *RES*, 6 (1955), 141–146; M. C. Bradbrook and M. G. Lloyd Thomas, *Andrew Marvell* (Cambridge, 1940), p. 45; Cleanth Brooks and Robert Penn Warren, *Understanding Poetry* (New York, 1952), pp. 293–297.

present state; it drives wedges between soul and object or, if the lover decides to send his soul on ahead, between the soul fixed in the object and the poor mortal it has left behind: either way, dissociation and Despair set in.

The personification of Fate completes the Petrarchan cast: despair, hope, and now the jealous lover. (The irony is continued in this and in a jauntiness of rhythm and sound, as in the rhyming of "fixt" and "betwixt" and in the internal half-rhyming of "union" and "ruine.")

V

And therefore her Decrees of Steel
Us as the distant Poles have plac'd,
(Though Loves whole World on us doth wheel)
Not by themselves to be embrac'd.

That the whole world of love whirls on the 'axis' of their separation, suspended between conjunction and opposition, is, of course, hyperbolic. But the cosmic imagery is introduced to define Love and to demonstrate that other lovers are in turn defined by this love, rather than simply to magnify the personal importance of particular lovers or to deflate conventions through exaggeration. "The first in every genus is the cause of the whole genus," Ficino writes ("cause" in the sense of "essence"); "for example, if the sun is the first among the light-bearing things it does not lack any degree of light." [3] And so other lovers may be more successful, but none are more perfect. As divine love sustains and moves the real cosmos, this love, first in its genus, sustains and 'causes' the world of love to 'be.'

As the definition emerges, its reliance upon, but free manipulation of, Platonic doctrine becomes clearer. Like Socrates' attempt to define love in the *Symposium* and Ficino's commentary upon that attempt, it is concerned with the essential nature of love as well as with its local manifestations, and it discovers both of these to be mixed blessings. For love, Socrates discovers, is of something desired but not possessed (200 A), or, in terms of the semi-humorous myth of Aristophanes, is a desire of the incomplete self for union with its other half (189–191). Diotima of Mantineia, "a woman wise in these and many other kinds of knowledge," has demonstrated love to be neither foul nor fair, evil nor good: "He is a

[3] From the *Theologia Platonica*, quoted by Paul Oskar Kristeller, *The Philosophy of Marsilio Ficino,* Virginia Connant, trans. (New York, 1943), p. 147. Marvell's use of Neoplatonist doctrine is discussed extensively by Ruth Wallerstein in *Studies in Seventeenth-century Poetic* (Madison, Wis., 1950), pp. 150 ff.

great spirit (δαίμων), and like all spirits he is intermediate between the divine and the mortal" (202 D).[4] And only he can bridge the chasm dividing mortal from immortal: "For God mingles not with man; but through Love all the intercourse and converse of God with man . . . is carried on" (203 A). Diotima's Love is born of plenty and poverty rather than of despair and impossibility, but, as her account of his activities shows, any set of oppositions would have done equally well: ignorance and knowledge, mortality and immortality, beauty and ugliness. Only the beloved is truly beautiful; love itself can never be (204 A): the object may be high, but love is only a process of desiring it. As long as the soul desires the good and the beautiful it seeks for what it does not, and cannot, have; actual possession of the good and the beautiful yields happiness, which is a static, or rather an ecstatic, condition, not a process as love is, seen in all its activities.[5]

The similarity of love's intermediate condition to that of the soul is noticed by Plotinus in his commentary upon Diotima's myth. The (All) Soul, directing its vision towards Kronos, the "Intellectual Principle," brings forth Eros, an outpouring of itself held firmly to itself, through which it looks towards Kronos. "Love, thus, is ever intent upon that other loveliness, and exists to be the medium between desire and that object of desire" (*Enneads,* III.5.2), as the soul in the Middle Platonists is intermediate between the indivisible and the divisible realm of the body.[6] The soul, like love, upholds the world and makes it possible. It subsists between the One and the many, is fixed firmly in both, and is partly defined by its position between them. And so Ficino and Pico declare that the soul "is all things together. . . . Therefore it may be rightly called the center of nature, the middle term of all things, the series of the world, the face of all, the bond and juncture of the universe" —the same definition Ficino had formerly given of love itself.[7] Because

---

[4] *The Dialogues of Plato,* B. Jowett, trans. (New York, 1937).

[5] Writing poetry, for example, is a passage of non-being into being, a creative 'making' (205 B). In fact, Socrates concludes, "all desire of good" in any human activity "is only the great and subtle power of love."

[6] See Philip Merlan, *From Platonism to Neoplatonism* (The Hague, 1953), p. 11. Plotinus is quoted from the translation of Stephen MacKenna as revised by B. S. Page (London, 1917–1930).

[7] *Marsile Ficin: Commentaire sur le Banquet de Platon,* Raymond Marcel, trans. (Paris, 1956), pp. 200 ff. (VI. 2): love "est un sentiment intermédiaire entre le beau et son contraire. . . . C'est certainement la raison pour laquelle Diotime, pour en venir à elle, appelle l'Amour démon [spirit], car, de même que les démons sont intermédiaires entre les choses célestes et les choses terrestres, ainsi l'Amour est un intermédiaire entre la beauté et la laideur" (p. 201). Cf. Kristeller, *Studies in Renaissance*

man's soul is a vital intermediary link in the great chain, it holds the world in line with God; because love is a conjunction of mind, it holds the lovers' world together.

Mounting a ladder from love of particulars, to love of universals, to love of "beauty absolute, separate, simple, and everlasting" is not, of course, what interests Marvell; rather, he is concerned with the dialectical interplay and tension between the poles Socrates first describes, and concerned with those both as definition and as personal experience, the two being vitally related. Love is formed by the taut attraction of equal forces, between which man is suspended as between two exactly equal magnets. Total conjunction would involve the collapse of the universe into a dimensionless plane:

> VI
> Unless the giddy Heaven fall,
> And Earth some new Convulsion tear;
> And, us to joyn, the World should all
> Be cramp'd into a *Planisphere*.

Like Herbert's spiritual exercises, love gives "temper" by stretching one from here to the impossibly high. The cosmic demonstration is impressive from an imagistic standpoint, but the geometrical imagery has greater finality:

> VII
> As Lines so Loves *oblique* may well
> Themselves in every Angle greet:
> But ours so truly *Paralel*,
> Though infinite can never meet.

The kind of love which allows lovers to meet at the corner gratifies the desire for union, but the implication is that, though loves not parallel have this minor advantage, they also soon part. Geometrical universals have their own irresistible laws, necessarily true at all times, and so love must have. The "bond and juncture" of love has in Fate, then, and in its own nature when perfect, a divisive obstacle which can prevent all union but that of minds. Like the Demiurge of the *Timaeus*, who has no luck persuading matter to be reasonable, the mind cannot conceive of any way to overcome recalcitrant stars, though, by the same token, the

---

Thought and Letters (Rome, 1956), p. 268; Pico, *Oration on the Dignity of Man*, Elizabeth L. Forbes, trans., in *The Renaissance Philosophy of Man*, Ernst Cassirer, ed. (Chicago, 1948), pp. 215 ff.; Plotinus, *Enneads*, IV.8.7. See also Castiglione, *The Book of the Courtier*, Charles S. Singleton, trans. (New York, 1959), p. 356 (IV.70).

marriage of true minds admits no impediments. Thus both conjunction and disjunction: a true and irreconcilable parallelism.

Though in pursuing this line, Marvell would seem to have used Platonic doctrine only as a vantage point from which to explore the psychological and metaphysical implications of love, Ficino's definition may have further relevance worth conjecture. In the commentary on the *Symposium,* Ficino connects the intermediate condition of the soul and of love, which are exactly analogous as we have seen, to the concept of man as the "third essence" or central link in a chain of essences. As the middle essence, man subsumes angelic and godlike, vegetative and animal, attributes, and thus holds the hierarchy together and apart. To fulfill love erotically, after the manner of the Venus of desire (*"Vénus vulgaire"* [8]) is to destroy the stability of the chain by descending egoistically to a lower element, by abandoning the crucial middle state. But Marvell implies further that to achieve a complete union with the high object in the manner of the *"Vénus céleste"* would also be to become something other than man. "Aspiring to be Gods, if Angels fell, / Aspiring to be Angels, men rebel," Pope will write: ". . . 'tis plain / There must be, somewhere, such a rank as Man." Sliding off the sharp edge of the paradox implied by his own definition of man and by the Socratic definition of love, Ficino finds no very formidable barrier to the soul's reaching what it loves (VI.7); but in "The Definition of Love," Hope's angel-like flapping of unangelic tinsel wings is born of a full recognition of the special human dilemma. To achieve complete identity would be to turn the heavens "giddy" and to destroy the very structure of things. Hence only "imperfect" love, fostered by the spirits "intermédiaires entre la beauté et la laideur" (VI.5), is proper to man.[9]

But I think Marvell finds the matter still more complicated than this: the cosmic and geometric imagery read in the context of Ficino's definition of love suggests a second possibility. The Platonic chain of being with its fixed intervals and distances is a metaphor stressing the discreteness of individual essences, each of which has its own station which makes it incapable of being lost in a love-identity. But the presence of the One in the many and of all things in "The Mind, that Ocean where each kind / Does streight its own resemblance find" requires another meta-

---

[8] *Commentaire,* VI.5.
[9] Cf. *Phaedrus* 249 D: when the philosopher sees the beauty of earth, he "is transported with the recollection of the true beauty; he would like to fly away, but he cannot; he is like a bird fluttering and looking upward. . . . And I have shown this of all inspirations to be the noblest and highest . . . and that he who loves the beautiful is called a lover because he partakes of it." Cf. also 252 C.

phor. Like Plotinus, Augustine, Dante, Castiglione, Donne, and others
in the Platonic tradition. Ficino turns to the circle to express this iden-
tity-within-difference.[10] And likewise, while Marvell's imagery of the
poles suggests disjunction, love, of course, is also an "infinite" conjunction. I find the emphasis gradually shifting, in fact, from an incompleted,
continuous yearning to a closed and "defined" experience. For this reason, I am tempted to visualize the parallel lines of stanza seven as circles
rather than straight lines stretching toward infinity. Like other theories
on the parallel lines, this one is relatively minor and not easily proved.
But the paradoxical mystery of love is that, while it demands separation,
while by definition it necessitates otherness and lack of identity, it also
'encompasses,' as one circle may encompass another and remain un-
joined. For love to achieve pure identity, its perfection would have to
be shattered, "cramp'd into a *Planisphere*." Recognizing this more
clearly, Marvell moves toward a wider and wider perspective, away from
Fate as an interfering meddler toward Fate as part of a sustaining order,
inexorable but detached and impersonal, the Fate of the stars.

The ambiguity of love is so carefully sustained up to the last stanza
that it becomes a special mode of discipline and grace in itself. The loved
"object" is both definite and intangible, something beyond grasp and yet
precisely placed; "strange and high" suggests both transcendence and
alienation. This is not, I think a game of words on Marvell's part, but
an attempt to find just the right words to define the experience. The
emotional blur of strangeness predicts the *pathos* of despair, while the
linear distance and clarity of the high object, in a sense, are attributes
of that *logos* which is reflected in the wit throughout the poem; together
they lead inevitably to further de-finition, to an establishing of limits,
boundaries, and essences, both of the object and of the lover's emotional
response to it. And this tension in the early part of the poem, however
difficult it is to pin down, clearly foretells the sharply defined contest
between fate and the painfully human desire to destroy it, to cross lines
and collapse spheres to achieve union, whether with a mistress or with
something more transcendent. The impulsive existence of the self is tempered only if one cleaves to the paradox of conjunction and opposition.
Love cannot survive either the sacrifice or the indulgence of selfhood.

Perhaps with this preparation we can describe more fully Marvell's

[10] See, *e.g.*, Augustine, *De Quantitate Animae* in *Patrologiae Cursus Completus, Series
Latina*, J.-P. Migne, gen. ed., 32: 1035 ff.; Ficino, *Commentaire*, II.3, VI.3; Castiglione,
The Book of the Courtier, p. 342; Dante, *Vita Nuova*, XII and *Paradiso* 27: 106 ff.,
28: 41 ff., 33: 115 ff.

final reaction to the paradox. Full concession has been made to love's undesirable family tree and to the human condition reflected in it. Yet the manifold moods which have had their moments in the poem—the lyric, the flatly declarative, and the satiric—give way to resignation in the last stanza:

VIII

Therefore the Love which us doth bind,
But Fate so enviously debarrs,
Is the Conjunction of the Mind,
And Opposition of the Stars.

The definition here arrives at a clarity and finality it has not had in previous stanzas. It is sealed as a definition and as a logical proposition by "therefore" and by the exactly delineated *genus* (love = conjunction and opposition) and *differentia* (of the mind, of the stars).[11] Though founded upon union and opposition, love is one thing encompassing both. Because minds can be joined, Fate is still envious; but stars are not unworthy enemies of love. It is the recognition of this that brings resignation; but if the definition concludes in a static opposition, it is a dynamic stasis: love becomes understandable through the dialectical process.[12]

Through analysis, satire, and irony, then, Marvell gives romance definitive clarity; without sacrificing awareness of its absurdities, he achieves 'oneness.' Though all irony collapses a multiple awareness into one idea, Marvell's works vertically, reconciling things of different levels; through it, Marvell purges the complexity of attitudes encompassed by the poem and adjusts to the order of things, an order embracing fate, love, minds, and stars. Involved through love and detached through irony, he is resigned through their inter-working.

The 'style' of "The Definition" is second nature to Marvell; he will sometimes use it even without a comparable subject matter, sometimes in humorous contradiction to his serious poems. "Ametas and Thestylis

---

[11] In the *Defense of John Howe*, 1678, Marvell writes that a definition "always consists, as being a dialectical animal, of a body, which is the genus, and a difference, which is the soul of the thing defined": in *The Complete Works in Verse and Prose*, Rev. Alexander B. Grosart, ed. (London, 1875), IV, 183; cf. Milton's *Art of Logic*: "For genus and form (which are as it were the body and mind of the definition) constitute the whole essence of the thing," in *The Works*, Frank Allen Patterson, gen. ed. (Columbia University Press, 1935), XI, 263.

[12] Cf. John Wheatcroft, "Andrew Marvell and the Winged Chariot," *Bucknell Review*, 6 (1956), 42–43; Lawrence W. Hyman, "Ideas in Marvell's Lyric Poetry," *History of Ideas News Letter*, II (1956), 30; F. W. Bradbrook, "The Poetry of Andrew Marvell," in *From Donne to Marvell*, Boris Ford, ed., p. 198; Bradbrook and Thomas, p. 46.

making Hay-Ropes," for example, progresses through a dialectical battle
of wits solely for the sake of battle. Ametas believes that opposition must
be entirely dissolved because "Love unpaid does soon disband: / Love
binds Love as Hay binds Hay." But Thestylis realizes that parallel lines
never meet:

> Think'st Thou that this Rope would twine
> If we both should turn one way?
> Where both parties so combine,
> Neither Love will twist nor Hay.

Which means that she will not agree, but neither will she disagree.
Love must be "taken," not weakly consented to. And so they split the
last stanza between them, combining and opposing simultaneously, agree-
ing and disagreeing, and ending, one supposes, kissing in twisted opposition *in* "the Hay." They can do so because their dialectic is a game and
their love does not demand quite all their talents.

Marvell never totally forgets that such dialectical combat is a sport,
an *agon* conducted according to definite rules. A mind as finely tempered
as his had to work in a gentlemanly way or become tortured, perhaps
paralyzed, as Donne's sometimes is. Ordinarily, of course, his dialectic
and exploratory irony have a more serious duty to perform than in
"Ametas and Thestylis." As in *The Rehearsal Transprosed* in which the
court wit defends the plain non-conformist, they enable him to tread a
narrow line between levity and seriousness and to hold together a head
and heart which, as F. W. Bateson writes, tend to want different things.[13]
Perhaps more important, they allow the Puritan-Platonist to explore his
relation to nature without becoming too deeply entangled in it. This can
work two ways, either to put off Created Pleasure or to justify a limited
enjoyment of it; but in either case, the complex, self-reflective process
requires these structural and stylistic tools for full development.

[13] *English Poetry, A Critical Introduction* (London, 1950), pp. 99 ff.

Marvell and Horace

by John S. Coolidge

Marvell labels his poem on Cromwell's return out of Ireland as an imitation of Horace. The label has drawn remarkably little attention. In an essay that has become something of a classic, Cleanth Brooks set up the question, "What is the speaker's attitude toward Cromwell?" as a challenge to critical method, and the debate which followed between Brooks and Douglas Bush established the reputation of the poem as a test of critical equipment.[1] Although critics and scholars have approached it one after another with one or another kind of key,[2] yet the one key that Marvell himself may fairly be said to have suggested has largely escaped attention, in the manner of the purloined letter, by being conspicuous.[3]

"Marvell and Horace" by John S. Coolidge. From *Modern Philology*, LXIII (November, 1965), 111–20. Copyright © 1965 by The University of Chicago. Reprinted by permission of The University of Chicago.

[1] Brooks's "Literary Criticism," *English Institute Essays 1946* (New York, 1947), pp. 127–58, has been reprinted in *Seventeenth Century English Poetry*, ed. William R. Keast (Oxford, Galaxy, 1962) and in *Explication as Criticism: Selected Papers from the English Institute* (New York, 1963). The controversy between Brooks and Bush is in *Sewanee Review*, LV (1947), LX (1952), and LXI (1953).

[2] In a symposium on how to read a poem, *Interpretations*, ed. John Wain (London, 1955), L. D. Lerner uses the poem to demonstrate close reading in the manner of William Empson. J. A. Mazzeo argues that Machiavelli supplies the proper prolegomena to the "Horatian Ode" (see n. 29 below). John M. Wallace, in "Marvell's Horatian Ode," *PMLA* LXXVII (March, 1962), 33–45, fits the poem into a formal scheme of oratorical composition prescribed by Cicero. This is a somewhat inconclusive exercise in itself, but Wallace wishes to show by it that the poem is not so much a working out of conflicting thoughts and affections as it is a craftily designed instrument of political persuasion: "Thus each section of the ode finds Marvell inventing subject-matter which will be suitable for its position in the scheme, and disposing it to convey his political meaning, often with ironic overtones." Wallace's method for discovering that predetermined political meaning is the study of the intellectual milieu, although his arbitrary manner of finding ideas in pamphlets and forcing them onto the poem does not represent the method at its best.

[3] The only extended discussion in print of what is Horatian about the "Horatian Ode" is that of R. H. Syfret in "Marvell's 'Horatian Ode,'" *RES*, N.S., XII (May, 1961), 160–72. Syfret conjectures that "If we could know just what Marvell included

If we approach Marvell's poem as an imitation of Horace we are offered the prospect of a double benefit. By placing the complexities of
the poem in the perspective indicated by the title, we may grasp the elusive consistency of Marvell's attitudes; at the same time, this approach
may alert us to an element of interest in Horace's work akin to that
which twentieth-century critics have found in Marvell's. Horace had
fought at Philippi against the "forced Pow'r." He came to look back on
that time with a certain self-deprecating humor (Odes, II, vii) that was
not without a pang of regret ("cum fracta virtus" [4]), and he never dis-
claimed the cause that was lost in that defeat. His latter-day readers have
too often been content, as Louis MacKay has complained, to see in Horace simply "a poet of a type with which in later Western civilization they
had been only too familiar—the venal court poet." [5] But Marvell, under
the pressure of events in mid-seventeenth-century England, seems to have
found in Horace the classical model of a poet maintaining a difficult
kind of integrity in a time of great change. Marvell's "Horatian Ode"
may be seen to combine the essential elements of a thoughtful *apologia*
derived from the Roman poet.

First, Marvell's general manner of using his Roman model needs to be
understood, and in particular to be distinguished from another possible
method which he scorns. In his verses on "Tom May's Death" he takes
the author of *The History of the Parliament of England* to task for comparing figures in contemporary England with figures from Roman history:

---

in his adjective 'Horatian,' perhaps there would be no unsolved problems about the
meaning of his Ode." She notices that commentary on Horace sometimes registers
an uncertainty about the poet's attitudes which is suggestively similar to that shown
in recent criticism of Marvell's poem, and she briefly suggests some points of comparison between the two poets which are supported by the present discussion. In an
unpublished doctoral thesis, "A Study of Marvell's Horatian Ode" (Syracuse University,
1956), William Raymond Orwen lists various things about the "Horatian Ode" and
about Marvell's situation when he wrote it that bear comparison with Horace's Odes
or with Horace's circumstances (pp. 16–24). However, he considers Marvell's imitation
of Horace to be a merely formal matter. John M. Wallace, in the article cited above,
suggests that in Marvell's poem "the mystery of the Horatian tone is in part derived
from the effacing of personality." By this he means the setting aside of personal ideas
of right and wrong in order to celebrate an accomplished fact; but the present discussion will attempt to show that the Horatian attitude adopted by Marvell is
valuable precisely for avoiding the pious acclamation of successful power simply as
such.

[4] Quotations from Horace are taken from the Oxford Classical Text.
[5] "Horace, Augustus, and *Ode*, I, 2." *American Journal of Philology*, LXXXIII
(April, 1962), 170.

> Go seek the novice Statesmen, and obtrude
> On them some Romane cast similitude,
> Tell them of Liberty, the Stories fine,
> Until you all grow Consuls in your wine.
> O thou *Dictator* of the glass bestow
> On him the *Cato,* this the *Cicero* . . .
> Foul Architect that hadst not Eye to see
> How ill the measures of these States agree.
> And who by *Romes* example *England* lay,
> Those but to *Lucan* do continue *May.*[6]

Taken simply, these lines might well seem to condemn not only May's "Romane cast" similitudes but Marvell's own in the "Horatian Ode" as well. However, Marvell's historical allusions work differently from May's, and the apparent inconsistency between his practice in the one poem and his precept in the other disappears if we suppose his condemnation to apply not to historical similitudes generally but to May's use of them. For example, when May compares the Earl of Strafford with Julius Caesar's agent, Curio, his explicit grounds of comparison are merely that both were able and potentially good men whose evil careers testify to the corrupting atmosphere of their times.[7] He quotes Lucan's character of Curio—ostensibly in order to make this point. But if the reader is thereby caused to think of a further comparison between Strafford's master, Charles, and Curio's master, the villainous Caesar portrayed by Lucan, that implication is clearly not accidental. The secondary implications of May's comparisons always "check out." Whatever the immediate grounds for the similitude, there always turns out to be a further implication to the effect that Charles I is like one or another tyrannical Roman emperor. The motto on May's title page is "Tempora mutantur, Mutantur Homines. Veritas eadem manet," and he clearly understands that to mean that circumstances and men come and go but the characteristics of tyranny recur consistently. Thus, like Dryden in *Absalom and Achitophel,* he looks for extended correspondences between events and persons of one historical era and those of another in which the same basic phenomenon occurs. Marvell's mind works differently. Every similitude, he remarks, must have "though not all, yet some likeness." [8] Apparently

---

[6] Quotations from Marvell's poetry are taken from *The Poems and Letters of Andrew Marvell,* ed. H. M. Margoliouth (Oxford, 1927).

[7] *The History of the Parliament of England* . . . (London, 1647), Book I, pp. 20–21.

[8] *The Rehearsal Transpros'd* in the *Complete Works in Verse and Prose of Andrew Marvell,* ed. Alexander B. Grosart (Fuller Worthies' Library, 1873), III, 107.

he belonged to that school of thought which held it to be positively desirable for a simile to call to mind points of dissimilarity as well as points of likeness between the items compared.[9] Each of his suggested comparisons between English and Roman history, if pursued beyond the immediately obvious grounds of comparison, leads to a reminder of "How ill the measures of these States agree."

Thus the opening lines of the poem seem to echo the lines in which Lucan describes the reactions of the youth of Ariminum, on the Italian side of the Rubicon, when they learned that Caesar was upon them.[10] Were we to extrapolate from this implicit comparison, we would gather that Cromwell is like Lucan's Caesar, returning from victory abroad to make himself tyrant at home. At the same time, however, this "Horatian Ode" on Cromwell's return after taming the wild Irish is likely to suggest comparison with Horace's Ode celebrating the victory of Actium,

---

[9] Jean de Sponde's analysis of the first epic simile in the *Iliad* (II, 87–93) concludes: "Neque enim fieri potest, ut undiquaque similia sint res, cui comparatur, & res quae comparationis vicem obtinet: hoc est, quod vulgò dicitur, Similitudinem uno pede semper claudicare. Itaque diligenter observanda est ilius mens, qui comparationes usurpat. Nam si ea inter se omnino responderent, falleret illud axioma, Nullum simile est idem" (*Homeri quae extant omnia . . .* [Bâle, 1583], p. 31.) George Chapman picks up the phrase, "quod vulgò dicitur," in a note which he makes into a kind of manifesto of the opposition: ". . . But much the rather I insist on the former Simile, for the word ἰλαδὸν, *catervatim* or *confertim,* which is noted by Spondanus to contain all the ἀπόδοσις, reddition or application of the comparison, and is nothing so. For though it be all the reddition Homer expresseth, yet he intends two speciall parts in the application more, which he leaves to his judicial reader's understanding, as he doth in all his other Similes, since a man may pervially (or as he passeth) discerne all that is to be understood. And here, besides the throngs of souldiers exprest in the swarmes of Bees, he intimates the infinite number in those throngs or companies issuing from the fleete so ceaslesly that there appeared almost no end of their issue; and, thirdly, the everie where dispersing themselves. But Spondanus would excuse Homer for expressing no more of his application, with affirming it impossible that the thing compared and the comparison should answer in all parts, and therefore alledges the vulgar understanding of a Simile, which is as grosse as it is vulgar, that a similitude must *uno pede semper claudicare*—his reason for it as absurd as the rest, which is this: *si ea inter se omnino responderent, falleret illud axioma, nullum simile est idem,* as though the generall application of the compared and the comparison would make them anything more the same or all or one, more than the swarmes of Bees and the throng of souldiers are all one or the same, for answering most aptly. But that a Simile must needs halt of one foote still showeth how lame vulgar tradition is, especially in her censure of Poesie. For who at first sight will not conceive it absurd to make a Simile, which serves to the illustration and ornament of a Poem, lame of a foote and idle?" (*Chapman's Homer,* ed. Allardyce Nicoll [New York, 1956], I, 69–70).

[10] Both Syfret and Wallace make this observation. Syfret lists other parallels with Lucan, and Orwen discusses at length possible recollections of Lucan in Marvell's poem (pp. 155–80).

where Caesar Octavian taught "true fears" to a wild rout of Egyptians (I, xxxvii). These two comparisons seem to carry contradictory implications concerning Cromwell's role in English history, and either of them is difficult to reconcile with the reference a few lines later on to Charles I as Caesar.[11] May's historical similitudes invite extrapolation; Marvell's deliberately frustrate it. Secondary implications do function in Marvell's poem, but not as a means of indirect persuasion. They are to be held in suspended conflict in the reader's mind as he attends to the points of comparison which are being indicated primarily.

The primary similarity between the situation described in the opening lines of Marvell's poem and that described in the lines he echoes from Lucan is that a time of war is succeeding a time of peace. That similarity is worth dwelling on for its own sake, because the difference between a time of war and a time of peace is something on which Lucan is a notable authority. The determining fact about the wretched world that Lucan portrays is that the laws have been silenced by war ("leges bello siluere coactae" [12]), leaving the poem to be dominated by Fortune, particularly, of course, by the notorious Fortune of Julius Caesar. It is the condition, almost the definition, of war in Lucan that Fortune replaces Justice. Caesar figures in the poem as the agent and beneficiary of that force in the world which is incompatible with law and to which the world is given over in time of war. He is "the Wars and Fortunes Son." Lucan's response to these conditions is a shrill, recurrent cry of pain. He allows the common people, at least, to cry to the gods "with vulgar spight"— "plurimaque in saevos populi convicia divos" (VII, 725)—and the poet himself is hardly less abandoned to frustrated rage at the "crime of the gods" (VIII, 799–800). At the death of Pompey, however, the great man's determination to maintain the dignity of his fame—a sense of personal decorum, in fact, like that which Marvell's "Royal Actor" observes—

[11] Wallace attempts to turn this difficulty to account. On the basis of the echo from Lucan he asserts that the opening lines of the poem are a call to all good men to take up arms against Cromwell-Caesar. He then argues: "Cromwell once, having taken his corslet from the wall at the start of the civil war, had succeeded (unlike the youths in Araminum [sic]) in successfully opposing a Caesar's tyranny; and in so blasting Caesar through his imperishable laurels, he had became [sic] Caesar and acquired his honors. It was inevitable that having once defeated a tyrant single-handed, Cromwell should now himself be able to tyrannize, but his achievement of the seemingly impossible proclaims the providential nature of his power . . . The moment has arrived for a youth to oppose Cromwell, as Cromwell had once opposed Charles. In 1650 the idea was of course unthinkable, and, in rejecting it outright, readers are forced to concede that Cromwell's eminence is secure, and must therefore be accepted" (p. 35).

[12] I, 277. Quotations from Lucan are taken from the Housman edition (Cambridge, Mass., 1926).

tempers the tone of the poem, and produces a deeply moving description which, as has long been recognized, seems to have inspired Marvell's passage on the death of Charles.[13]

Horace, too, has the Roman awareness of the awful power of Fortune, but his attitude toward it is less like Lucan's heroic desperation than it is like the fear of God. He associates Fortune with another vaguely mythologized abstraction, Necessity (Odes I, xxxv). This figure "goes before" Fortune, as in a procession, holding in her brazen hand significant and ambiguous emblems: she carries nails "to be fixed to the beam" ("clavos trebalis"), wedges, a "stern" or "harsh" hook ("severus uncus"), and molten lead. These are all identified with the building trades, so that Necessity appears as the original architect. However, the "severe" hook is also the instrument by which condemned criminals are dragged along; and Necessity fastens those nails to the high rafters of the houses of those to whom she brings ruin and death.[14] She is well named "grim Necessity," [15] then, and appropriately associated with the frightening power of Fortune; yet she is also the great builder.

This Horatian figure of Necessity seems to have made a deep impression on Marvell's mind. The "iron wedges" which Fate drives between the lives of the lovers in "The Definition of Love" seem to be the same

---

[13] See Margoliouth's notes.

[14] Odes III, xxiv, 5-8. In the note on Odes I, xxv, 7-8, in his Oxford edition of 1874, E. C. Wickham remarks: "The old mistake of the Comm[entator] Cruq[uianus], who took all the expressions of instruments of torture, has found no recent defender except Ritter [1856]." More recent annotated editions ignore the "old mistake" altogether and so avoid the complex idea of Necessity that might have formed in the mind of a thoughtful student reading such a comment as that of Lambinus: ". . . cuneis insertis non solum res perrumpuntur, & finduntur, ut lib. Georg. *Nam primi cuneis scindebant fissile lignum:* & Tuscul. 2. *Hos ille cuneos fabrica crudeli inserens, Perrupit artus:* sed etiam continentur, ut intelligere licet ex Vitruvii lib. 10. cap. 10. . . . unco utebantur antiqui ad cruciatus, et maleficorum poenas. M. Tull. Philip. 1. *uncus impactus est fugitivo illi.* Suet. in Tiber. *Putant Neronem ad voluntariam mortem coactum, cum ei carnifex, quasi ex Senatus auctoritate missus, laqueos, & uncos ostentaret.* Iterum M. Tull. in orat. pro C. Rabirio. *nos à verberibus, ab unco, à crucis denique terrore neque res gestae, neque acta aetas, neque nostri honores vindicabunt?* utebantur olim uncis etiam ad adstringendum & continendum plumbo liquido addito, itémque nos hodie utimur. sunt enim tales unci, hami quidam ferrei, quibus saxa & caementa firmissime inter se devinciuntur & continentur, praesertim plumbo adiecto. . . ." (*Dionysii Lambini . . . in Q. Horatium Flaccum . . . Editio postrema* [Frankfurt 1577], p. 83). That the liquid lead had painful associations as well as architectural ones is stated by a scholion: "Nam et resoluto plumbo rei puniri consueverant" (*Scholia in Horatium,* λφψ, *Codicum Parisinorum Latinorum 7972, 7974, 7971,* ed. H. J. Botschuyver [Amsterdam, 1935], p. 72).

[15] "I am sworn brother, sweet, / To grim Necessity, and he and I / Will keep a league till death" (*Richard II,* V, i, 20-22).

which Horace's "saeva Necessitas" carries in her brazen hand,[16] and some twenty years after the composition of these poems the *clavi trabales* turn up again in a discussion of Necessity in Marvell's *Rehearsal Transpros'd*. Marvell's opponent in that Restoration controversy, Samuel Parker, has a great deal to say about the powers which it is absolutely necessary for the king to have. Marvell replies with his greatest passage of prose, an extended conceit on the "family" of the Necessities:

> For though necessity be a very honourable name of good extraction and alliance, yet there are several families of the Necessities, . . . and though some of 'm are patrician, yet other are plebian. There is, first of all, a necessity that some have talk'd of . . . that was pre-eternal to all things, and exercised dominion not only over all humane things, but over Jupiter himself and the rest of the Deities, and drove the great iron nail thorough the axletree of Nature.

Since Parker has been dogmatically laying down the law for kings and for nations, Marvell takes it that he considers himself to be that great primal Necessity in person:

> For what can you be less or other, who have given an absolute and unlimited power to princes . . . who have obliged Providence to dispense power to the magistrate according to your good pleasure, and herein have claim'd to yourself that universal dictatorship of necessity over God and man, though it were but *clavi figendi causa,* and to strike thorow all government, humane and divine, with the great hammer? [17]

Marvell constantly accuses Parker of taking delight in persecuting people; and so his phrase, "though it were but *clavi figendi causa,*" shows that he understands those emblems of Necessity in Horace to be instruments of cruelty. But that magnificent Marvellian phrase, "and drove the great iron nail thorough the axletree of Nature," reminds us again that this cruel companion of Fortune is the world's great builder. Marvell's point against Parker, of course, is that it is absurdly presumptuous for a human mind to claim such an identity between its own ideal constructs and Necessity. He is not denying the king's rights. Indeed, this passage on Necessity is the preamble to his explicit statement of belief in those rights. Nevertheless, like Horace, writing of Fortune and Necessity on the eve of a military adventure by Augustus, he is reminding the ruler that those forces which threaten his man-made order are themselves part

---

[16] This is Grosart's observation. Margoliouth does not mention it.
[17] Grosart, III, 365–66.

of the great, incomprehensible order of the world. It was, Marvell says
in another place, *"Necessity,"* that first made *Kings."* [18]

The opening lines of the "Horatian Ode," then, call to mind a great
deal of ancient political experience. The reader who looks in them for
clues in a game of historical charades will be baffled, because Marvell is
putting his reading to much better use. Recollections of Horace and of
Lucan serve to evoke Roman responses to the ambiguities of power and
right.

Those ambiguities center on the name of Caesar, which stands once
in Marvell's poem for the legitimate ruler, as it does in Horace's Odes,
and once for the irresistible scourge of nations, as it does in Lucan. Even
May shows this curious double reference of the name of Caesar, although he does not make knowing use of it as Marvell does. As has been
seen, May's own view is simple: it is Charles I who is "Caesar," and he is
to be seen as Lucan sees Julius Caesar, the usurper. Yet at one point May
quotes without comment a Latin epigram that was circulated among
royalists at Oxford, and in which "Caesar" stands quite naturally for
Charles as the legitimate ruler.[19] This is the legitimate "Caesar" in Marvell's poem whose head the "three-fork'd Lightning"—Cromwell—"did
through his Laurels blast"; "restless Cromwell," on the other hand, is
clearly likened to Julius Caesar, the usurper, as Lucan portrays him:
"nescia virtus stare loco" (I, 144–45). However, when Marvell says that
Cromwell "has his Sword and Spoyls ungirt, / To lay them at the Pub-
lick's skirt," it is the memory of Augustus Caesar that he is invoking,
and Cromwell is again like the beneficent "Caesar" of Horace.

· That occasion when Octavius Caesar resigned his "Sword and
Spoyls" (his various offices and powers) to the Senate of Rome signalized
the transformation of the·one kind of "Caesar" into the other; for the
Senate, not surprisingly, handed right back to him his former powers,
or the equivalent of them, now decently legitimized and with the addition of a new name, Caesar Augustus.[20] Young Octavian had risen to

---

[18] "The Character of Holland," l. 37.

[19] ". . . Nihil relictum est / Britanicum domare Caesarem / Ni νεομαινομένου preces
Gregis" (Book III, pp. 90–91).

[20] "In his sixth and seventh consulates C. Julius Caesar Octavianus went through
a painless and superficial transformation. The process was completed in a session of
the Senate on January 13th, 27 B.C., when he solemnly announced that he resigned
all powers and all provinces to the free disposal of the Senate and People of Rome.
Acclamation was drowned in protest. The senators adjured him not to abandon the
Commonwealth which he had preserved. Yielding with reluctance to these manifestations of loyalty and patriotism, the master of the whole world consented to assume a
special commission for a period of ten years. . . .

"Three days later the Senate met, eager and impatient to render thanks, to confer power as Julius Caesar's heir and avenger. He was wholly the creature of the Caesarian mystique, of those very forces, that is, which were irresistibly battering down the ancient structure of the Roman Republic. His achievement was, first of all, to draw those forces to himself. Octavius became Caesar. His second achievement, however, was to make himself the embodiment of all the ancient ideals of Rome, of that very structure of values which the relentless tide of Caesarian power was sweeping away. Octavius Caesar became Caesar Augustus; "the Wars and Fortunes Son" became the restorer of temples. Thus the name of "Caesar" came to epitomize both the ancient rights and the "forced Pow'r" that was by its origin destructive of them. It is the most ambivalent name in history, and its ambivalence corresponds to that which Marvell found in the Horatian figure of grim Necessity.

"Veritas eadem manet." The specific institutions, personalities, and political histories of England and of Rome are simply not comparable, but the enigmatic relationship between legitimacy and force is of all time. The idea of that relationship is a unique and elusive concept, an uneasy suspension of the mind between two conflicting realizations. From the beginning of the poem the reader's mind is held in suspense between responses prompted by recollection of Lucan and those prompted by recollection of Horace's Actium Ode. Similarly, the very name of Caesar functions as a "concrete universal," giving rise not so much to a clear idea as to a unique process in the mind. Marvell turns to Roman history, not to manipulate allusions to it as part of a tendentious rhetorical strategy, but to evoke the complex Roman experience of the ambiguities of power and right. The vocabulary of Roman history, as Marvell uses it, enables him to achieve a difficult political *prise de conscience*.

---

honours upon the saviour of the State. . . . He had founded—or was soon to found —the Roman State anew. He might therefore have been called Romulus. . . . But Romulus was a king, hated name, stained with a brother's blood and himself killed by Roman senators, so one legend ran, before his assumption into Heaven. That was too much like Caesar the Dictator. . . . A veteran politician, the consular L. Munatius Plancus, proposed the decree that conferred on Caesar's heir the appellation of Augustus" (Ronald Syme, *The Roman Revolution* [Oxford, 1939], pp. 313–14). This is clearly the event referred to in a passage which Wallace quotes from a seventeenth-century tract, supposing it to refer to Julius Caesar: "*Sir*, I have heard that one of the bravest Generals that ever commanded the *Roman* Legions, after he had victoriously asserted the peoples liberty, and put an end to a Civil war, offered up his power and Commission to the then assembled Senate by whom he was re-invested and gratified with more triumphant dignities. Here was a fair and honorable correspondence. And this procured a present and lasting peace to that Empire, and rendered it flourishing and formidable" (Anthony Norwood, *A Clear Optick* . . . [1654], Wallace, p. 42).

Beyond that, Marvell's Roman model helps him to define a *prise de position*. The concept of Necessity complicates the requirements of loyalty and integrity; it does not annul them. On the contrary, it is precisely in times when laws have been silenced by war and justice pleads the ancient rights in vain that the poet's duty to assert them becomes most clear:

> When the Sword glitters ore the Judges head,
> And fear has Coward Churchmen silenced,
> Then is the Poets time, 'tis then he drawes,
> And single fights forsaken Vertues cause.
> He, when the wheel of Empire, whirleth back,
> And though the World's disjointed Axel crack,
> Sings still of ancient Rights and better Times,
> Seeks wretched good, arraigns successful Crimes.

These lines from the poem on "Tom May's Death" have been read as expressing a simple revulsion from the position Marvell had taken a few months earlier in the "Horatian Ode." [21] But if that position was as carefully tempered and acutely conscious as it has been shown to be in other respects, it is hard to believe that it was so ill-considered as to be subject to rather hasty reversal with respect to its central concern, the poet's political stance. As in the matter of "Romane cast" similitudes, an apparent contradiction between the two poems should make us look all the more carefully for an underlying consistency between them. In order to grasp Marvell's political consistency, the concept of Necessity must be understood together with a set of conceptions concerning constancy and change which are central to Horace's books of Odes and which can be seen to be reflected in Marvell's imitation of Horace.

Horace's Odes begin, after the dedicatory piece to Maecenas, with his famous declaration of peace—"Iam satis": enough of war—while Marvell's poem begins by announcing that a long period of peace has ended and it is time to take up the attitudes of war. Although the immediate circumstances to which the two poets refer are opposite in this respect, both poets express the same conception of a kind of decorum of war and peace. "Nunc est bibendum," begins the Actium Ode (I, xxxvii)—"Now it is time to drink." And Horace then accomplishes his "flashback" to the time of war just ending by saying that before this it was "nefas" (forbidden, unthinkable) to break out the wine from the ancestral cellars.

---

[21] For an account based on this kind of explanation see Lawrence W. Hyman, "Politics and Poetry in Andrew Marvell," *PMLA*, LXXIII (December, 1958), 475–79.

Wine is one of the things that belong to peace (Horace describes the mind of Cleopatra while at war as being drunk with Mareotic wine, which makes the point negatively); other things that belong to peace in Horace's world are love songs and the cool shade of trees. Marvell's phrase, "Nor in the Shadows sing / His Numbers languishing," evokes those shades or shadows—those *umbrae*—in which the Horatian figure of the poet, like the Vergilian shepherd, sings his unambitious songs, celebrates his *otia sacra*.[22] Both these *umbrae* and this *otium*—this leisure, or, from another point of view, this sloth—are heavily charged ideas, and they are charged ambivalently. They are, after all, the end in view of all striving; they are the final good without which all the strenuous Roman virtues would be pointless and even barbarous. On the other hand, they tend to sap the spirit of the "forward Youth" and produce the languishing decadent.[23] In time of war one attitude is appropriate toward wine, shades, and *otium*. It is the attitude which Marvell's "languishing" suggests. In peace another attitude is called for.

The very arrangement of Horace's books of Odes suggests that these two opposing attitudes toward *otium* are interdependent. Heroic odes and odes of statecraft stand in places of honor, supporting, as it were, and at the same time complemented by, amatory odes and odes celebrating wine and pleasure. The two attitudes and the things associated with them contrast and correspond to each other in Horace's Odes as they do in Homer's description of the shield of Achilles. Each attitude has its place in the complete life of humanity, and neither is rightly understood without recalling the other. This idea of the interrelation of successive motives in life can be seen as Horace's *apologia pro vita sua* and, in fact, the unifying principle of the books of Odes. The personality of the poet as it is created in the Odes is itself bound up with this theme. If he dis-

[22] This is the title of Mildmay Fane's volume of poetry published in 1648. Marvell's "Hortus" is a celebration of "Otia sana" (1. 57). On *otium* in the context of Roman political ideas see Ch. Wirszubski, *Libertas as a Political Idea at Rome During the Late Republic and Early Principate* (Cambridge, 1950), pp. 92–94. Needless to say, the Epicurean Lucretius speaks favorably of "otia dia," which he associates with singing and dancing in the woods much as Horace does (V, 1384–87). For other notable examples of the favorable attitude, see the whole of Horace's Ode II, xvi (the commentary of Eduard Fraenkel on this poem, *Horace* [Oxford, 1957], pp. 211–14, is helpful) and the famous line in Vergil's first Eclogue, "O Meliboee, deus nobis haec otia fecit."

[23] Recall the lines toward the end of Vergil's last Eclogue: "surgamus: solet esse gravis cantantibus umbra, / iuniperi gravis umbra; nocent et frugibus umbrae." Compare this with Horace, Ode II, xv, 9–12 (although the word itself is not used here): "tum spissa ramis laurea fervidos / excludet ictus. Non ita Romuli / praescriptum et intonsi Catonis / auspiciis veterumque norma."

claims for himself both the impetuous ardor of passionate love and the strength to deal militantly with the great matters of the world, it is with an implicit recognition that such things are the highest glories of life; but their time is past for him, just as the time of war and the high-hearted struggle for liberty is past for Rome; and now it is time to realize to the full the *otium cum dignitate* of the succeeding age. The decorum of war and peace corresponds, in Horace's own life, to the decorum of the successive ages of man:

> aetatis cuiusque notandi sunt tibi mores,
> mobilibusque decor naturis dandus et annis
> [*Ars Poetica,* 156–57].

The poet is not what he was "consule Planco," in the time of Philippi.[24] When Marvell announces that it is time for the "forward Youth" of mid-seventeenth-century England to relinquish peace for war, he is thinking in the same terms as the middle-aged (the professionally middle-aged!) Roman poet who announces, after roughly a century of civil war, that it is time for peace.

The Horatian art of time-serving, to give it a name acknowledging its moral dangers, calls for a kind of mental poise among the changing possibilities and impossibilities of life. What is no longer possible is not renounced but relinquished. Marvell evokes this sense of the relations of times at the outset of his "Horatian Ode," and together with the sense of the nature of war and of Necessity which he also evokes from his Roman models, it indicates his attitude toward Cromwell and the martyred Charles. Horace does not deny the cause for which he fought under Brutus when he makes his peace with the later age and celebrates its different gifts, chiefly the gift of peace itself. And Marvell still affirms the ancient rights of the Royal cause when he turns to face the Necessity of a time of civil war.

Like Lucan, he sees the time of civil war as one in which the cry for justice goes up in vain; but like Horace, he sees that terrible disorder as evincing a larger order in which force and right, war and peace still have their changeless, fitting relationships. The failure of a good and just king, such as the poem assumes Charles to have been, shows a disjunction between these aspects of life from one side; the success of a mere usurper would show such a disjunction from the other; but Cromwell

---

[24] Odes III, xiv. Commenting on this phrase Steele Commager observes: "Horace views his political shift in terms of a comprehensive decorum of age and natural change" (*The Odes of Horace: A Critical Study* [New Haven, Conn., 1962], p. 227).

appears in Marvell's poem as a man in whose mind the things of war and the things of peace are properly related. It is this quality in the man, Cromwell, that makes it possible to hope that in rallying to him the poet can remain true to the tradition of just and civilized humanity. There is in his manner of approaching his Caesar a respect of the most sincere and cogent sort, similar to that which should be paid to a thunderbolt; yet there is also a more human appreciation, combined curiously with a distinct note of calculated policy:

> So when the Falcon high
> Falls heavy from the Sky,
> She, having kill'd, no more does search,
> But on the next green Bow to pearch;
> Where, when he first does lure,
> The Falckner has her sure.

The last lines of this arresting simile read almost as an aside. With proper handling this extraordinary bird of prey can be, shall we say, hoodwinked. If this quiet hint does not seem quite so scornful as that, it is because it recognizes that the element in the man's nature which gives promise of such amenability is a modest desire for civilized peace. Marvell's "green Bow" evokes again some of the same ideas as the *umbrae* and *otia* of the Augustan poets:

> Hic tamen hanc mecum poteras requiescere noctem
> fronde super viridi . . .
>
> > [Vergil, Eclogue I, 79–80].

He sees in Cromwell, then, not only the unaccountable power that emerges in a time of civil war, but also a civilized man whose warlike virtue began and will end in the arts of peace.

Much is due, indeed, to the character of the man Cromwell. It is only that which makes it possible for the poet to wager, so to speak, on this Horatian reading of the signs of the times. Echoes from Lucan in the "Horatian Ode" provide a ground note of warning that the stakes in the wager are high. It is not so much Lucan's hatred of Caesar that should be a warning as it is the desperation permeating his poem on the Civil War. The restored harmony between power and justice depends entirely on the character of the new man of power. If it ceases to exist in his mind, it disappears from the world he rules, and liberty and justice become mere terms of rhetoric, either hollow or desperate. Whether or not Marvell read Lucan's attacks on Caesar as having been covertly directed against Nero,[25] the mere fact that the Augustan poet's rejoicing was destined to give way to the macabre virulence of the Neronian poet is itself enough to caution the English poet against easy confidence. It may always turn out to be the poet who has been hoodwinked.

This cautionary note only serves to emphasize an element of reserve which Marvell must have recognized in Horace himself. Horace's characteristic manner of addressing the ruler is hortatory praise. It could even be described as conditional praise. One of the Odes, for example, places Augustus first among the heroes of Roman history and concludes by saying that he is second to Jove himself (I, xii); the poem is extraordinary praise, but it is also an admonition against the emperor's assuming deity, for it carefully delineates the difference between his earthly dominion and Jove's heavenly power (53–60). Augustus agreed that Romans should not deify a mortal ruler, and Horace knew that he agreed, so that the poem expresses an allegiance that is happily mutual. It is a kind of compact, the ruler committing his power to the civilized tradition that is the poet's trust, and the poet bringing to the regime the needed sanction of that tradition. The poet speaks as one conscious that there is something in his power to withhold.[26] Marvell's success in reproducing the tone of Horace's odes to Augustus derives from his well-considered adoption of this Horatian stance. It is both a diffident and a proud stance, and to define it is one of Horace's most impressive achievements. It recognizes the force of Necessity and the rare quality of the man who can draw that force to himself. It is not simply a pious fatalism, however, for the ground on which the poet praises the ruler is always his own.[27] If the ruler addressed falls off from the terms in which—and on which—the poet praises him, the praise will come to read, as Marvell's "Ode" does to readers who dislike Cromwell, as cruel, quiet irony.

Marvell can rally to Cromwell and yet not cease to cast himself in the role of the poet who

[25] This is the traditional interpretation, although a careful sifting of the evidence in the poem does not appear to support it. See Gerald Kenneth Gresseth, "The Politics of Lucan" (unpublished dissertation, University of California, Berkeley, 1951).

[26] Suetonius' account of how the *Epistle to Augustus* came to be written reflects this relationship between the ruler and the poet. The Emperor "post sermones vero quosdam lectos nullam sui mentionem habitam ita sit questus: 'Irasci me tibi scito, quod non in plerisque eius modi scriptis mecum potissimum loquaris; an vereris ne apud posteros infame tibi sit, quod videaris familiaris nobis esse?' "

[27] "By 27, Horace was willing to see in Augustus the exceptional man who alone could pull and hold Rome together; he was willing to support, admire, and praise him, but not without reservation, and always on his own terms" (MacKay, *loc. cit.*, pp. 175–76).

> . . . when the wheel of Empire, whirleth back,
> And though the World's disjointed Axel crack,
> Sings still of ancient Rights . . .

Similarly, Horace can describe the man whom, "iustum et tenacem propositi,"

> si fractus illabatur orbis,
> impavidum ferient ruinae,

and not feel, obviously, that his own response to the ruin of the republican cause disqualifies him as the poet to celebrate such constancy. He goes on to apply the description to Augustus, and then, by one of his apparently arbitrary transitions, he brings in the goddess Juno and has her deliver a warning to the Romans not to rebuild Troy. If Troy is understood to stand in a general way for the old Roman Republic,[28] the poem appears as a unified composition celebrating the kind of constancy to the Roman tradition which Horace claims for the Augustan program and setting that constancy off from the attitude of those who, "nimium pii," might think of disturbing the Augustan settlement by yet another effort to restore the original Republic. The Principate claims to restore and perpetuate the traditions of the Republic, although with differences corresponding to the new relations of power and the new necessities of Roman life. In the same way, Rome itself claims to perpetuate Troy, though on different soil.

> sed bellicosis fata Quiritibus
> hac lege dico, ne nimium pii
> rebusque fidentes avitae
> tecta velint reparare Troiae.

[28] For another argument generally supporting this interpretation of this much discussed reference to Troy in Odes III, iii, 57 ff., see L. P. Wilkinson, *Horace and His Lyric Poetry* (2nd ed.; Cambridge, 1951), pp. 73–75. Eduard Fraenkel (pp. 268 ff.) says: "The speech of Juno, when properly taken in its own setting, refuses to be turned into a piece of Augustan propaganda." But he is referring to the now generally rejected interpretation of the speech as a literal warning against a supposed project to rebuild the actual city of Troy. He does not consider the possibility of reading it as "a piece of Augustan propaganda" in a less specific sense, and he is willing to settle for a reading of the poem that leaves the introduction and the rest of the poem quite disjoined (p. 270). Steele Commager interprets the speech as "the mythical expression of a political mood" (p. 221), and observes: "Though the figures and symbols of the various passages differ, one theme remains constant: Rome's break with the past" (p. 223). The evocation of Rome's past, however, is as conspicuous as the theme of the break with the past. The two conflicting ideas are brought together in the poem, and the balance between them can be seen as its unifying principle.

Troiae renascens alite lugubri
fortuna tristi clade iterabitur . . .

To attempt to restore the Republic as it was before the cataclysm will not serve the ancient rights but only bring about a renewal of civil war and the abandonment of all things to Fortune. This Augustan idea of the relationship between the old state and the new may well account for Marvell's political evolution during this period.[29] If the English monarchy has joined the Roman Republic among the ruins of time and of war, it is the poet alone who can preserve the integrity of his civilization through the time of social convulsion. That is a kind of preservation of the ancient rights: the poet can maintain them, though not in force; and, given an Augustan disposition in the power that emerges from the civil wars, he may be able to come into the new state bearing the *lares* and *penates* of the old.

[29] Later, as J. A. Mazzeo has shown, Marvell's thought evolved "from a predominantly secular conception of Cromwell to a profoundly religious one," culminating in the association of the Protector with the biblical figure of David ("Cromwell as Davidic King" in *Reason and the Imagination: Studies in the History of Ideas, 1600–1800*, ed. J. A. Mazzeo [New York and London, 1962], p. 55). However, Mazzeo characterizes the "predominantly secular conception" by saying that "In the *Horatian Ode* Marvell's 'frame,' so to speak, was Machiavellian." It should rather be called Horatian. (Mazzeo's argument for Machiavellian influence is presented in "Marvell's Machiavellian Cromwell," *JHI*, XXI [January–March, 1960], 1–17, and criticized by Hans Baron in "Marvell's 'An Horatian Ode' and Machiavelli," *JHI*, XXI [July–September, 1960], 450–51).

Marvell, St. Paul, and the Body of Hope

by Geoffrey H. Hartman

Stanzas V and VI of "The Garden" have become the cruxes of many contemporary interpretations of the poem.[1] Starting with an analysis of their difficulties, I would like to come to a more adequate reading of both "The Garden" and the Mower Poems. My first section will be a purely contextual study of V and VI, but I shall seek help, after that, from the relations of seventeenth-century poetry to religious thought and to emblem techniques.

I

The poet in stanza I of "The Garden" ironically supposes man to run after the part (Palm, Oak and Bays) instead of the whole (the repose of all flowers and all trees), where the whole does not even need running after. He himself retreats from the world and enters a garden (st. II ff.) where he finds what he desires: repose, innocent love, solitude. But stanza V shows his quiet love for nature reciprocated with alarming intensity:

> What wond'rous Life in this I lead!
> Ripe Apples drop about my head;
> The Luscious Clusters of the Vine
> Upon my Mouth do crush their Wine;

"Marvell, St. Paul, and the Body of Hope" by Geoffrey H. Hartman. From *ELH*, XXXI (1964), 175–94. Copyright © 1964 by The Johns Hopkins Press. Reprinted by permission of the author and the publisher.

[1] See, *inter alia*, W. Empson, *Some Versions of Pastoral* (New Directions, n.d.), pp. 119–132; H. W. Smith, "Cowley, Marvell and the Second Temple," *Scrutiny*, XIX (1953), 184–205; L. W. Hyman, "Marvell's *Garden*," *ELH*, XXV (1958), 13–22. Others give attention to these stanzas within the frame of wider *explications de texte:* Ruth Wallerstein, *Studies in Seventeenth Century Poetic* (Madison, 1950), pp. 318–335; W. Klonsky, "Guide through the Garden," *Sewanee Review*, LVII (1950), 16–35; M. C. Bradbrook and M. G. Lloyd Thomas, *Andrew Marvell* (Cambridge, 1940), pp. 59–64; M. S. Røstvig, "Andrew Marvell's 'The Garden,' A Hermetic Poem," *English Studies*, XL (1959), 65–76; George Williamson, "The Context of Marvell's 'Hortus' and 'Garden,'" *MLN*, LXXVI (1961), 590–98.

The Nectaren, and curious Peach,
Into my hands themselves do reach;
Stumbling on Melons, as I pass
Insnar'd with Flow'rs, I fall on Grass.[2]

This is too solicitous a solitude, and the poet's mind returns to itself (stanza VI):

Mean while the Mind, from pleasure less,
Withdraws into its happiness:
The Mind, that Ocean where each kind
Does streight its own resemblance find:
Yet it creates, transcending these,
Far other Worlds, and other Seas;
Annihilating all that's made
To a green Thought in a green Shade.

The mind's new creation links repose to a vision of a world beyond this world, to which the garden is no more than a porch. Perhaps "perch" is the better word, since in the next stanza (VII) the poet slips his body off, and his soul flies up, not beyond the garden, but into the boughs. Thus the soul still ends in a tree (cf. ll. 27–28), and the final stanzas emphasize its "garden-state," rather than its anticipation of ultimate flight and metamorphosis. We are left with the image of an artful, this-worldly garden, a mimesis of Eden, in which the soul's labor of waiting is rewarded by what it sought in the first stanza, the transforming of time into "all Flow'rs and all Trees."

Three major queries attend the central stanzas. How do we interpret the curiously erotic fruits of stanza V? How is the mind's withdrawal, described in stanza VI, related to their ardor? And what precisely is the meaning of VI, with its suggestion of a two-rung Platonic ladder, which seems to reach far beyond the Garden, yet also ends in something "green"?

Whether or not these fruits are sexual, they effectively "lessen" the poet in some way, and so stand again his emphasis on the garden's holistic nature ("All Flow'rs . . ." "Two Paradises . . . in one" "hole-some Hours.") Again, if the poet withdraws into the mind it is to pursue that for which he originally entered the garden, having withdrawn from a too busy world: wholeness and repose. But the mind does not immediately satisfy this desire, being also crowded—with the ideal correlatives of natural things. It may, however, imagine worlds transcending the

---

[2] All quotations are from the Muses Library text of *The Poems of Andrew Marvell*, ed. Hugh MacDonald (London, 1952).

consciousness of ideal "kinds" (i.e. species or sexes),[3] worlds entirely beyond duality.[4] The final lines of the stanza suggest an intuition that fuses the real and the mental garden into one whole and reposeful entity.

Their paradox, however, remains: that to know this imaginary body of things the mind must annihilate or make into nothing "all that's made" (perhaps the "ea quae facta" of Romans i. 20). The paradox is strengthened by a doubling of "green" which suggests that the things which are *not* made are conceived within the context of a thing which *is* made, the garden. The succeeding stanzas enforce this impression of an inescapable relation between the garden and the poet. His mind may "annihilate" it, his soul be ever on wing to leave it—the garden still stands between him and his greatest hope, his desire for wholeness. To understand this "between"—both obstacle and mediation—we call on a source familiar to Marvell.

II

I have anticipated it by a reference to Romans i. 20. This is one of two exceptional passages in Saint Paul dealing with nature's eschatological aspect. The other is Romans viii. 19 ff. Both were commonplaces,

---

[3] OED s. v. 7, but especially s. v. 10c: "A class (of human beings or animals) of the same sex; a sex (in collective sense)." This usage is common as late as Dryden and Pope.

[4] "Resemblance" (l. 44), is probably colored by Christian Platonism, and could bear both an ontological and an amatory meaning. The former is commonplace—Spenser uses it in the "Hymn in Honor of Beauty," ll. 120–21 ("faire soules, which have / The most resemblaunce of that heavenly light")—but the OED does not quote, and I could not find a pure example of the word used metonymously for "the (ideally) resembling person or sex." Empson takes this meaning for granted when he writes (op. cit.) "the *kinds* look for their *resemblance* . . . out of a desire for creation." It is true, on the other hand, that a Platonist like Ficino, who remains untranslated in the 17th Century, uses the Latin *similitudo* (and sometimes *simulacrum*) in the double meaning here attributed to "resemblance"; see Raymond Marcel, *Marsile Ficin Sur le Banquet de Platon ou de l'Amour* (Paris, 1956), pp. 206, 251, and 252. The potential richness of "similitudo-resemblance" comes from its being used by two different yet constantly merging philosophical traditions: the essentially Christian of the "speculum" of creatures, and the Platonic of "Amorem procreat similitudo" (Ficino), of the lover drawn via the beloved to the "most resemblance" with God. See Wallerstein, *op. cit.*, "The Various Light"; and cf. "God made the Universe and all the Creatures contained therein as so many Glasses wherein he might reflect his own Glory . . . *Remotiores Similitudines Creaturae ad Deum dicuntur Vestigium; propinquiores vero Imago* . . . Good Men . . . find every Creature pointing out to that Being whose image and superscription it bears, and climb up from those darker resemblances of the Divine Wisdom and Goodness . . . till they sweetly repose themselves in the bosom of the Divinity. . . ." John Smith, *Select Discourses* (London, 1660), pp. 430–31.

proof-texts giving nature an essential place in the scheme of salvation. Augustine remembers them in one of the most moving episodes of his *Confessions*.[5] Romans i. 20, associated with Platonic discipline raising the mind from visible to invisible things,[6] says that God, though invisible, is clearly revealed in nature: "Ever since the creation of the world his invisible nature, namely his eternal power and deity, has been clearly understood in the things that have been made."

The second passage from Romans justified even more strongly a Christian, or even mystical, consideration of nature.[7] It reads:

> For the creation (creature) waits with eager longing (earnest expectation) for the revealing of the Sons of God; for the creation was subject to futility (vanity), not of its own will but by the will of him who subjected it in hope; because the creation itself will be set free from the bondage to decay and obtain the glorious liberty of the children of God. We know that the whole creation has been groaning together until now; and not only the creation, but we ourselves, who have the first fruits of the Spirit, groan inwardly as we wait for adoption as sons, the redemption of our bodies. (RSV 19–23; KJV in parentheses.)

Paul says that nature fell because of man, not of its own fault, and will be redeemed with man, not of its own power. Hence it looks to man with eager longing, and groans, and man also groans, because he too is waiting, like nature, for redemption, though he has the first fruits of the Spirit, i.e., the knowledge, through Christ, of the redemption of the body (cf. I Cor. xv. 20).

I propose to read stanzas V and VI in the light of these *loci classici*

[5] Bk. IX. xxiv–xxv. Cf. X. ix–x. Both recall an *ascensus mentis* from the "things that are made" to an intuition of the Wisdom "per quam fiunt omnia ista." (Wisdom, or Sapientia, has its own theological history, cf. Milton's "Omnific Word," *P.L.* vii. 217.) When Crashaw wishes to hymn "The Name above every Name, the Name of Jesus," he calls on Nature and Art, "All Things that Are / Or, what's the same, / Are Musical." The Hermetic τὰ ὄντα may be implicated.

[6] *Confessions*. the all-important Bk. VII, in particular xxiii–xxvi. See also W. R. Inge, *Christian Mysticism* (1st ed. 1899) whose two chapters on nature-mysticism carry Romans i. 20 and viii. 19 as epigraphs. Ruth Wallerstein, after quoting Tertullian who relies on Romans i. 20, observes: "Symbolic thought is thus rooted for the Christian tradition in the epistles of Paul. It will be noted that Plato stands beside Paul." (*Seventeenth Century Poetic*, p. 31).

[7] See Henry Vaughan, "And do they so? have they a Sense / Of ought but Influence? / Can they their heads lift, and expect, / And groan too?" The poem is prefaced by Romans viii. 19, quoted as "Etenim res Creatae exerto Capite observantes expectant revelationem Filiorum Dei" (*The Works of Henry Vaughan*, ed. L. C. Martin [Oxford, 1914] II, 432). G. M. Hopkins' poem to the Ribblesdale landscape, "Earth, sweet Earth . . ." is prefaced by the same text (*Poems of G. M. Hopkins*, ed. R. Bridges [New York, 1948], p. 240).

on nature. The first statement becomes, in theology, one of the major proof-texts for the concept of *lumen naturale,* or the "light of nature," developed by Thomas Aquinas from beginnings in Augustine.[8] The Romans, says Paul, are inexcusable in not accepting the new faith, because like nature itself they have a purely natural capacity for recognizing what is divine. They must be blinding themselves to Christ. In later developments the polemical context of the passage becomes often less important than the idea in it that both man and nature possess an inherent source of illumination. If St. Paul could be in the mind of a poet dealing seriously with nature (and especially this passage which played an important role in the Platonic-Christian synthesis), then the simple and well-known idea of the "light of nature" may aid significantly in interpreting "The Garden" and similar poems.

In stanza V, for example, nature seems more knowing and intense than the poet in his strange naivete ("What wond'rous life in this I lead!"). Exactly what nature 'knows' as if by its own light Paul's second statement will explain. Paul sees nature and man joined in their hope of attaining the same glorious end, a "redemption of the body," and it is the creature which looks earnestly to man for its liberation (either because man will be the cause of it, or, more probably, because he is the dial and chronometer of its hope).[9] Stanza V might therefore be read

---

[8] Fuller documentation of the historical development may be found in Rudolf Eisler, *Wörterbuch der philosophischen Begriffe,* 4th ed. (Berlin, 1929), II, 67–69. Rom. i. 20 is introduced by Milton at exactly the right point in *P.L.,* when Adam and Eve hymn the works of God at dawn (V. 154–59). It enters again at VIII. 273–79, when Adam by the light of nature deduces the great Maker from his creation. The quotation from John Smith (note 4 above) refers implicitly to Rom. i. 20, and goes on to make the allusion explicit: ". . . they sweetly repose themselves in the bosom of the Divinity: and while they are thus conversing with this lower World and are viewing *the invisible things of God in the things that are made* . . . they find God many times secretly flowing into their Souls. . . ." In Dante the concept plays an exceedingly important role as Charles Singleton has pointed out in his lucid "The Three Lights," *Dante Studies* 2 (Cambridge-Mass., 1954); and the idea of the "light of nature" is, in my opinion, one of the important links between Medieval, Renaissance and Romantic views of Nature: it does not designate simply reason, or the inner light, but generally reason kindled by a contact with creatures. The most eloquent seventeenth-century formulation I know is Donne's Sermon preached on Easter Day 1628, *The Sermons of John Donne,* eds. E. M. Simpson and G. R. Potter (Berkeley and Los Angeles, 1953–62) VII (1956), 219–36. Grotius, at Rom. i. 21 ("for although they [i.e. the Romans] knew God"), remarks: "Naturali iure, non familiari"; and goes on to quote the Church Fathers on the two "notitiae gradus," *Annotationes in Novum Testamentum,* Paris, II (1646), 178–79. Andrew Willet, in his *Hexapla* . . . (Cambridge, 1611), says at i. 19: "They had the knowledge of God by the light of nature, and by the light of the creatures."

[9] Cf. Willet, *Hexapla,* pp. 367–69, and Grotius, *Annotationes,* pp. 259–60.

as a witty emblem of Man hunted by nature into one body with it. Nature is, in a sense, the wrong body, as we shall point out later on. But the gods of stanza IV also pursue their prey *in order that* it metamorphose and become Tree, Laurel, Reed. They chase Ovid's women with (at least in point of syntax)[10] an eschatological purpose. The aggressive fruits of stanza V, which show an analogue of that eager longing mentioned by Paul, also seem to wish to hasten redemption, to mingle their life with the poet's because his and theirs is ultimately intertwined. At the end of the stanza ("Insnar'd with flow'rs, I fall on Grass") the poet is near to being transformed, like the women of IV, into a green body.[11]

From a purely literary standpoint what Marvell does is to take a Pauline figure of speech literally. This 'taking literally' is, as we shall see, a common device in Marvell, and may extend here to yet another scriptural metaphor. Stanzas IV–VI all depict metamorphoses of something human into something green, and many readers have felt that the "I fall on Grass" of V may mockingly echo a Biblical proverb—*All flesh is grass* (e.g. Isaiah xl. 6). It has not been observed, however, that the fruits of V, which are given the passions of flesh, suggest the converse of this thought, namely *"All grass* (viz. fruit) *is flesh."*

Stanzas IV to VI become, through this, a variation on one eschatalogical theme. All flesh is grass; but the "green" thought to which the poet sacrifices all things (ll. 47–48) may well be its redemptive converse, pictured in ll. 33 ff. and hinted at by st. IV: "All grass is flesh." It is his hope in a redeemed body, and a love in accord with it, for which he (imaginatively) destroys "all that's made."

Perhaps the reading here advanced is possible even without reference to St. Paul. It may be unnecessary to harmonize "All grass is flesh" with Romans if one is attentive to the quicknesses of Marvell's mind. Yet the Christian source may actually suggest one reason why this poetry is not

---

[10] Remembering the ambivalence of the Latin *ut* construction, which may introduce either a purpose or a result clause, Marvell here effects a synecdochal substitution of the first for the second (*"Apollo* hunted *Daphne* so / Only that she might Laurel grow").

[11] Stanza LXXVII of "Appleton House," to which V of "The Garden" has occasionally been compared, also contains, in the image of the "courteous *Briars"* urged by Marvell to nail him through, a hint of the redemptive relation of poet and nature. Both stanzas, moreover, suggest an ambivalence in this relationship to which I refer later: the ensnared poet is man reduced to a divine steadfastness of imagination by overhasty or foreshortened means. The similarity of "Bermudas," ll. 21 ff., probably comes through a common tradition of 'ideal landscape' (*locus amoenus*), but it is the function which each picture has in its poem that is important.

more overtly Christian. However complex the thought through which he passes, Marvell, *wearing the pastoral mask,* realizes it by "the light of nature." [12] The hope in redemption so wittily expressed is also literally a *green* thought, as if nature itself possessed it or brought it forth. The question why Marvell should wish to put on the pastoral mask cannot be answered at this point: he has, we suggest later, a religious reason related to his knowledge of the precipitous nature of hope and his desire to chasten hope into diffidence.

One thing, however, is clear. The special theological basis of the "light of nature" may actually have helped to make Marvell's poem more than theological in mode. The modern reader is tempted to take it as entirely secular or humanistic. The poem is certainly a step toward the Neoclassical, which shuns the direct treatment of the 'mystery' part of religion, and toward the Romantics, who revive the 'mystery' as an integral part of the human, rather than divine or enthusiastic, imagination. What Paul calls *Hope* becomes in them *Imagination;* and its dialectic is, in the main, freed from theology. Yet if "The Garden," by its curiously literal use of the idea of the Light of Nature, points forward to later poems, its continuity and inner logic remain linked to Pauline thought. I would now like to show that "The Garden" is essentially about the precarious relation of man's hope to his hope in nature. Behind it lies the disparity between nature and grace, continually overcome, continually reasserted.

III

According to St. Paul faith or hope is based on the evidence of things not seen (Hebrews xi. 1). The pasture of the religious soul is a world beyond this one, although the first fruits of that world may be tasted here. Marvell, however, at the beginning of his poem, seeks the garden to make his hope directly visible, as in "The Mower's Song," where the mower's mind

[12] There is no need to bring in the iconographic tradition to help with the significance of "green." But at least nothing in it contradicts Marvell's use of the color to denote (roughly) 'a hope involving or expressed by nature.' Alciati has hope dressed green in emblem 94; emblem 117 explains that "Nos sperare docet viridis"; Whitney's *Choice of Emblems* (1586) picks up the reference in the emblem "In Colores"; and Peacham's *Minerva Britanna* (1612) says of Repentance; "The cullar greene, she most delightes to weare, / Tells how her hope, shall overcome dispaire." Ripa's *Iconologia* also has hope dressed in green. Cf. D. C. Allen, "Symbolic Color in the Literature of the Renaissance," *PQ,* XV (1936), 81–92, esp. 86, and R. Wallerstein, op. cit., pp. 159 ff. and 321 ff.

in the greenness of the Grass
Did see its Hopes as in a Glass.[13]

The poet who enters the garden *sees* his hope in its plants, sees its innocence and repose as a kind of heaven on earth:

Your sacred Plants, if here below,
Only among the Plants will grow.

The "if" is the only remnant of uncertainty. Yet while his imagination
turns to the garden, he perceives that its imagination is turned toward
him! As lovers are star-crossed, so man and nature are hope-crossed. The
garden that in sts. II–IV was likely to embody his hope, in st. V projects
its own hope—man—to the poet. In this way nature paradoxically reminds him that his hope cannot be turned to nature, that he must re-
nounce visibility and turn into himself.

Stanza VI then shows the poet withdrawing into the mind, beginning
to hope for what he cannot see. "Who hopes for what he sees? But if
we hope for what we do not see, we wait for it in patience." (Romans
viii. 24–25). The dialectic between sight and a hope always transcending
sight is pushed to its last conclusions. The mind, that ocean mirror,
contains the ideal image (the Narcissus) of every species. It is, nevertheless, unsatisfied, and annihilates, supremely, all visibles, all quicksilver
bodies.[14] Instead of continuing to mirror natural species it creates "far
other" worlds, purely imaginary.

The Pauline context illumines, finally, the action of the entire poem.
As in the Horatian Ode and "Upon Appleton House" Marvell is deeply
concerned with the question of the redemptive use of Time. His concern
touches, yet goes beyond, the Classical debate between the active and the
contemplative life. And it is, very directly, the time-sense of the poem
which first charms and then continues to hold the reader. Marvell's *tim-
ing* is best described by comparing it to Saint-Amant's, a poet whose influence has been noted but not interpreted.[15] The stanzas of Saint-
Amant's "La Solitude" and "Le Contemplateur" are neat and leisurely
units, whose continuity is almost peripatetic. The French poet provides
a personable series of tableaux; he wants to intensify our sense for the

---

[13] There is a commonplace reference here to I Cor. xiii. 12.
[14] Empson (op. cit.) suggests that "streight" in l. 44 is not only or necessarily an
adverb of time: one could read 'Does find its own resemblance [to be] streight,' i.e.
too narrowly circumscribed. Either way of reading the word could harmonize with
the present interpretation.
[15] See R. Wallerstein, op. cit., pp. 318–355.

mind's freedom vis-a-vis time and nature. Marvell's "Mean while," introducing st. VI, avoids like Saint-Amant's "tântot" the impression of strict sequence; all his transitions, in fact, explicit or implicit, evoke a similar mood of casual rather than causal progression. But if Marvell imitates the libertine meanderings of his French source, it is to counterpoint an inner hastiness. His poem begins with the theme of haste, and he knows only too well that hope, whether political or spiritual, also contains haste, in the form of a deep hate of medial time. While Saint-Amant makes free with time, the poet of "The Garden" is always on the point of an untimely vaulting over it.

It is this tendency, or temptation, which brings us back to the Pauline context. The deceptive movement of "The Garden" is from the haste mentioned in stanza I to repose, but even within the garden haste reappears because integral to hope. Though man's mind should be purified of haste, of the too active urging of its object, the poet who retires into his *hortulus* finds that the quiet plants of stanza II become the precipitous wooers of stanza V, and he himself continues to objectify his hope in visible terms, to seek the "divine body" of imagination (I borrow the term from Blake). Thus the spiritual combat never ends because hope has in it a tragic or ironic flaw by which it defeats its own expectation by anticipation. I said previously that nature, in stanza V, hunts man into one body with it, which perhaps is the wrong body. The rococco fall pictured there points to a foreshortening of the Pauline travail of patience. The fruits are given the passions of flesh, but only succeed in turning flesh (the poet stumbling) to grass. If Marvell expresses less a particular eschatology than the form of eschatological thinking as a whole, one could say that the poet in st. V is in danger of being trapped by the illusion of an earthly paradise. Insnared, he may not get beyond the upper point of Dante's Purgatorio, or what Blake calls the lower paradise (Beulah), marked by innocence, sensuous passivity, and the acceptance of contraries.

The poet escapes this temptation but only by (paradigmatically) skirting a second. I think Marvell, in st. VI, portrays himself 'falling' in a different way, this time upwards. The temptation he suffers is that of pure hope, of an absolute transference of hope to a world beyond this world. Just as nature had sought to hasten redemption (st. V), so he too seeks to hasten it by the obverse means. Stanza VI retains a hint of haste, of the poet's undue mental violence in the opposite direction (against "all that's made"). Only in VII is haste clearly put off, and a true image of Paul's "waiting in patience" given. The picture of the soul in VII stands over against its previous evocations. Instead of being insnared (as in V) it here does its own snaring—waves a "various light" in its wings as if to transform time into wing-power.[16] The soul will not leave the garden by a premature ecstasy, as in VI; it stays there to gather strength for its eventual flight, perhaps to turn the "various" into a constant light. The "garden-state" (VIII) is this stasis,[17] the roosting place of the resolved soul, resolved not so much against created pleasure as against false bodies of hope. Though still divided from its true body, nothing (no Eve) stands between it and the substance of things hoped for.

The last stanza then recalls the garden as a *res facta* and work of patience:

> How well the skilful Gardner drew
> Of flow'rs and herbes this Dial new. . . .

Marvell implies the relation of faith and works, for here the gardener cooperates with nature to anticipate redemption. This last picture of the garden is marked by an emphasis on time and labor, but a flower-time and a flowering-labor. The new-drawn dial is at once temporal and floral, so that the victor's wreath (st. I) becomes now a circle of time against time, a living garland of plants. It records an unhasty growing of creation into its true body, the redemption of nature with man, of all in all. But it remains, nevertheless, a symbolic gesture, an artifice, and recalls that the best our poet (like the gardener) can do is to gather us up into the "artifice of eternity."

IV

My close use of Paul's text need not argue a similar procedure on Marvell's part. Hope's paradoxes were a commonplace, the Pauline texts

---

[16] The image has been enriched by Wallerstein's chapter, "The Various Light." Hyman suggests an allusion to Genesis i. 14 (op. cit., p. 21) which enforces, if correct, the idea of the soul's action within or on time. The image seems to me a fit emblem for Paul's "waiting in patience." A striking parallel to both Marvell's thought and emblem is found in John Smith's *Select Discourses*, pp. 156–57: "And because all those scatter'd *Raies* of Beauty and Loveliness which we behold spread up and down all the World over, are onely the *Emanations* of that inexhausted *Light* which is above; therefore should we *love* them all in that, and climb up alwaies by those Sun-beames unto the Eternall Father of Lights: we should look upon him and take from him the pattern of our lives, and alwaies eying of him should . . . (as *Hierocles* speaks) polish and shape our Souls into the clearest resemblance of him."

[17] For other connotations of "Garden-state," see Bradbrook and Lloyd Thomas, pp. 59–64.

their natural scaffolding. The poet could range among them as seriously and wittily as Crashaw and Cowley.[18] It is not important, moreover, to recognize Paul behind Marvell because it is *Paul:* there may be, as is usual in a writer of the Renaissance tradition, an implicit harmonizing of several sources. What is essential to recognize is the peculiarly *textual* quality and response of the poet's mind. The reader who sees Galatians v. 17 behind "A Dialogue between the Soul and the Body," or who catches Romans viii. 19 and a play on Isaiah xl. 6 in stanzas IV and V of "The Garden," gains more than a religious commonplace, more even than a new link between letter and spirit. He sees that Marvell has wrought a device or emblem for the scriptural text.

The emblem was commonly defined as a mute poem, or one which speaks to the *eye*.[19] It was praised, above all, for its economy, for the very thing that commends metaphor and image to the modern poet: "Toutes les richesses de la Nature sont en petit: toute sa majesté, comme parle Pline, est reserrée et à l'étroit." [20] No emblem really lived up to

---

[18] See Cowley's verses on "Hope" and Crashaw's answer "For Hope" in *Steps to the Temple* (1646) and *Carmen Deo Nostro* (1652). Cowley also has his own "For Hope." I should add that Hope, one of the three theological virtues, was generally distinguished from Faith with some clarity. Faith, based on assent, did not of itself satisfy man's desire for truth. He needed, in addition, Hope, that "taster of eternity" (Crashaw), which yielded a preview of heaven to sustain the believer in this life. ". . . even when we have faith, there still remains in the soul an impulse toward something else, namely, the perfect vision of the truth assented to on faith . . . stirrings of hope arise in the soul of the believer that by God's help he may gain possession of the goods he naturally desires, once he learns of them through faith"—Thomas Aquinas, *Compendium of Theology,* tr. C. Vollert, S.J. (St. Louis and London, 1947), p. 313. In the Renaissance emblem-books Hope is generally represented with a cross-shaped anchor (cf. Spenser, *F.Q.* I. x. 14), and sometimes with a spade. This conception has not, as far as I know, been discussed: it involves a linkage of patient labor and hope (cf. the last stanza of "The Garden"; also Ripa's comment on "Agricultura" in the *Iconologia*), and may indicate that hope is the virtue keeping man faithful to the earth. The anchor-cross expresses perhaps Christ's example, and the expectation of a final journey, but is derived textually from Hebrews vi. 19—see Picinelli, *Mundus Symbolicus,* tr. Aug. Erath (Cologne, 1687), Lib. XX, cap. i.

[19] "An emblem is but a silent parable . . ." says Quarles in his *Emblemes* (1635). "Les Emblemes sont des discours muets, une Eloquence des yeux, une Morale en couleurs . . ." François Menestrier, *L'Art des Emblemes* (Lyons, 1662), also appropriating Horace's "Ut pictura poesis." Emblems were not, of course, a truly pictorial mode but strongly literary in conception, and employed (especially by Catholics) as illustrated primer morality. The idea behind the mode was, nevertheless, quite serious and often mystical, and surpassed each individual attempt to realize it as the idea of the epic its various seventeenth-century embodiments (Milton excepted). For the influence of emblems on literature, see *inter alia* M. Praz, "Emblems and Devices in Literature," *Studies in Seventeenth Century Imagery* (London, 1939), I, 108–207; R. Freeman, *English Emblem Books* (London, 1948); and Elbert N. S. Thompson, *Literary Bypaths of the Renaissance* (New Haven, 1924), pp. 29–67.

[20] Pere Le Moine, *De L'Art des Devices* (Paris, 1666), quoted by Praz, *Studies,* I, 52.

this eulogistic description, which defines the ideal not the fact. Yet how apposite to Marvell, when transferred from visual to verbal! His verse seems a renewal of the spirit of the Greek Anthology, of its epigrams so closely connected to lapidary and pictorial inscriptions.[21] Verses used to accompany emblems as a dependent aid or as their "soul." Marvell's poems, however, are autonomous emblems in verse, approaching the compactness of pictorial form and even implying, at times, a scripture text for motto.[22]

To prove an exact relationship is somewhat difficult. The poems having no explicit epigraphs like the emblems, we must keep, for the most part, to internal evidence. Austin Warren, in his study of Crashaw, has pointed to the ingenuity of the baroque emblem-makers, whose designs translate scriptural metaphors into exact visual terms: " 'I sleep, but my heart waketh' takes form in the recumbent figure of a virgin who, though the eyes of her body are closed, holds at arm's length a large heart centrally occupied by a large and wide-open eye. . . . An art of bizarre ingenuity, the sacred emblem does not hesitate to translate into visual form any metaphor offered, in poetry, to the ear." [23] Marvell, I suggest, performs a similar feat of wit. He also paints (but in words) little scenes which project *literally* certain scriptural metaphors. A text, or its central

[21] Praz remarks that of Alciati's emblems roughly 50 out of 220 are imitated or translated from the Greek epigrams of the *Planudean Anthology* (*Studies*, I, 20 ff.). The epigrams were, in fact, superscriptions, or a derived genre, conceits illustrating objects or events. The exact relation of Marvell's poems, in point of genre and style, to the epigrammatic tradition has not been discussed. They seem to be an exceptional blending of the "naïve" and "pointed" epigram which James Hutton distinguishes so well in his *The Greek Anthology in France* (Ithaca, 1946). Only H. H. Hudson, as far as I know, discusses the question of how the 17th Century lyric might have developed from the epigram in his unfinished *The Epigram in the English Renaissance* (Princeton, New Jersey, 1947).

[22] Herbert and Quarles are, of course, Marvell's forerunners, but his specific difference is implicitly suggested by Miss Freeman's comments on them: "In Quarles' Emblems the poetry simply deduces ideas from a given image; it consequently requires the presence of an actual picture for the verse to analyze in detail and build its argument upon. Herbert's poetry brings its pictures with it. It remains primarily visual, but the images presented have already been explored and when they enter the poem they enter it with their implications already worked out" (op. cit., pp. 154–55). Considering Marvell's poetry as the third step in this liberation of the poem from the picture-emblem, we can say that the image of the Mower has not been explored previous to the poet: it is he who works out its implications within the poem, relying nevertheless on an understanding nourished by emblems. R. Wallerstein has seen the debt Marvel's poems owe to emblems (op. cit., pp. 151–180) but she did not specify his difference within the tradition. See also Jean H. Hagstrum's analysis of English iconic poetry in *The Sister Arts* (Chicago, 1958), pp. 112–120.

[23] *Richard Crashaw, A Study in Baroque Sensibility* (Ann Arbor, 1957), p. 73.

notion, is translated into a rebus, a special form of the emblem representing words by things. In Marvell's use of the rebus, the text is projected by the 'picture' or action of the particular stanza.

An obvious analogue to the rebus in st. V of "The Garden" is st. L of "Upon Appleton House." Isaiah says, All Flesh is grass, and Marvell gives body to the words in a micro-scene:

> With whistling Sithe, and Elbow strong
> These Massacre the Grass along:
> While one, unknowing, carves the *Rail*,
> Whose yet unfeather'd Quils her fail.
> The Edge all bloody from its Breast
> He draws, and does his stroke detest;
> Fearing the Flesh untimely mow'd
> To him a Fate as black forebode.

Does this not paint the words of scripture literally, or as Marvell himself puts it, "impart hearing to the eyes?"[24] But the stanza depicts, in addition to the scripture text, the movement of the mower's mind toward it. Here a further resemblance to "The Garden" appears. The mower discovers that "All flesh is grass" by moving through its converse, "All grass is flesh." The converse is already implicit in the poet's metaphor of "massacring" the grass; a metaphor which becomes literal almost at once when the Rail is "carved"; and this word, by the way, which likens the cut of the scythe to that of a neat table-knife, also becomes near-literal in the next stanza, where Thestylis "forthwith means on it [the Rail] to sup." The proleptic use of metaphor (the unapparent movement from the metaphoric to the literal) and the use of the converse are among the defining traits of Marvell's poetry,[25] and to speculate on their ulti-

---

[24] "Insinuare sonos oculis," *The Poems of Andrew Marvell*, p. 67. Marvell's Latin epigram is a retranslation into Latin of a part of Georges de Brebeuf's translation of Lucan's *Pharsalia* (*La Pharsale de Lucain*, 1655; v. H. M. Margoliouth, *The Poems and Letters of A. M.*, I, 228). It is interesting to observe that Menestrier in his *L'Art des Emblemes*, pp. 15–16, cites the French verses which Marvell retranslates into Latin, and praises them as an elegant definition of what happens in emblems. I hope to collect, in another essay, evidence of Marvell's playfulness with regard to the emblem tradition. Hagstrum, *The Sister Arts*, p. 95, has noted the link between Brebeuf and Menestrier, but not that between Marvell and Brebeuf. The theme of the transposition of eye and ear is characteristic of emblematic speculation, and might be linked to what Hagstrum terms "the one element that is new, or at least that received greater emphasis in the century of the baroque than in the Renaissance . . . the notion that in the union of body and soul, picture and word, sense and intellect, there was some kind of interpenetration" (p. 97).

[25] I use the term heuristically to indicate figures that could include 'inversion' and

mate role would need a further essay. But they are clearly signatures of an intensely eschatological mind. Marvell uses both to reverse relations —especially of man and nature or of figurative and literal—with a quasi-divine ease of manner. The world he creates is a precarious realm which mirrors the dialectic of hope, the drama of the believer's search for redemptive acts or evidences, yet he himself remains strangely uninvolved, a gay artificer. A glance at his most original creation, the Mower, should bear this out.

"The Mower's Song" depicts a midget catastrophe, which seemingly inverts the lesson of Romans viii. 19, for it shows man involving hopeful nature in his fall instead of in his redemption. Here are the first four stanzas:

> My Mind was once the true survey
> Of all these Medows fresh and gay;
> And in the greenness of the Grass
> Did see its Hopes as in a Glass;
> When *Juliana* came, and She
> What I do to the Grass, does to my Thoughts and Me.

> II
> But these, while I with Sorrow pine,
> Grew more luxuriant still and fine;
> That not one Blade of Grass you spy'd,
> But had a Flower on either side;
> When *Juliana* came, and She
> What I do to the Grass, does to my Thoughts and Me.

> III
> Unthankful Medows, could you so
> A fellowship so true forego,
> And in your gawdy May-games meet,
> While I lay trodden under feet?
> When *Juliana* came, and She
> What I do to the Grass, does to my Thoughts and Me.

> IV
> But what you in Compassion ought,
> Shall now by my Revenge be wrought:
> And Flow'rs, and Grass, and I and all,

'reversal.' The wittiest mottos of the emblem books were generally conversions in this sense, e.g. "Qui captat capitur," and the form is beautifully used in many poems of the Greek Anthology, as in the following epigram (trans. Grotius): "Ex viva lapidem me Di facere. Sed ecce / Praxiteles vivam me facit ex lapide."

Will in one common Ruine fall.
For *Juliana* comes, and She
What I do to the Grass, does to my Thoughts and Me.

The poem's relation to st. V of "The Garden" and st. L of "Appleton House" is evident. The refrain again projects the thought that "All flesh is grass." This combines with the idea of the "mower mown," which is the neatest example of the converse in Marvell's poetry, and basic to the whole series of Mower poems.[26] It is *the* emblem of apocalypse, a figure of divine ironies, of unpredictable reversals. The Mowers of "Appleton House" (sts. XLIX–LIII) also move in this lucid realm of perplexities. Passing, like the Israelites, through the sea (a sea of grass), they are clearly redemptive harvesters, yet their cutting-down of the green may suddenly become a cutting-off, and turn this green sea red.

"The Mower's Song" is Marvell's nearest approach to a verse-emblem.[27] Its refrain, which has been rightly said to recall the sweep of a scythe, links it to the class of figure poems, a well-known but limited way of

[26] In the final line of "Damon the Mower" ("For Death thou art a Mower too"), death is a redemptive figure healing Damon's wound by a more ultimate wound. But he is redemptive only *if what he does to Damon will be done to him* (Death, the mower, will be mown: cf. I Cor. xv. 54–55). Quintillian's distinction between 'figures of speech' and 'figures of thought' is very hard to maintain in the case of Marvell. Image reversals, synecdochal substitution, conceptual metonymy (st. I of "The Garden") and such witty transpositions as All flesh is grass—All grass is flesh, inform most of his poems.

[27] Unless we chose "The Mower to the Glo-Worms." It is certain, in any case, that the Mower Poems as a group (excluding, perhaps, the more discursive "The Mower against Gardens") are conceived in the spirit of emblems, and stand midway between the more dependent emblem-poem of Mildmay Fane or Herbert and the free myth-making of modern poetry. The glow-worm has an emblematic tradition clearer than that of the mower, who is almost completely Marvell's new emblem. May it suffice to point for the mower to George Wither's *A Collection of Emblemes Ancient and Modern* (London, 1635), Bk. I, illustration xxi (motto: "initium mors vitae") and Bk. IV, illustration xlviii (motto: "omnis caro foenum"). These are pale though true foreshadowings of Marvell's conception, which is found more explicitly in Picinelli's *Mundus Symbolicus*, s. v. *Gramen* (Liber X cap. xxi): "Gramen, ut laetius crescat, falce demetitur, et humo tenus considitur. Symbolo subscripsit Philotheus . . . LAETIUS UT SURGAT." As to the glow-worm, it was *inter alia* an emblem for prudence, being associated with the proverbial ant, to which it gives light in Mildmay Fane's poem, "The Fallacy of the outward Man," *Otia Sacra* (1648). But prudence itself may be associated with the Light of Nature in the theological sense explained in note 6 above—which makes the emblem even more relevant to Marvell. See Picinelli, s. v. Cicindela, Lib. VIII, cap. vii. Another tradition stresses the Plinyan micro-character of the glow-worm, which makes it a fit marvel for the poet's world of "unfathomable grass" as in Saint-Amant. "Le Contemplateur" (1629), st. XXIII. For an especially exquisite use of the glow-worm emblems, see Thomas Stanley, *Poems* (1647 and 1651).

imitating emblems in verse. The refrain, moreover, acts as an invariant motto (the "mower mown") and caps each stanza's tenor with the same mysteriously joyous highpoint. The poem is clearly a song of hope, yet the hope in it ironically linked to this destructive sweep of the scythe, a conjunction also emphasized by the change from the past tense ("When *Juliana* came") to the present ("For *Juliana* comes"), which suggests that the havoc wrought by the lady is not final enough for the mower: he seems to hope for a Second Coming as strong as that of Death itself, the greatest mower of them all. "For now we see through a glass, darkly; but then face to face: now I am known in part; but then shall I know even as also I am known."

Such strange alliance of hope and death is also reflected by the mower's Orlando-fury. This fury, is it not the "annihilating all that's made" magnified into a superb emblematic action? The mower's pique is, in any case, given a resonance and amplitude no less than cosmic. Marvell's aggrandizement of pastoral clichés reminds one of Donne's exploitation of Petrarchan conceits, except that the 'mower eclogues' must maintain the mask of the naive singer.[28] The mower's fury and the temptation of hope seem to me related: hope may deny too quickly this world for the world beyond, and despair, in Marvell, is really a greater form of hope.[29] Milton's Adam is taught that "in contemplation of created things / By steps we may ascend to God," [30] but Marvell views this ladder (the "scale of nature") with a post-lapsarian eye. He evokes, in fact, less a ladder or a progress than a precarious dialectic which sets ultimate hope catastrophically against hope in nature. And this holds true of all the Mower poems, in which the contradiction between nature and grace finds a deeply oblique, an unsacrilegious form. Their theme is the *labor of hope.*

The mower recalls Vergil's "agricola," and in the emblem-books this spiritual peasant always labors "in hope": *agricolas spes alit.*[31] Marvell,

---

[28] The term 'mower eclogues' is my own. J. C. Scaliger recognizes "mower pastorals" in Bk. III, ch. 99 of the *Poetices*: "Pastoralia continent . . . Bucolica, Arationes, Messes, Foenisecia, Lignatoria, Viatoria, Capraria, Ovilia, Holitoria: quibus magnus vir Sanazarus ex Theocrito etiam addidit piscatoria: nos etiam Villica." I have not been able to find a Classical or Neolatin example of "Foenisecia"; and but for this passage in Scaliger would have thought Marvell an inventor, like Sannazzaro. The absence of dialogue would not disqualify his Mower poems as eclogues; Scaliger thinks the amorous monologue came before the dialogue forms of pastoral (*Poetices,* Bk. I, ch. 4).

[29] "The Definition of Love," sts. I and II.

[30] *Paradise Lost* V. 511–512.

[31] Peacham, *Minerva Britanna*, emblem 32, pp. 126–129; Wither, *A Collection of Emblemes,* Bk. II, illustration xliv.

however, shows hope in nature frustrated by love or by the very strength
of hope. The mower's revenge is clearly an "untimely" harvesting, or
hastening of the end: what he had cultivated in hope he now destroys
in hope. Yet this might well be the anagogical ministry of love, for the
"annihilating" again ends in something green. Revelation, the seeing of
one's hope face to face, or redemption, the reunion of man and nature,
is pushed, not without irony, into death:

> And thus, ye Medows, which have been
> Companions of my thoughts more green,
> Shall now the Heraldry become
> With which I shall adorn my Tomb;
> For *Juliana* comes, and She
> What I do to the Grass, does to my Thoughts and Me.

Here the device or emblem enters the poem formally, to express on the
tomb the mower's hope, which remains with nature or the green body
of ultimate rebirth. Love ("the greatest of these . . .") shows its great-
ness in a mysterious way. To achieve man's redemption it works catastrophically against hope, which is premature, tinsel-winged. Only love
causes such mowing-madness unto death, an outmoding of childish hopes,
a happy fall.

V

A few additional comments may forestall misunderstanding of what
I have wanted to say in this essay. "The Garden," as I see it, is dialectical
rather than merely progressive in structure. It is true, but not all the
truth, that the poet progresses from the vanities of the world to the
pleasures of the garden, and finally to a garden within this garden—
to the Eden which the soul is enabled to foresee in this, its earthly state.
It is likewise true, but not all the truth, that the main contrast in the
poem is between the worldly fruits (of fame and love) and the sensuous
yet innocent fruits which the garden offers; between, in short, the con-
trasty red and white and the unified amorous green. To see a progression
of thought that is dialectical rather than linear completes rather than
denies these views of the poem, and modifies them only insofar as the
poet is shown to be respectful of certain inherent (Pauline) paradoxes.
Not only does the garden stand against the world, but within the garden
a new opposition arises, engendered by hope itself, and turning the poet
inward. He enters a mental garden, this again is surpassed in the light
of greater hope, but this hope remains tinged by the color, and is con-

ceived within the context of, the earthly garden—it is a "green Thought
in a green Shade." Both views, the dialectical-progressive and the linear-
progressive, are relevant; but I feel that the first subsumes the second
and follows more closely the inner turns and surprises of Marvell's poem.

I would also urge that while Marvell thinks within a Pauline context
his poetry expresses less a particular eschatology than the form of eschatological thinking as a whole. His figure of the "mower mown" might well
be compared to Milton's the "gatherer gathered," and though a protestant background may explain them in part, it does not wholly.[32] The
strength of Blake's poetry is likewise in its unfolding of a highly abstract
eschatological scheme, belonging less to one religion than (as Blake says)
to all religions insofar as derived from the Poetic Genius. Blake and
Milton, however, claim and clothe an ultimate illumination. They move
us, with irony and caution, toward a precise image of the last things.
The specific subject of "The Garden" is also related to one of the last
things; the poem prospects the redemption of the body, or nature's para-
dise-body. Yet Marvell evokes no sustained image of Eden, only the
tastings and testings of hope by the individual mind. A morphology of
hope is given us in miniature.

This miniature quality is of great interest, and related to the sophisticated naivete of Marvell's poems, which I have touched on *ambulando*.
It may be fruitful to explore in how far Marvell's miniaturism of mood
and mode represents emblem-techniques fully adjusted to poetry. Perhaps Marvell is constructing a poetic kind of heraldry, not unrelated to
the very personal symbol-making of the modern poets. If the miniature
quality prevails more strongly in Marvell, it could be because, unlike
modern poets, he scruples to avail himself of his full creative autonomy,
or because he makes an at once literal and ironic use of the idea of man
as a little world or microcosm. His Damon, a diminutive Adam, instead
of redeeming the world whose image in sharp he is, alienates himself
from it through the mystery of hope.[33]

My main thesis, that Marvell is concerned with the 'body of hope' has
been variously anticipated. The amorous or even androgynous vegetation
of "The Garden" has been traced to a Kabbalistic myth concerning the
unfallen Adam, though it could also be derived from Aristophanes's

---

[32] F. R. Leavis notices the pattern in *P.L.* IV. 268 ff., *Revaluations* (London, 1949),
pp. 62–63. Is it not present in *P.L.* IX. 426 ff. also? The situation of little T.C. is
similar, or perhaps of "the nipper nipped." Donne's "spyed Spie" (*Satyre* IV) also
belongs here.

[33] On the poet's alienation from nature, cf. J. H. Summers, "Marvell's 'Nature' "
ELH, XX (1953), 121–135. [Reprinted in this volume. See p. 42—Ed.]

story in the *Symposium*—Renaissance Platonism had already associated the two myths.[34] What matters is, in any case, that both are speculations on the same subject, the form of man's true or redeemed body. Marvell's use of the concept of metamorphosis has also been interpreted in this fashion.[35] It is certainly true that the Garden, in its most general aspect, appears as a place of various metamorphoses, or changes of body. All are redemptive; yet some less than others. But none, not even those depicted in sts. IV and V, suggest that the 'body of hope' is in the image of a nature which reabsorbs man. What they prefigure is a body or a love that stands beyond the division of nature and man, or of the sexes:

> Such was that happy Garden-state
> While Man there walk'd without a Mate. . . .

The beautiful lines

> No white nor red was ever seen
> So am'rous as this lovely green

suggest likewise not an expulsion of sexual love but rather its absorbed perfection, the passion and the duality overcome. Yet if, in Christian theology, the exact nature of the redeemed (resurrection) body is in dispute, and not a matter of doctrine, and if the imagination remained, in this respect, relatively free, the poet still knew himself in the presence of a mystery not to be profaned.[36] Marvell confronts the mystery obliquely, through the mask of Platonic thought, the concepts of microcosm and metamorphosis, and other Pastoral or Classical guises. His oblique—the oblique of poetry—is more sensuous than the direct could ever be.

[34] E.g., Leone Hebreo, in his *Dialoghi d'Amore*, published posthumously in 1541; see Richard Benz, *Der Mythus vom Urmenschen* (Munich, 1955), esp. 31–49. For the commonplaceness of the conjunction, cf. Henry More, *Conjectura Cabbalistica* (London, 1653), pp. 123 and 157 f. (But More rightly considers Plato's version to be a parody of the myth.) The archetype recurs, perhaps via Böhme, in Blake's poetry, also fundamentally concerned with the redemption of Man's original body, and has a strong emblematic revival in some of D. H. Lawrence's animal poems.

[35] Bradbrook and Lloyd Thomas, "Marvell and the Concept of Metamorphosis," *Criterion*, XVIII (January 1939), 236–254. In particular: "The concept of Metamorphosis, the basis of the poem, fuses the modern psychological idea of sublimation and the modern [!] theological idea of transcendence into something more delicate" (p. 243).

[36] See "On Mr. Milton's Paradise Lost" for Marvell's scruples that poetry might ruin "The sacred Truths to Fable and old Song."

This Sober Frame: A Reading of "Upon Appleton House"

by M. J. K. O'Loughlin

I don't speak of the putting off of one's self; I speak only—if one has a self worth sixpence—of the getting it back. The place, the time, the way were, for those of the old persuasion, always there—are indeed practically there for them as much as ever. They can always get off—the blessed houses receive.

Henry James, "The Great Good Place"

"O! let me not," (quoth he) "then turne againe
Backe to the world, whose joyes so fruitlesse are;
But let me heare for aie in peace remaine,
Or streightway on that last long voiage fare,
That nothing may my present hope empare."
"That may not be," (said he) . . .

The Faerie Queene, I.x:lxiii

Though Marvell will always be best known for the poised complexity of the shorter poems, more of his readers should enjoy discovering that, like the place they describe, the seven hundred seventy-six lines of "Upon Appleton House" exhibit work of no foreign architect. Happily, the poem's distinction no longer seems to be the best kept secret in seventeenth century literature.[1] To the increasing number of readers willing

"This Sober Frame: A Reading of 'Upon Appleton House' " by M. J. K. O'Loughlin. Unpublished essay. Copyright © 1968 by Prentice-Hall, Inc. Published here by permission of the author.

[1] Revaluation of the poem began with the chapter by Don Cameron Allen in his *Image and Meaning* (Baltimore, 1960). In such fascinating background studies as Ruth Wallerstein's *Studies in Seventeenth Century Poetic* (Madison, 1950) and Maren-Sofie Røstvig's *The Happy Man* (Oslo, 1954; 2nd. rev. ed. New York, 1962) it had been seriously considered, but more as a document in the history of ideas than in its own terms. Yet even Allen seemed finally less concerned with poetic coherence than with those evocative and allusive dimensions which, in his encyclopedic way, he could describe so impressively. Recently however the poem has begun to receive the kind of

to read it carefully it offers not only an experience unique in the literature of the age, but one almost certain to enlarge our estimate of a poet capable of far more scope than his usual reputation leaves room for. Such at least are the impressions I wish to confirm in this essay. If it does not pretend to do full justice to the poem's extraordinary richness of implicative detail, the following account of its theme and genre, idiom and structure, and especially of its imagery and tone (or *persona*) may serve to introduce it precisely as a poem, one with its own complex way of dramatizing the large and perennial human question that was raised for the poet by the decision of Thomas Fairfax, Lord General of the parliamentary army, to resign from that position and retire to the Yorkshire estate which gives the poem its title.

In a heroic sonnet celebrating the victory at Colchester Milton had once summoned "Fairfax, whose name in Europe rings" to the nobler task of reconstructing the state which his military prowess had preserved. That, however, was before the execution of the king and the planned invasion of Scotland drove the Lord General to withdraw from the ambiguities of power, to cultivate his garden, and to prepare to serve another city. No theme exercised the imagination of Andrew Marvell more than that embodied in the situation of Fairfax. Throughout his most impressive lyrics the tension between a state of contemplative detachment and a life of active engagement amid the exigencies of history and the erosions of time is enacted again and again—and from shifting perspectives. One thinks of the other-worldly contemplative yearning of "On a Drop of Dew" or the hymn to those Edenic isles of the blessed, the Bermudas, "Safe from the Storms and Prelat's rage," but there is also the felt pressure of time and historical force upon the world of his love poems and pastorals, as poignantly as in "The Picture of Little T.C. in a Prospect of Flowers," or as ironically as in "The Nymph complaining for the death of her Faun." The same poet who wrote in "The Garden" the most memorable English expression of Horatian retired

---

scholarly "new criticism" that has canonized Marvell's lyrics. See for example Joseph Summers's remarks on "the most interesting and entertaining long, non-dramatic between *The Faerie Queene* and *Paradise Lost*" in the introduction to his edition of Marvell in the Laurel Poetry Series (New York, 1961), p. 17, as well as the fuller readings of Harold Toliver, *Marvell's Ironic Vision* (New Haven, 1965) and Harry Berger, Jr., *Southern Review*, I (1965). Most significantly, perhaps, so gifted a poet as John Hollander has imitated its form and translated its concerns in "Upon Apthorp House," commemorating the master's residence of Adams House, Harvard, and teaching us, incidentally, not a little about how to approach his model (*Movie-Going*: New York, 1962).

leisure could also write "An Horatian Ode" in judicious tribute to a "restless" Cromwell who, leaving his private garden, could climb "To ruine the great Work of Time."

In his lines on the Fairfax estate, Marvell seems to me to have been able to draw together his manifold awarenesses of this issue and dramatize them in an organic imaginative whole. To this end he adopted a tradition of seventeenth-century poems in praise of the great house which was peculiarly suitable to his complex theme. In this tradition, ranging from Ben Jonson's lines "To Penshurst" to Pope's "Epistle to Burlington," the rural location of the great house and its typical activity and sense of history provide the poet with what might be called a "georgic" emblem of the good society, one which has its roots in earlier literatures in "the fairest thing there is" enjoyed by Odysseus in the gardens and feasts of Alcinous, in the transfiguration of rustic labor in Vergil's *Georgics,* and in the perfection of the active life imaged in the earthly paradise that crowns Dante's mountain of Purgatory. The special accomplishment of "Upon Appleton House," however, is its transformation and renewal of these generic expectations. Here the house's cultivation must be confronted not as the emblem of its surrounding culture, but as an alternative to it. The visit of James to Penshurst is the consummate instance of the civic quality of the leisure enjoyed there, but the execution of that king's son has driven Fairfax to a private station, leaving the poet who tutors his daughter to reconstitute a vision of civic leisure in language that he—and she—might comprehend.

The distinctive idiom of "Upon Appleton House" is probably the feature that most impresses us in our first reading. Subtly and pervasively it diffuses an air of playfulness and free time which we gradually discover to be not only the particular élan of the poem but nothing less than what it is most profoundly about. From the opening stanza we begin to notice the curious effect, at once riddling and conversational, of these tetrameter couplets with their elliptically contorted or pleonastic syntax, their conspicuous enjambment, and yet their ruminative, even Spenserian pace, their casual inclusiveness. Orphic yet urbane, such a style is the perfect instrument for the *homo ludens* whose poetic game enacts in miniature the recreation of his patron. This playful spirit is most striking of course in the poem's "outrageous" displays of metaphysical wit, as in the famous last stanza. These conceits have become curiosities of literary history, seeming all the more eccentric when excerpted and censured even in Mr. Eliot's wise essay. Yet considered in the poem's own spirit, whimsically portentous, self-consciously arch, these Clevelandisms, as Mr. Alvarez shrewdly observes, might remind us of the wit of Lewis Carroll and be enjoyed in that vein.[2]

Long before we reach the last stanza, however, this impression of playfulness has already begun to blend with another quality likely to attract the reader, and here too an intuition of the poem's manner yields a revealing insight into the matter it deliberates. For the note of playfulness is accentuated by the poem's apparently desultory pace and random structure. We loaf and invite our souls as we follow the poet in what seems to be merely a loose and rambling tour of the great house, its past history, and its grounds. But it is worth noting that though we move back and forth over a century in time, and though we amble in our inspection of the estate's topography through gardens and meadows, into a grove and alongside a river, there is remarkably little sense of the passage of time. Instead there is the deepening consciousness of a continuous moment "now." One feels it in the insistent use of the present tense (especially in the narrations), or in the way each "section" is introduced by a transitional passage which dissolves a clock-time sequence into a ruminatively expanded moment of personal duration "now." The singular effect of this liberation from linear time is that it does not (as might be expected) relax the poem's structure, but rather that it draws into one central focus those very parts which have seemed so unrelated that they have even been taken for separate poems.[3]

"Upon Appleton House" has its own claim to the structural integrity which its first ten stanzas commend in buildings and men. To describe the architecture of the poem, especially after those opening stanzas, we might begin by noticing how variously yet persistently it ponders the theme of contemplative detachment and public involvement. Then we might notice that the coordination of these perspectives seems anything but accidental.[4] The polemical history of the convent which once stood on the grounds has its function, in the economy of the poem, to expose

---

[2] A. Alvarez, *The School of Donne* (New York, 1961), pp. 118–120.
[3] Allen, p. 117.
[4] As my interpretation of the poem tries to define more coherence among its parts than has previously been conceded (or may be apparent at first glance), I offer the following outline of the dialectical relationship of the parts of each sequence to one another and of one sequence to the other.

The contemplative life is found wanting. (The Cistercian convent)	The active life is found wanting. (The mowers and the flooded meadow)
The necessity of the active life—yet dramatizing the value of reflection. (William Fairfax's rescue of Isabel Thwaites)	The necessity of the contemplative life—yet dramatizing the pressure of action. (The poet's withdrawal to the grove)

that perversion of the contemplative ideal still apt to seduce us (and Fairfax) as it did Isabel Thwaites. Her predicament elicits in turn the exemplary activity of Sir William Fairfax's invasion of the convent, a use of violence which is all the more dramatically compelling because it seems to spring from a reflective disposition which honors important values to which the active life should be subordinate. Finally, in a playful synthesis of the two possibilities just traced in the stories of Isabel and William, we view the present recreation of the formerly active general. If there is a certain dialectical logic to this triad of meditations, the same might be said of the other sequence which leads to the evening walk of Mary Fairfax. As the first sequence began with an indictment of the contemplative life and dramatized the problematical necessity for action, the second sequence will begin with a grisly parody of the active life (the mowing and flooding of the meadow), which in turn elicits the speaker's contemplative withdrawal to the grove, the tone of which, as I hope to demonstrate, is anything but an unqualified endorsement of retirement. Finally, just as the first sequence concluded in Fairfax's garden with a retrospective resolution of past activity and present contemplative play, the second sequence will conclude with a celebration of Mary Fairfax's present recreation seen under the aspect of her future engagement.

Those of us disposed to praise poems with the formula that the author "has it both ways" could find, perhaps, no more inclusive range of interrelated attitudes than the double dialectical configuration which gives this poem's argument its extraordinary coherence. What may not yet be apparent is the rich metaphoric texture which transforms this deliberative structure into a vision of historical process in which the opposed possibilities of retirement and involvement can be imaginatively "married"—if I may introduce a term which is not only an apt description of the poem's method, but would seem to be the governing metaphor of the metamorphic imagery which embodies its sense of history. Appropriately,

---

| The symbolic resolution of past activity and present contemplation. (The Lord-General in his garden) | The symbolic resolution of present contemplation and future activity. (Mary Fairfax's evening walk) |

Readers recognizing the kind of "Hegelian" synthesis that often informs Marvell's poems might also consider the influence here of the meditative tradition which Louis L. Martz describes in his magisterial *Poetry of Meditation* (New Haven, 2nd. ed., 1962). Remembering that the mowers act out historical events, one finds the use here of memory, intellect and will for recollection, analysis and "colloquy." On the use of time cf. the discussion by Lowry Nelson, Jr., in *Baroque Lyric Poetry* (New Haven, 1961).

the process is most evident in the accounts of the two girls whose histories enclose the poem, affirming in each case a state of virginal innocence and a marital destiny in which the early state must be destroyed in order to be renewed, as it is indeed from Isabel to "our Thwaites," Mary. But there is also a broader sort of "marriage" informing the poem's imagery, one which often implicates the language of sexual union, but which also enacts its own creative dialectic of retirement and involvement in the terms of art's relationship to life such as we might expect in a poem concerned with architectural styles and religious rituals, formal gardens and formless meadows, the intricate light mosaic of a contemplative grove and the "vitrified" world envisioned after the flood. Here the condition corresponding to the virginal state of innocence is the aesthetic and ethical norm of the "sober frame" announced in the opening line and exemplified soon enough as the reader begins his meditation at home, so to speak, with the poem and the building, with all things "composed here,"

> Like Nature, orderly and near:
> In which we the Dimensions find
> Of that more sober Age and Mind,
> When larger sized Men did stoop
> To enter at a narrow loop;
> As practising in doors so strait,
> To strain themselves through *Heavens Gate*. (26–32)

Insistently described in the language of contraction, the architectural dimensions of the place perfectly express the "sober" English Protestant alternative to those vacant and expansive styles sarcastically dismissed at the start of the poem. Yet important as these values are in reenacting an age of innocence and preparing for a heavenly destiny, it is crucial to an understanding of the poem to see that they are not ends in themselves but rather find their fulfillment in what might be called their "marriage" to history. For all its contractile emphasis the passage just quoted is also charged with an expansive civic resonance in the first of the poem's many evocations of the *Aeneid*: the legend of a "larger-sized" Hercules visiting the Arcadians, as described by Pallas to Aeneas, who, significantly, would in time recreate that heroic past with his own settlement in the same hills.[5] Similarly, when the dwarfish confines of the house are compared to the "bee-like cell" of the *casa Romuli*, the simile

---

[5] See *Aeneid*, VIII.362–67. Beginning here, the poem's allusions to this epic insinuate the civic significance of the rural estate. See also 40, 577, 739 (cf. *Aeneid*, VI.205–07).

(with its georgic emblem) puts our awareness of size and style in the context of history, in the presence of the Roman past or in the future significance of the English present to the later generations that will return here "in pilgrimage." Indeed, as we learn soon enough in the ninth stanza, the final significance of these doors lies not in their humble narrowness, but in their charitable openness. What ultimately justifies the house itself is not its sober stability but the utility which is the function of its impermanence; in the transience of history, it exists only as an inn "to entertain / Its Lord a while, but not remain." [6]

To dramatize affirmatively the openness of the house to history, these first ten stanzas introduce what I take to be the normative metaphoric (or metamorphic) action of the poem in which, typically, the terms of art dissolve into and are perfected by those of life: a stately frontispiece of poor, daily new furniture of friends. This is why, conversely, the poem begins by scorning the evacuation of life into artifice as in the bizarre metamorphosis of a head whose human features have been "architecturalized" by the great design it stretched "in pain" to conceive. With this compare the vividly humanized architecture which results from Fairfax's entrance into his sober frame:

> Yet thus the laden House does sweat,
> And scarce indures the *Master* great
> But where he comes the swelling Hall
> Stirs and the *Square* grows *Spherical;*
> More by his *Magnitude* distrest,
> Then he is by its straitness prest. (49–54)

What is most striking of course is the fact that as a result of its *human* configuration the house attains a more perfect *architectural* form, the central cupola where, transcending geometry, a circle has been immured in a quadrature.

We are now perhaps in a position to appreciate the full significance of the language used to describe Isabel's confinement in the convent and her liberation when "young Fairfax through the walls doth rise." For the convent is tenaciously and inventively exposed precisely as the work of a foreign architect, one in which the poem's normative meta-

---

[6] Perhaps there is an allusion here to Fairfax's own poem on his house as but an inn on the way to one not built with hands; cited by H. M. Margoliouth from the Bodleian MS Fairfax 40 in his edition of *The Poems and Letters*, I, 2nd ed. (Oxford, 1963), 231. If so it is important to see how even here Marvell begins to shift the direction of the metaphor away from absolute quietism. Hence, at least, the epigraphs for this essay.

morphic process is persistently inverted. Unlike the house with its furniture of friends, the convent, we might say, made friends of the furniture. Thus, for example, instead of the humanized architecture just noted in the swelling hall, the walls, bars, gates, and grates of the convent merely maintain an empty space, ironically "enclosing" outwards that greater thing they should contain (and will indeed when Fairfax rises through them). This displacement of life by artifice reticulates every odious image in the Cistercian bower of bliss, whether it be the subtle nun's own artfully woven words, the superstition of the convent's dedication to sacramental "works" or the cunning infantilism of their cult of virginity. When young Fairfax invades the convent therefore, the triumph of action and marriage over contemplation and virginity also enforces the larger reassertion of the poem's sense of history—and in language informed by its characteristic metamorphosis: "Twas no *Religious House* till now", until it ceased to be a religious house as such. For if these are perhaps the most charming stanzas in the poem, their special enchantment is precisely the dissolution of artificial charm into a reality more fabulous for being humanly true. The sacramental instruments of the Virgin Amazons are no match for the more authentic romance of history: the glad youth who, rescuing the child as if from Gypsies, frees the castle from the enchantment that had possessed it. In a more profound way history's metamorphic process realizes the typology which the nuns had merely played at in their touching of "Our Lady" in Isabel. For just as "Our Lady" 's virginity is most meaningful when linked to her motherhood, so, in a sense they cannot comprehend, the nuns' Mariology has an ironic validity in presaging the final fulfillment of Isabel in history, in the glorious progeny to come from that blessed bed and especially in the latest issue of the Fairfax line, the nubile "Mary" in whom her promise is renewed at the end of the poem.

At the present moment, however, the Lord General would seem to have found his own resolution of detachment and engagement in his retired gardens laid out "in the just Figure of a Fort." And yet, given the thrust of past events, Fairfax's present recreations may seem something of a disappointment for all their charm. Indeed, what distinguishes Marvell's presentation of the scene here is precisely the tone of voice which allows such a possibility to be entertained, the delicate accent of reproof which hovers over the hyperbolical language of celebration. How "just," we may begin to ask ourselves, is this floral figure of a fort? Does it, like the metamorphic account of the house's cupola, in every figure equal man?

The most delicate and yet the most necessary critical enterprise for the reader of this poem is to gauge the effect of its tone upon its normative metaphoric process. One must be careful not to minimize the very real attraction of this floral fortress, the way in which this least humane of "arts" has been dissolved and perfected into a state of natural innocence, as in the way a typical day begins with its own version of reveille:

> Then Flow'rs their drowsie Eylids raise,
> Their Silken Ensigns each displayes,
> And dries its Pan yet dank with Dew,
> And fills its Flask with Odours new. (293–96)

Compared to the martial play of the nuns in their unnatural garden this sweet militia enlists us immediately. It is emblematic too of a lost Eden and a lost England when the gardener had the soldier's place, before the island garden was devastated by the "planting" of ordnance and the "sowing" of powder.

These are the values of Fairfax's gardens, as indeed he might have seen them, and they are considerable. But what they neglect to take into account is the aching irony of who Fairfax is:

> And yet there walks one on the Sod
> Who, had it pleased him and *God,*
> Might once have made our Gardens spring
> Fresh as his own and flourishing.
> But he preferr'd to the *Cinque Ports*
> These five imaginary Forts:
> And, in those half-dry Trenches, spann'd
> Pow'r which the Ocean might command. (345–52)

In these, perhaps the most moving lines of the poem, the incongruity which has been tactfully available in the fanciful celebrations becomes poignantly apparent. Presenting Fairfax's retirement from his own point of view ("him and *God*"), Marvell simultaneously evokes the larger context which would have justified a different course of action. Sorrow for the country's wasted garden tugs under the witty deference to imaginary forts and half-dry trenches. Had Fairfax taken up the sword perhaps the nation might have beaten swords into plowshares. The gardens delight us as a playful vision of history's goal, but not as the means to this end. In Vergil's *Georgics,* it is worth recalling, the nation's restoration was to issue from the unlikely means imposed by history: the soldier who makes war to have peace becoming the farmer whose hard work achieves a new golden age. By substituting his private version of the end for the means of history, Fairfax has made the realization of the end impossible. William Fairfax destroyed a convent to build a religious house, but now only "the invisible artillery" of contemplation is aimed at the nearby castle of an ambitious prelate. The telling irony of these gardens turned to forts is their poignant evocation of what Fairfax might have done instead—turned forts to gardens.

And yet the very tact of such a summons to involvement seems to manifest on the poet's part what might be called the rhetorical equivalent of Fairfax's political withdrawal. It is, so to speak, the kind of summons that might have been expected from a poem which has so far been much more at home with gardens and nunneries than with that inchoate world from which Fairfax retired. If the second sequence of meditations (in the structure I have outlined) engages us as the more memorable half of the poem, this is because it confronts that world. The lines which remind Mr. Alvarez of the manner of Lewis Carroll might remind us as well of the matter of Melville's "little lower layer," of Conrad's "destructive element":

> And now to the Abbyss I pass
> Of that unfathomable Grass,
> Where Men like Grashoppers appear,
> But Grashoppers are Gyants there:
> They, in their squeking Laugh, contemn
> Us as we walk more low then them:
> And, from the Precipices tall,
> Of the green spir's, to us do call.

> To see Men through this Meadow Dive,
> We wonder how they rise alive.
> As, under Water, none does know
> Whether he fall through it or go. (369–80)

This ominous yet eerily beautiful reversal of perspectives intimates a transformation of the poem's typical metamorphic process which is to become more and more apparent in the increasingly brutal imagery of the "massacre" of the grass, the slaying and eating of the birds sheltered there, the wasted landscape of haystacks and stubble and finally the flood which "makes the Meadow truly be / (What it had seemed before) a Sea." To contemplate the dissolution and perfection of art into life in the context of great houses, convents and gardens is one thing; it is another here where that metamorphosis is taken radically and literally and the life which displaces art seems but nasty, brutish and short. If, for

example, we have discerned a normative process in the house's "furniture
of friends," what are we to make of this kind of absolute dissolution of
the first term:

> For to this naked equal Flat,
> ' Which *Levellers* take Pattern at,
> The Villagers in common chase
> Their Cattle, which it closer rase (449–52)

What are we to make indeed of the miniature version of English history
which has just been "acted" out, leading us from an Egyptian world of
artifice to the brutal naturalism of this promised land? Evoking the
parliamentary army's own image of providential history, the militant
pilgrimage of these "Israelite" mowers enacts the raw violence which has
driven its Lord General to retirement.

> With whistling Sithe, and Elbow strong,
> These Massacre the Grass along:
> While one, unknowing, carves the *Rail,*
> ، Whose yet unfeather'd Quils her fail.
> The Edge all bloody from its Breast
> He draws, and does his stroke detest;
> Fearing the Flesh untimely mow'd
> To him a Fate as black forebode.

> But bloody *Thestylis,* that waites
> To bring the mowing Camp their Cates,
> Greedy as Kites has trust it up,
> And forewith means on it to sup:
> When on another quick She lights,
> And cryes, he call'd us *Israelites;*
> But now, to make his saying true,
> Rails rain for Quails, for Manna Dew. (393–408)

The mower who first "untimely" cuts the bird has all the decent reservations of the reflective man committed to make common cause with the
true believer, Thestylis, whose fanatical use of scripture sanctions activity which seems as mischievous as the withdrawal sanctioned by the
nuns' mariology.[7] Or so it seems at least to the narrator, whose *persona,*

[7] Citing U. Aldrovandus, *Ornithologia* (Bologna, 1637), III, 455–56, Allen, in a richly
suggestive note, observes that "Marvell certainly knew that the 'rallus crex' was known
to the Italians as 're di quaglie' and to the French as 'roi des cailles.' The bird is
the king of quail, though not a quail itself. . . . The Bird is also neutral. It is sometimes a wading bird and sometimes it comes to the fields and lives with the quails,"
p. 137.

it is important to notice, is itself becoming the dramatic focus of the poem. For in the more radical probing of this second sequence of meditations the meaning of historical involvement is dramatized not in the exemplary figures of an Isabel or William Fairfax, but in the poet's own acting out of the kind of experience which has driven the Lord General to withdrawal from action. The performance is most moving perhaps in the speaker's address to the slaughtered victims whose retirement could not save them:

> Unhappy Birds! what does it boot
> To build below the Grasses Root;
> When Lowness is unsafe as Hight,
> And Chance O'ertakes what scapeth spight? (409–12)

In the same perspective "the pleasant acts" of the rustic victory celebrations will be hyperbolically described with a Flaubertian irony. Finally, drawing together all the previous intimations of the dissolution of order, the flood whelms over the scene with an (apparently) catastrophic metamorphosis of nature and history into chaos.[8]

In poems as diverse as "Cooper's Hill" and *Paradise Lost* the image of the flood with its virtually archetypal mixture of destructiveness and creativity reveals the purposefulness immanent in the drama of history. At this moment in the poem, however, the speaker will seek his revelation not in the terms of history's dialectic but out of history.

> But I, retiring from the Flood,
> Take Sanctuary in the Wood;
> And, while it lasts, my self imbark
> In this yet green, yet growing Ark. (481–84)

The account of the speaker's contemplative play in this retired scene is perhaps the most famous portion of the poem; to many readers it would seem to be its climax, a looser and more curious way perhaps of acting out the condition celebrated more concisely and perfectly in "The Garden." Here I would like to suggest that there is a reason for the distinctive quality of this treatment of a favorite Marvell theme, one which should point up not only the circumstances and the character of the role which the speaker has assumed but also those limitations of his point of view which the reader begins to perceive. More so even than in

---

[8] See Horace, *Carmina*, I.ii.13–20, as Allen notes, pp. 133, 139. It is important to perceive, however, that Horace uses the symbol of the flood not to advocate withdrawal but to celebrate the order which Augustus has brought in expiating the sins of the past and redeeming the community (29–40).

the description of Fairfax's floral fortress, the metamorphic imagery of this green yet growing ark must be gauged by a discriminating sensitivity to tone. To use the terms of the lines just quoted, it is important to distinguish the grove as a sanctuary, which the speaker will increasingly cherish, from the grove as an ark, in which perspective we (especially after our first reading) may take the measure of the speaker's ecstasies. Indeed it could be argued that it is quite misleading for the speaker to identify himself with Noah "retiring" from the flood in the first place; instead one might say more accurately that, in the literal sense of a well-worn metaphor, Noah rode the crest of history. Especially as the type of a later carpenter, he exemplifies the active life, the pattern of destruction as a means of recreation which characterizes the Christian and georgic sense of history.

The speaker's innocence of such connotations is the typical (and most irresistible) feature of the experience acted out in the grove. It is this note of innocence which deftly undercuts the speaker's hermetic exclusion of couples from the ark or his attention to the Corinthean porticoes of the sanctuary. It is nicely manifest too when the speaker begins to observe the birds within the grove, but not, it would seem, to perceive their significance. The reader meanwhile, enjoys the rather matter-of-fact description by the bird-watcher, but he also begins to perceive an instructive progression from the solitary nightingale whose *locus amoenus* is perfectly suited to the wish fulfillment of the amorous pastoral to the "sadder yet more pleasing sound" of the doves who seem to have confronted the world of experience and who, even in their contemplative yearning, are conspicuously a married pair (with all the resonance that union has in the poem's metaphoric structure). The distinction between the nightingale and the doves has its analogue in the next stanza's presentation of the throstle and the heron:

> Then as I careless on the Bed
> Of gelid *Straw-berryes* do thread,
> And through the Hazles thick espy
> The hatching *Thrastles* shining Eye;
> The *Heron* from the Ashes top,
> The eldest of its young lets drop,
> As if it Stork-like did pretend
> That *Tribute* to its *Lord* to send. (529–36)

The last lines attribute to the heron the stork's habit (according to Dutch folk lore) of gratefully leaving one of its young behind when it abandons its nest in a house. Reminding us that a nest too is but an inn, and this grove but an ark, the incident is merely narrated by the "careless" speaker who, characteristically, finds the charms of a nest far more fascinating to contemplate. The haunting adjectival details recorded there intensify a certain child-like delight, but they leave little sense of that larger perspective enjoyed by the heron whose willingness to "let drop" its young signals a more impressive carelessness than that in the strawberry beds.

The climax of this dialectical progression towards engagement is, of course, the exemplary georgic activity of the hewel or woodpecker.

> But most the *Hewel's* wonders are,
> Who here has the *Holt-felsters* care.
> He walks still upright from the Root,
> Meas'ring the Timber with his Foot;
> And all the way, to keep it clean,
> Doth from the Bark the Wood-moths glean.
> He, with his Beak, examines well
> Which fit to stand and which to fell.
>
> The good he numbers up, and hacks;
> As if he mark'd them with the Ax.
> But where he, tinkling with his Beak,
> Does find the hollow Oak to speak,
> That for his building he designs,
> And through the tainted Side he mines.
> Who could have thought the *tallest Oak*
> Should fall by such a *feeble Strok'!*
>
> Nor would it, had the Tree not fed
> A *Traitor-worm*, within it bred.
> (As first our *Flesh* corrupt within
> Tempts impotent and bashful *Sin.*)
> And yet that *Worm* triumphs not long,
> But serves to feed the *Hewels young.*
> While the Oake seems to fall content,
> Viewing the Treason's Punishment. (537–60)

With all the manifest political and religious significance of his georgic involvement the hewel might well persuade us to revise the speaker's earlier indictment of the militant mowers' activity, an indictment which, we recall, focused on the pathos of the slain landrail whose nest could not escape the mowers' blades "when Lowness is unsafe as Hight" (411). In the hewel's search for his nest in a tree which he fells, we have however the symbolic reconciliation of the necessity of the mowers' action and the pathos of the landrail's plight. The hewel is, so to speak, both a mower and a nester. Like the swarm of bees in Vergil's slain bullock, the hewel's nest in the fallen oak enacts the perennial georgic metamorphosis, perfectly expressing the need of destruction for regeneration, of war for peace, of work for leisure, of action for contemplation.

If the climax of the speaker's contemplation of the creatures reminds us therefore of the necessity for action, how then are we to take the incipient metamorphosis of the next stanza with its celebrated apostrophe?

> Thus I, easie *Philosopher,*
> Among the *Birds* and *Trees* confer:
> And little now to make me, wants
> Or of the *Fowles,* or of the *Plants.*
> Give me but Wings as they, and I
> Streight floting on the Air shall fly:
> Or turn me but, and you shall see
> I was but an inverted Tree. (561–68)

We are not to take it, it seems to me, as solemnly as the mere identification of its allusions might suggest. Professor Røstvig has proposed, for example, that the speaker's blending into nature here evokes the Plotinian union of contemplating man and contemplated creation which, in Christian terms, characterized the original state of innocence.[9] One might add that the dream of the contemplative life as a return to paradise (in Adamic harmony with the beasts) can be traced back to the desert fathers. But this hardly seems to do justice to the tone of the speaker's willingness to play such a role by floating in the air or standing on his head. Indeed, as in Fairfax's garden-fortress, the reader will delight in these metamorphic high jinks precisely to the extent that he sees them as a playful image of man restored to innocence and not, as the speaker would have it, as the means to this end. For if "conferring" with the birds has taught anything to the reader it is the cost of easy philosophy, the necessity of a leisure earned by activity while walking "still upright from the Root/Measuring the Timber with his foot."

It is this mixture of enjoyment and suspicion of the speaker's play which gives the stanza's famous last line its special complexity. The image of man as an inverted tree derives from the Platonic notion that man's soul, located at the summit of his body, continually aspires towards the celestial place where it originated. Man is thus a plant whose

[9] Røstvig, I, 183.

roots are not on earth but in heaven.[10] At the risk of schematizing what is itself a delightfully comic subversion of the systematic by the vital, I would point out that no previous use of the *arbor inversa* metaphor contains Marvell's request to be turned upside down. The reason is evident: the tree must remain inverted (man must remain upright) to illustrate the metaphor: the root within the mind must be closer to heaven. Consequently the inverted tree which Marvell invites the reader to visualize by standing him on his head is not at all the spiritual one which he "was." It is, in effect, simply the one which he would be if upside down with his hair dangling and his feet (his less Platonic "roots") now branching upward in the air. In this posture the speaker might seem really to be saying "I *am now* 'but an inverted tree.' " To invert the inverted Platonic tree is to bring the otherworldly seer's root literally "down to earth" in the very act of flamboyantly demonstrating his inversion.

This blend of tones suffuses the concluding "acts" in the grove, enabling the speaker to kick up his heels in increasingly more fanciful postures while, enjoying the display in the limited way I have described, the reader also ponders the summons to history dramatically revealed in the connotations of the very language of retired celebration.

> And see how Chance's better Wit
> Could with a Mask my studies hit!
> The Oak-Leaves me embroyder all,
> Between which Caterpillars crawl:
> And Ivy, with familiar trails,
> Me licks, and clasps, and curles, and hales.
> Under this *antick Cope* I move
> Like some great *Prelate of the Grove*. (585-92)

If it recalls the Laudian Prelate previously contemplated from the garden fortress, the last line might well warn the reader to his own kind of vigilance. Like the studies he is trying to describe, the speaker's masquing habit suggests both the "antic" liberation of innocent play and the hazards to the free soul in the "antique" organization of contemplative experience which has not been justified by right action. Like

[10] The seminal statement is in Plato's *Timaeus* (90a). See A. B. Chambers, " 'I was But an Inverted Tree': Notes toward the History of an Idea," *Studies in the Renaissance*, VIII (1961), 291-99, and Røstvig, I, 183. The meaning of the line is readily apparent if one speaks it giving "was" and "inverted" the strongest possible emphasis. As I shall suggest, however, it is significant that most readers interpret the line as if the speaker were actually describing the inverted position of his body.

the cope itself, the rhetorical fabric of the stanza swarms with sinister innuendoes in its most minute verbal details. Both, one suspects, require the inspection of the hewel. Rather than overtly pronounce the distinction that would seem to be required here, Marvell chooses to dramatize the necessity for discrimination. Of course the reader may be expected to discern that in a sense the speaker's pleasures are as innocent as Fairfax's retired amusements. But that they are innocent, that they are not as prelatical as, say, the amusements of the nuns is only ironically apparent in the very theatricality with which they are overplayed. Marvell leaves the reader, especially perhaps Fairfax, to determine the sense in which retirement can be justified and to reflect on the perils of play.

Such perils are soon intimated in the speaker's increasing restlessness, probingly dramatized in his very overplaying of the playful role. Languishing with ease and tossing on the moss, too insistently grateful perhaps for his declared relaxation, he can also use quite violent and uncontemplative language to proclaim his new found security. "How safe, methinks, and strong, behind/These Trees have I incamp'd my Mind" (601–02). If the punning verb recalls the original "embarking" from the flood into the sanctuary of the green yet growing ark, its strenuousness belies the promised liberation of the earlier lines and lacks, as well, the insouciance of Fairfax's garden-fort. The pressure of history is felt even in the contemplative's insistence on its being subdued: the mind which has "incamp'd" itself behind the trees has not only lodged itself in a field but adapted a curiously militant stance. Safe from the world, he will not only securely play "on it," but ride its riders, "gaul its Horsemen all the Day" (608). What the speaker finally acts out is the impossibility of dismissing history. Even to stand outside it is to stand in relation to it and even in contemplation he must share the language of the committed.

In this way the climax of the retirement to the wood dramatizes the necessity of engagement in its very insistence on an absolute withdrawal from the world.

> Bind me ye Woodbines in your 'twines,
> Curle me about ye gadding *Vines*,
> And Oh so close your Circles lace,
> That I may never leave this Place:
> But, lest your Fetters prove too weak,
> Ere I your Silken Bondage break,
> Do you, *O Brambles,* chain me too,
> And courteous *Briars* nail me through. (609–16)

Once again Professor Røstvig's learned interpretation cogently defines the critical issue. Here, she writes, the retired speaker offers himself in a sacrifice imitating the passion of Christ. He dies to the old Adam, to put on the new one in Christ; he undergoes a baptism from the flesh to the spirit which has its parallel in the release of the mind from the passions in Platonic and Hermetic lore.[11] An evocation of the crucifixion seems to be demonstrable, but one is less sure how to apply the allusion to the speaker's situation. After all, it is also true that Christ's crucifixion in the city was one of the most *public* acts of his career, as was the salvation which it made possible. To invoke the crucifixion as a typological justification for absolute withdrawal from history is rather like the nuns' invocation of Mary for being a virgin instead of the mother of God. Nowhere more than in this crucial stanza must one gauge the import of the speaker's lines by the metaphoric quality of his language and the dramatic circumstances of its utterance. One might begin by noticing the curiously painless and artificial connotations of such words as "curle," "lace," "silken," and "courteous,"—language which one might associate with the weaving of the Prelate's embroidered cope, or, less whimsically, with the kind of crucifixion of the self which the self-indulgent nuns might practice in their needlework. Of course one must concede a certain heightened urgency to the tone of this passage full of apostrophes and imperatives. And yet the very desperation of its almost masochistic insistence would seem to expose the incompleteness of the solitary state from which it arises. What the poet's self-dramatization reveals is as relevant to the situation of Fairfax as it would have been indecorous in the actual description of his gardens. It is the impoverishment of contemplation if it is not married to history.

The liberation sought in the grove-as-sanctuary will be found upon leaving the grove-as-ark and as a result of the unlikely means of the flood. The events which had driven the speaker to retirement are seen now under the aspect of their final cause, the renewal which seems to justify this miniature version of history's dialectical process. If there is a hint of infantile self-satisfaction and Narcissism in the characterization of the meadows and river, it would seem a pardonable innocence in the newborn. Bunyan—or Blake—might have called the present state of being "Beulah." To the speaker it offers more refreshment than one feels he ever found in his postures in the grove.

---

[11] Røstvig, I, 183.

Oh what a Pleasure 'tis to hedge
My Temples here with heavy sedge
Abandoning my lazy Side
Stretcht as a Bank unto the Tide;
Or to suspend my sliding Foot
On the Osiers undermined Root,
And in its Branches tough to hang,
While at my Lines the Fishes twang! (641–48)

The lines have all the childlike charm of a scene from *The Compleat Angler* or *Huckleberry Finn,* but it is characteristic of the conclusion of this poem that an idyll of rebirth should not be seen as an end in itself. Attractive as it is in one way, the speaker's pleasure springs from a dissolution of his distinctively human identity. With his temples hedged with sedge, stretched "as a bank," he has yet to define himself as separate from nature, to stand upright and on firmer footing.

As the young Maria walks tonight along the river, one part of the meaning of the poem's concluding stanzas is just such a making firm of the world reborn. The other part is the consciousness that such a condition too must be open to history in a growing up and a growing out of this new world, this house, this poem. Together, their equilibrium creates an ineffable "evening" mood, a conclusion which is also a transition and is itself beautifully announced by the twilight transformation of the halcyon's flight, suffusing the interlude between the fresher green after the flood and the darkness of night with "Mary's" color, blue. Many critics tend to find the conclusion somewhat anticlimactic after the excitement of the mowing and flooding and the ecstasies in the grove; to this reader at least it is the fullest and richest statement of the poem's metamorphic image of history (or marriage). It is true that compared to the previous scenes Mary's world is more chastened, but this should be the very reason why her performance should command a kind of serious response which was never elicited by those exhibitions. For her "loose" nature recollects itself into a sober frame rather like her own virginal silence. Not only does the "viscous" air suck the halcyon's azure dye to become the *"Saphir-winged Mist,"* but as the last adjective connotes, a crystallization is also effected: the "gellying" stream now "compacts" to "fix" the bird's reflected image. In the pure intensity of her contemplation Maria compacts and informs the world just as her father had shaped his house: "but by her *Flames,* in *Heaven* try'd,/*Nature* is wholly *vitrifi'd.*" Suggesting density and hardening, *"vitrifi'd"* nature is thus transformed into something like that unchanging "fifth element" which the poet had sought in the grove (502). The whole world is now such a sanctuary, not because of what it is, but because of whom it contains or, more accurately, whom it reflects, "vitrifi'd" as it is like the river into her glass.

Contracting our focus to the lesser world that contains the greater, we next behold the particular effects of Maria's presence here where she becomes the genius of her place and (in stanzas whose very chiastic rhetoric embodies compactness) infuses the four sections of the topography with their distinctive natural graces even as she enjoys their transformation into the carpets, crowns, mirror and screen that in every figure equal man. Instead of the conversation of the easy Philosopher with the birds and trees (and with his strenuously hyperbolic apostrophes), one may now ponder the noiseless *"Wisdome"* of *"Heavens Dialect,"* the ineffable plenitude of meaning in the silence of the virgin who has just hushed the world. *Felix qui potuit rerum cognoscere causas . . . fortunatus et ille deos qui novit agrestis.* He who was the "thrice-happy" reader of nature's mystic book learns more here contemplating the contemplation of the artless girl.

And yet, true to the poem's sense of history, the most moving aspect of these lines is not so much their contractile "recollection" of loose nature, but their registered consciousness that she who is already "the *Law*/of all her *Sex*, her *Ages Aw*," must yield, not to be destroyed but fulfilled. Along the safe but roughest way of her sober parents Maria has been preserved from the Petrarchan artifice of the amorous shot and cannon of tears and sighs. Yet the very use of such imagery reminds us that, like Isabel among the nuns, Mary too must someday yield to the attack whose triumph heralds renewal when some other Fairfax through the wall does rise. Like the young heron she must be "let drop." As in her domestic heaven she now enjoys the fulfillment of contemplation, so she must someday be uprooted from her *hortus conclusus,*

> Hence *She* with Graces more divine
> Supplies beyond her *Sex* the *Line;*
> And, like a *sprig of Misleto,*
> On the *Fairfacian Oak* does grow;
> Whence, for some universal good,
> The *Priest* shall cut the sacred Bud;
> While her *glad Parents* most rejoice,
> And make their *Destiny* their *Choice*. (737–44)

The stanza is inexhaustible to meditation. Druidical folklore here expresses a simple native English piety which is the opposite of the exotic prelatical ritual of the grove. The mistletoe is, of course, green through the winter, and as its deciduous host shows the signs of seasonal change, it reveals, as at Christmas time, the promise of regeneration even in the wintry world. As in the title of Frazer's famous book the mistletoe recalls "the golden bough" guiding Aeneas through the descent to death with the promise of rebirth, and in the Christian tradition it is obviously suggestive of the god whose triumph over death on the "tree" of the cross offers the same deathless liberation to the believer. It may not be too much to say that the retired poet's yearning for "crucifixion" in the grove was a desire by being "chained" and "nailed" by brambles and briars to reach the timeless stasis of the mistletoe such as Mary enjoys now attached to the Fairfacian oak or as symbolized in the "viscous" air of this interlude. The crucifixion in the grove is important to recall here, for its insistently voiced private seclusion from time is precisely the opposite of the liberating deliverance which animates the public engagement with time symbolized by the cutting of the "sacred bud" from the tree. It is the perfect expression of the poet's georgic vision of the necessary interplay of private contemplative ease with active public involvement. The cutting off of the mistletoe is itself a practical horticultural example of the destruction necessary for transplanting. With its delicate suggestion of the defloration which must precede burgeoning it is also a poignantly intimate image of the nature of Mary's future engagement as another "blooming" Thwaites. Rather than grieve for the blight man was born for, Marvell envisions Mary's future as part of the age-old georgic mystery of destruction and regeneration at the heart of organic reality. The metamorphosis of the virgin to wife enacts the liberation in death of Christ on the cross. Marvell of course puts it less explicitly, indeed less sacramentally, but in his fashion he deftly intimates that a sacred bud, like a grain of wheat, will bring forth much fruit "if it die."

What finally gives Mary's Appleton House its special distinction among the blessed isles of literature is not its distance from the tempest but the imminent cutting of its timeless bud, immersion in time and acceptance of historical responsibility. As the past and the future are mastered in the present, so the World previously imaged in the "Gulfes, Deserts, Precipices, Stone" of the active life in the meadow is now transformed in the "lesser" world that can "contain" the greater precisely because it accepts participation in it, teaching us to view that world not as a rude heap but as potentially the decent order to which, in its scale, the house has attained.[12] Thus if the estate finally offers *"Paradice's only map,"* it does so still only as an inn, fitly reminding us how to earn that blissful seat —by leaving it.

In the same way it might be said that the poem itself was built to entertain its lord awhile, "but not remain":

> But now the *Salmon-Fishers* moist
> Their *Leathern Boats* begin to hoist;
> And, like *Antipodes* in Shoes,
> Have shod their *Heads* in their *Canoos.*
> How *Tortoise* like, but not so slow,
> These rational *Amphibii* go?
> Let's in: for the dark *Hemisphere*
> Does now like one of them appear. (769–76)

It is regrettable that most readers who have ever heard of "Upon Appleton House" know only that its last stanza is commonly regarded as a notorious instance of metaphysical wit at its most extravagant. Though a separate essay could be written explicating the stanza's intrinsic suggestiveness, perhaps it is most important to stress here that the conceit does not exploit local details at the expense of the poem's total structure. Indeed it is instructive to consider this conceit alongside the poem's other more remarkable flights of wit (e.g., 5–8, 49–56, 377–84, 561–68, 641–48) and discover (to use the terms they themselves employ) how it fills them out and turns them right side up. To do so would be to begin to perceive the extraordinary implicative power of these lines in which, from the slightest verbal details (*"Salmon," "moist," "Leathern"*) to the largest themes (the "amphibious" metamorphic resolution of work and contemplation, time and the timeless, death and life), the patterns of meaning I have tried to explain in the previous reading are here "in less contained." And if this very density should embarrass the poem (for the reputation of the stanza is not to be denied), it does so with an urbane kind of vexatiousness, to remind us aptly that the time for poetry is over, to tease us into thought—and action. The stanza too has its metamorphic sense of history: from its "inn" one simultaneously looks back over the poem as past event and beyond its end. It is a prospect to summon the critic at least to his own metamorphosis. Let the criticism

---

[12] Differing from Margoliouth, I interpret these lines to mean that the world is now seen no longer as "what it was" which was "but (appositively, meaning 'only') a huge heap." As Toliver points out, this reading is more evident in the editions of Cooke, Thompson and Grosart where a comma is placed after "world"; but as the next line shows, a semi-colon could also be used to separate appositional modifiers (p. 129).

of this poem admit that the only way it too can finally contain things greater is by emulating the poem's purposeful inconclusiveness which invites us "in" at the end to the sober frame which it celebrates in the beginning, to the domestic work of art whose consummation (as the poem's art has shown) is to lead us out to life. "Let's in."

Andrew Marvell and Cromwell's Kingship: "The First Anniversary"

by John M. Wallace

When Marvell accepted office under the Protectorate, and committed himself, for life as it turned out, to an active political career, he sold himself down the river as a poet and surrendered his independent critical mind first to a servitude under Cromwell, then to a slavery under the Whigs. "The First Anniversary of the Government under O. C." marks the beginning of his decline, for the poem reveals few of the tensions of the Horatian Ode, and thereafter his verse tended to scurrility and formlessness. So ran the familiar tale until a few years ago—it is not yet dead —but recently Professor Fogel has spoken up for "The Last Instructions," and Professor Mazzeo has implicitly argued that "The First Anniversary" is better than it has been taken to be, because Cromwell is there portrayed as a Davidic king.[1] In the future, when "The Last Instructions" has had the reading it deserves, when editors have admitted the evidence for Marvell's authorship of the libelous doggerel attributed to him to be extremely slight, and when it is generally recognized that his main contributions to the political and religious crises during the 'seventies are, in their own way, as good as anything he ever wrote, the integrity of Marvell's concept of himself as a writer will emerge, and will be found to conform very closely to the legend of his unbribable honesty as a Member of Parliament. It is not my purpose, however, to defend "The First Anniversary," but to show it defends itself once its deliberative intention is perceived. Even Mazzeo, who comes close to the heart of the matter, has mistaken a deliberative poem for a simple panegyric, and hence fails

"Andrew Marvell and Cromwell's Kingship: 'The First Anniversary'" [Abridged] by John M. Wallace. From *ELH*, XXX, No. 3 (September, 1963), 209–32. Copyright © 1963 by The Johns Hopkins Press. Reprinted by permission of The Johns Hopkins Press.

[1] Ephim G. Fogel, "Salmons in Both, or Some Caveats for Canonical Scholars, Part II," *Bull. N. Y. Pub. Lib.*, LXIII (June, 1959), 299–303; "Cromwell as Davidic King," in *Reason and the Imagination*, ed. J. A. Mazzeo (New York, 1962), 29–55.

to account for large sections of the verse, which he does not mention. If "The First Anniversary" is not read both carefully and in its immediate historical context, then (to be sure) Cromwell emerges as a Protector "sui generis"—a political freak whom Marvell praises, almost blasphemously, as a king—but the imagery then functions only to increase the hyperboles of Marvell's admiration, and we are back where we started with the poet's uncritical subservience to his new master. If, however, the poem is read as an argument that Cromwell accept the English crown and institute a new dynasty of kings, then the structure and imagery of the poem can be accounted for more completely than by presupposing their merely panegyric aim. Paradoxically, this exposes not Marvell's supreme flattery of the Protector, but his concern for the country's future; a concern which transcends private admiration, and manifests the serious calling to which Marvell felt himself elected as a political poet.

I

The first anniversary of the Protectorate was cause for some rejoicing. The year had been notable less for the improvement in domestic than in foreign affairs, but here the success was remarkable, and as a result Cromwell was at the height of his power.[2] The Dutch war had come to an end on terms which were to England's advantage; treaties had been concluded with Sweden, Portugal, and Denmark, and another with France was in preparation; minor Protestant states were being courted with emissaries, and envoys of tiny principalities from the North Sea to the Baltic were waiting to be heard in London. Since Cromwell was now the head of the greatest sea-power in Europe and a diplomat of proven ability, it was altogether appropriate for Marvell to terminate his poem with an address delivered by a foreign king, and to commence it with a comparison between Cromwell's activity and the sluggishness of ordinary monarchs.

At home, on the contrary, the difficulties had possibly increased, and Abbott records "it was beyond the ingenuity of even [Cromwell's] most devoted followers to evolve a constitutional argument for his assumption

---

[2] W. C. Abbott, *The Writings and Speeches of Oliver Cromwell* (Cambridge, Mass., 1937–47), III, 525. Henceforth cited as Abbott. His account of the Protectorate years surpasses any other in comprehensiveness. He reports (III, 523) that "By the end of November, 1654, the Protectorate at last seemed on the way to something like a permanent footing."

and exercise of supreme power and to make him seem a *de jure* ruler by any stretch of legal technicality." [3] The first parliament of the Protectorate was preoccupied almost exclusively from its first meeting in September 1654, and through the new year, with the Instrument of Government, thus proving constitutional problems were uppermost in the thoughts of public men, and their solution of paramount importance. The legality of the "Single Person" in the constitution was a battle which had been fought and won during the first weeks, but the means of choosing a successor to the Single Person were not settled. Some favored an elective, others a hereditary Protectorship, while a certain number hoped Cromwell would accept the crown. A good deal of evidence concerning the vitality of the kingship issue as early as 1654 can be found in the histories of the period (though never widely aired by historians), and more is available in the pamphlet literature.

Two of the most fully-reported meetings at which kingship was discussed took place even before the Protectorate began; one at Lenthall's house on 10 December 1651, the other a year later when Cromwell asked Whitelock the famous question "What if a Man should take upon him to be King?" [4] Yet another year later, in December 1653, Lambert and his fellow officers, when making an outline for the Instrument, had offered Cromwell the title of king, but he had refused.[5] By January 1654 some foreigners, including Queen Christina, were inclined to think Cromwell should have accepted the crown.[6] A little later, Hyde and the Venetian resident independently reported rumors of the title of Emperor.[7] In September Paulucci passed on the news that Cromwell had rejected the thought of kingship, but from 16–18 October there was a debate in parliament on the motion that the Protectorship be made hereditary.[8] The motion was lost by a heavy majority, but sixty or sixty-five members voted for it, and Bordeaux reported Cromwell had hoped to keep the

---

[3] III, 181.
[4] Abbott, II, 505–507 and 589 ff.
[5] C. H. Firth, "Cromwell and the Crown," *English Historical Review*, XVII (1902), 429, and S. R. Gardiner, *History of the Commonwealth and Protectorate* (London, 1903), II, 319.
[6] Abbott, III, 149.
[7] Abbott, III, 285. John Thurloe, *A Collection of State Papers*, ed. Thomas Birch (London, 1742), II, 614 has a letter of intelligence from Cologne, dated 29 Sept. 1654: "Here is a common report, of which your letters say noething, that the protector went into the parliament-house, and there had his peroration for an houre; and that after, the parliament with unanimous consent called his highness emperor; and his title they have written thus: *Oliver, the first emperor of Greate Britaine, and the isles thereunto belonging, allways Caesar, &c.*"
[8] Abbott, III, 482–483; Gardiner, *History*, III, 200–201.

title in his family. A similar decision was passed again in December without a division, but, at the same time, Broghill and Cromwell discussed a possible compromise with the Stuarts.[9] Two days before Christmas, when Marvell's poem may have been in the press, Augustine Garland, supported by Henry Cromwell and Sir Anthony Ashley Cooper, moved to have the Protector crowned, but this motion was also dropped after a short debate.[10] Dissolving parliament in January, Cromwell "went out of his way to protest against the idea that the government should be 'made a patrimony,' " [11] but within six months a crowd was assembling at Westminster expecting to hear Cromwell announce his acceptance of the crown, and the making of the Great Seal was delayed because (probably) his title had not been fixed.[12]

Defenses of the Instrument denied Cromwell would king it, or pointed out that while kings in the past had hindered the reign of Christ, wise kings did not. The dangers of an elective system were made the excuse for demanding negotiation with Charles II, and another writer asked why, if others had made profits from the war which they expected to pass on to their sons, the Protector's acquisitions should not be hereditary also.[13] One poetaster concluded a poem in a volume of tributes published at Oxford to celebrate the Dutch treaty with this suggestion:

> Rise now, by whom both *Arts and pollicy* stood,
> Thou one *Seth's Pillar* in a double *Floud!*

[9] Abbott, III, 524–526.

[10] Firth, "Cromwell and the Crown," p. 429; Abbott, III, 549; Gardiner, *History,* III, 225. Abbott, pp. 476–477, also believes that it was about this time that Wither presented his "Discourse" to the Protector, which suggested an alternative form of government to the hereditary rule Cromwell was supposed to favor.

[11] Firth, "Cromwell and the Crown," p. 430; Abbott, III, 589.

[12] Gardiner, *History,* III, 304.

[13] See *An Apology for the Present Government, and Governour,* sig. A2ʳ (All dates London, 1654); *The Grand Catastrophe, or the Change of Government,* esp. pp. 12–15; *An Admonition to my Lord Protector and his Council of their Danger; A Copy of a Letter Concerning the Election of a Lord Protector,* esp. pp. 6–8, 19–37. An important defense of the Instrument, i.e. of the status quo, was [Nedham?] *A True State of the Case of the Commonwealth.* The dissolution of the Nominated (Barebones) Parliament was defended by John Hall, *Confusion Confounded: or a Firm Way of Settlement Settled and Confirmed.* The (clearly accurate) attribution of this pamphlet to Hall occurs in John B. Shaw, "The Life and Works of John Hall of Durham," unpub. Ph.D. diss. at Johns Hopkins (1952), pp. 210–211. Defenses of a strong executive are to be found in *Sedition Scourg'd,* in *Somers Tracts,* ed. Walter Scott, VI, 297 ff., and *A Representation Concerning the Late Parliament, in the Year 1654. To Prevent Mistakes* (n.p., 1655), in which the author is nevertheless critical of the dissolution of the First Parliament. M[ichael] H[awke], *The Right of Dominion* (1655) is another strongly monarchical tract.

To thee we prostrate *Crowne* and *Booke*: with it
Rule *Champion* of our *State*, with *that* of *wit*.[14]

The most explicit proponents of monarchy I shall quote later. They
were Samuel Hunton, who wrote at least two tracts on the subject, and
John Hall of Richmond, whose *Of Government and Obedience* is one
of the lengthiest works on constitutional theory to appear during the
Interregnum. He refused even to consider aristocracy and democracy as
viable means of government, because multitudes cannot control themselves: "And therefore I should rather think, that the most rational
course that in this case [when a government has been overthrown] can
be taken to recover their former happiness and peace . . . that they
return to the same form of government and obedience under which they
formerly enjoyed them." [15]

In spite of parliament's unwillingness at this date to alter the thirty-
second article of the Instrument, the matter was once more to the forefront in May 1655, and again in July. Long before the issue became
the first item on the political agenda, and Cromwell was begged to take
the crown, the succession was clearly a topic which would neither lie down
nor (even) fail to be the subject of a serious political discourse celebrating
the Protectorate. On the other hand, the plea for kingship would by no
means command unanimous assent, and Marvell is cautious in making
it. To a contemporary reader, however, who was not limited to the inade-
quacies of a historical and rhetorical reconstruction, the message would
be plain enough.

II

Readers generally agree that the poem falls into seven clearly defined
sections, though Marvell has managed the transitions with sufficient skill
to leave the exact lines of demarcation in some doubt. An occasional
short passage may be thought to belong more properly to the section
which precedes or follows it, but clarity demands precise numeration
here: 1. The comparison of Cromwell with the "heavy Monarchs" (1–48);

---

[14] John Ailmer, in *Musarum Oxoniensium* (Oxford, 1654), p. 97.
[15] (London, 1654), p. 188; see also pp. 190–191. Arthur Barker, *Milton and the Puritan
Dilemma 1641–1660* (Toronto, 1942) in a long note on p. 382 argues that the absence
of references to the disadvantages of kingship in Milton's *Defensio Secunda* (1654) and
the *Pro Se Defensio* (1655) "can only be explained by the possibility that Oliver might
yet become king."

2. Cromwell's building of the harmonious state (49–116); 3. The advent of the millennium which Cromwell has brought nearer is postponed by man's sin (117–158); 4. The coaching accident (159–220); 5. A series of brief proofs that Cromwell has not employed his power arbitrarily (221–292); 6. A short diatribe against the Fifth Monarchists (293–324); 7. The tribute of foreign monarchs to Cromwell's astounding success (325–402).

The homogeneity of these diverse parts is assured not only by their relation to Cromwell but by their preoccupation with time. Obliterating, useful, and useless time in the first section; hoped-for millennial time in the third; destructive time (death) in the fourth; and restored time (the simile of the returning sun) in the seventh and last. Were mere eulogy his aim, Marvell lost an opportunity of proving the fulfillment of time had arrived, and the millennium (so conspicuously unrealized but so tantalizingly near in the poem) had been ushered in by the Protector's rule. Temporality, however, is but the context within which the drama of the Protector's achievements has been enacted, and, incredible though they are, they fall swiftly under the sentence propounded by the opening lines:

> Like the vain Curlings of the Watry maze,
> Which in smooth streams a sinking Weight does raise;
> So man, declining alwayes, disappears
> In the weak Circles of increasing Years;
> And his short Tumults of themselves Compose,
> While flowing Time above his Head does close.[16]

As ethical proof, these lines justify Miss Lloyd Thomas' and Miss Bradbrook's assertion that Marvell writes in full consciousness of the passing importance of his own labors.[17] Moreover, an irrefutable statement carries more weight than an exaggeration, and so Marvell's claim for Cromwell loses, not its essential truth, but the absolute value which it appears to assert: *"Cromwell* alone with greater Vigour runs, / (Sun-like) the Stages of succeeding Suns" (7–8). By employing the usual pun on sun-son, Marvell is at once calling attention to his real theme, as well as trans-

---

[16] All quotations from Margoliouth's edition. Ripples round a stone had been used in various ways. Vitruvius, V.iii.6 compares the spread of a voice to ripples, in which he is followed by Diogenes Laertius, *Dialogues,* VII.158 and Chaucer, "House of Fame," lines 782–792. Seneca, *Naturales Questiones,* I.ii.7 uses the simile for light in the air around a star, and Silius Italicus, *Punica,* XIII.24–29 for courage spreading outwards from the leaders to the common soldiers in the Carthaginian ranks. I have not yet found a usage similar to Marvell's.

[17] *Andrew Marvell* (Cambridge, 1940), p. 78.

ferring the traditional image of kingship on to the uncrowned Protector. In the remainder of the first section, the heavy kings, unlike stones in the water dropping rapidly out of sight, become heavy planets circling for aeons in a useless time. "Well may they strive to leave them [their "Projects"] to their Son, / For one Thing never was by one King don" (21–22). For the Christian all time is "useless" (41) unless redeemed, and Cromwell has set out to redeem it all he can, but as he "cuts his way still nearer to the Skyes" (46) one picks up the suggestion again of his future death. All the iniquities which Marvell attributes to monarchs contrast implicitly with Cromwell's virtues, but when he asserts "They neither build the Temple in their dayes, / Nor Matter for succeeding Founders raise" (34–35), is he not hinting that the world of "matter" or "things" (cf. 22, 43, 77) requires a new line of rulers when the old have proved themselves inadequate? Cromwell's eminence as a founder is indisputable, but the question of what happens to his work at his death is left suspended. If the "sacred Prophecies" are to be "perfected" (36), a beginning must be made, but Marvell deliberately insinuates that no single ruler would be able to complete them. So the world of time and its concomitant Things go on remorselessly, and the first section as a whole arouses the hope, which other parts of the poem are to exploit fully, that time will one day have a stop, this lower sphere will be tuned to the higher, and the great work which Cromwell has begun will be completed.

The description of Cromwell as Amphion is the most strictly panegyric section of the poem. The comparison had been made before by Cromwell's eulogists,[18] and on its acceptability the subsequent argument depends. If the new state were not harmonious and constructed on sound principles, its perpetuation could only be a mistake. Rhetorically it was necessary to describe the Protectorate, a kingdom in all but name, as a flawless pattern of a commonwealth, and in Amphion Marvell had a figure long renowned in the mythological books as the type of successful politician who by persuasive oratory could soften the hearts of the hardest men. He "persuaded those who lived a wild and savage life before," wrote the most imitative of all mythologists in his *Pantheon,* "to embrace the rules and manners of civil society." [19] One admirer of Cromwell, after exclaiming that not only war but love had conquered England, wrote "Thus a *sweet concord* do's *He timely* raise / From th' lofty *Treble* and

---

[18] Fitzpayne Fisher, in *Inauguratio Olivariana* (London, 1654), p. 15, and references to Cromwell's cithara in *Musarum Oxoniensium,* pp. 9, 16.

[19] Andrew Tooke, *Tooke's Pantheon of the Heathen Gods* (Baltimore, 1838), p. 324. Tooke, like Picinelli in *Mundus Symbolicus,* was following Boccaccio and Conti.

the humble *Base,*" and another came even nearer to describing the new state as Marvell saw it: "Away with Concord now, since that we see, / The loudest Discords make best Harmonie." [20] The law of *concordia discors* is the cosmological origin, as it were, of the mixed state, and the mixed state was the basic concept of the English constitution. Among political books in England, Malvezzi formulated the classic expression of the idea in the ninth discourse of his *Discourses upon Cornelius Tacitus,* but Marvell's passage in this poem ranks with *Cooper's Hill* as probably the most sustained utterance on the subject in English political poetry before Pope. The cardinal fact is that the building Cromwell has constructed, "Knit by the Roofs Protecting weight" (98), is an essentially royalist edifice, lacking nothing but the title to distinguish it from the princely state. Without the sovereignty of the roof, the walls would collapse into "a multitude . . . like a heap of stones, before they are cemented and knit together into one building," [21] or as another royalist, Sir Francis Wortley, once commented, the true English protestant "thinks it not fit to pull downe the Cantrell of an Arche till the key-stone be settled, and then the greater the weight is, the stronger it will be." [22] When the time came, on 24 March 1657, to discuss once again the offer of the crown to Cromwell, Colonel Bridge wrote "I was somewhat confident in the morning, that we should have laid the top stone of the great and noble structure we have been so long in framing before this time. But we have not been able to bring it to an issue." [23]

For the related imagery of the circular state with Cromwell as its center, there is evidence also that the most monarchical of Cromwell's supporters were thinking in these terms. Samuel Hunton "the kingling" (as the advocates of Cromwell-for-king were later derogatorily called) exclaimed "would you concentrize all your particular ends in the generals Centre, you would there meet, whereas now you are bemet with, and it

---

[20] John Ailmer, in *Musarum Oxoniensium,* p. 97, and J. Nethway, in the same work, p. 96.

[21] Dudley Digges, *The Unlawfulnesse of Subjects Taking up Armes* (n.p., 1647), p. 15.

[22] "Character of a True English Protestant" [1646], quoted in B. Boyce, *The Polemic Character 1640–1661* (Lincoln, Nebraska, 1955), p. 19.

[23] Quoted in C. H. Firth, *The Last Years of the Protectorate 1656–1658* (London, 1909), I, 147. For king as keystone of an arch, see Juan de Solorzano, *Emblemata Regio Politica* (Madrid, 1653), emblem 48, and Andres Mendo, *Principe Perfecto y Ministros Aiustados* (Leon de Franci, 1662), emblem 70. Sir James Harrington described his Oceana as a circle made up of orbs, and for the throne as a roof upheld by the walls of justice and mercy, see Thomas Fuller, *The Holy State and the Profane State,* ed. M. G. Walten, II, 352.

would render you powerfully defensive and offensive, so it's factions that fractions you, *and self-ends that divide and undo you.*" [24]

The Amphion myth offered Marvell further advantages; it allowed him to glide over a great many of the troubles of that anxious year, and indeed to pretend that the quarrels and disappointments of the republicans were a concordant discord, not a real threat to the state; it afforded an excellent illustration of that speed of action which so often caused Cromwell to be compared with Caesar (a comparison conspicuously missing in the poem); and it permitted him to allude to the military operations (of which the Western Design was the chief) and to the controversial new ecclesiastical settlement as elements of Cromwell's success. However, I doubt if any special significance should be attributed to the "Palace" which Amphion erected "with a Touch more sweet" (61), although it does suggest that palaces were not of themselves evil. The section concludes by bringing to the forefront the promise of the Fifth Monarchy which is crucial to the total argument.

III

The Fifth Monarchy, "a notion," said Cromwell, "I hope we all honour, wait, and hope for," [25] had an especially wide appeal in 1654–55, as the First Parliament was troublesome precisely on account of the large number of enthusiastic saints it contained. There was no more fruitful way of proposing still further changes in the constitution than by appealing to the hopes of the approaching millennium. Chiliasts were inclined to be precise in their demands for overturning, but vague about the kind of government they would institute. It would be a theocracy ruled by a single party, and if Christ appeared in person to reign (many doubted this) there would be no need for a temporal monarch. However, inherent in their schemes was a belief in the great captain who would lead the troops until Christ's arrival, and, until Cromwell had disappointed them, he was their natural choice.[26] Harrison in 1653 was reported to have

[24] *His Highnesse the Protector-Protected* (London, 1654), p. 7. The following year Hunton became yet more blatantly a kingling in *The King of Kings: or the Soveraignty of Salus Populi*—a pamphlet signed S. H. which can be certainly identified as Hunton's by a ref. on p. 5.

[25] Abbott, III, 437. For the conflicting hope and pessimism aroused by Fifth Monarchism, see Ernest Lee Tuveson, *Millennium and Utopia* (Berkeley, 1949), pp. 22–112, esp. 86 ff.

[26] Louise Fargo Brown, *The Political Activities of the Baptists and Fifth Monarchy Men in England during the Interregnum* (Washington, D. C., 1912), ch. III remains

envisioned, literally, some kind of monarchical rule, and seems to have favored himself for the office;[27] but John Rogers declared that thousands were looking to Cromwell as "our conqueror upon Christ's and the Commonwealth's account"; there existed also "a prediction, which says C. shall sound within the walls of Rome," [28] and John Spittlehouse humbly requested that "the Lord would so operate by his Spirit upon all our affections who claime an interest in the benefits that doe accrew unto us by the marvellous Acts of the same providence, as also instrumentally upon him, (*viz.* our present Deliverer, Generall, and Judge) whom the Lord hath been pleased to make use of." [29] Marvell's argument could draw directly, therefore, on an already well-established belief that Cromwell was destined to play a part in the arrival of the millennium: few doubted the times were approaching, and Cromwell himself speculated in public on their nearness.[30] Yet Marvell's appeal was not directed, as the later diatribe shows, to the lunatic fringe of this group, but to the sober-minded Christians who were content to wait for the indisputable signs of the glorious Day. He was voicing orthodox opinion in his statement "a thick Cloud about that Morning lyes, / And intercepts the Beams of Mortal Eyes" (141–42), for it was an abuse of providence to attempt to hasten God's designs, as John Goodwin reminded the faithful at this time.[31] Marvell's proposition does in effect seek to speed the day, so the modesty with which it is made is peculiarly important. Without more conclusive proof, neither Marvell nor England could be positive time's useless course was drawing to a close, and almost every sentence carries a qualification. No thesis was ever put more tentatively:

---

standard for this year. A convenient summary of their predictions is to be found in Thomas Richards, *A History of the Puritan Movement in Wales . . . 1639 to . . . 1653* (London, 1920), pp. 192–196; Arthur Barker, *Milton and the Puritan Dilemma* has a useful chapter, pp. 193–214, and, because of its full quotation, the appendix ("The Free Spirit in Cromwell's England") in Norman Cohn's *The Pursuit of the Millennium* (London, 1957) does much to show why the Ranters could be accused of all kinds of lasciviousness (to which Marvell later refers).

[27] Gardiner, *History*, II, 276.

[28] *Sagrir, or Doomes-day Drawing Nigh* [1654], in Edward Rogers, *The Life and Opinions of a Fifth-Monarchy Man* (London, 1867), p. 77.

[29] *A Warning-Piece Discharged* (London, 1653), p. 24. Cromwell as the British Moses was a common analogy; see, e.g., Spittlehouse's *The First Addresses to His Excellencie the Lord General* (London, 1653), sig. A2ᵛ.

[30] Abbott, III, 436. C. A. Patrides, "Renaissance and Modern Thought on the Last Things: A Study in Changing Conceptions," *Harvard Theological Review*, LI (1958), 170–173 documents the belief that the times were near.

[31] *Sugkretismos, or Dis-satisfaction Satisfied* (London, 1654), p. 16. For the moderate millenarian view, see Thomas Goodwin, *The World to Come, or, the Kingdom of Christ Asserted* (London, 1655).

> O *would* they rather . . .
> How *might* they under such a Captain . . .
> *If* gracious Heaven to my Life give length . . .
> What we *might* hope, what wonderful Effect
> From such a wish'd Conjuncture *might* reflect . . .
> That *'tis the most* which we determine can,
> *If* these the Times . . .
> And well he therefore does, and well has *guest* . . .
> And *knowing not* where Heavens choice may light . . .
> But Men alas, *as if* they nothing cared . . .

Cautious though he is, Marvell was not challenging God's plan if he envisaged all Europe (or all Protestant Europe) united in a war against Anti-Christ, and the possibility of such a crusade seemed much nearer in 1654 than it had in 1650, when Marvell concluded the Horatian Ode with a similar threat to "all States not free." The princes, however, were "Unhappy"—that is, "infelix," unblessed by fortune[32]—and Cromwell remains splendidly and desperately "alone" in his struggle against the forces of evil. Kings and "Men" cooperate to frustrate the work Cromwell has begun. England should lead the vanguard of the Church Militant, but something is lacking, and "Hence landing Nature to new Seas is tost, / And good Designes still with their Authors lost" (157–58). Marvell claims no certainty in diagnosing either the cause or the remedy for the discrepancy between Cromwell's achievement and its perfect fruition, but he does suggest them both in the lines which carry the most explicit avowal of his theme:

> Hence oft I think, if in some happy Hour
> High Grace should meet in one with highest Pow'r,
> And then a seasonable People still
> Should bend to his, as he to Heavens will,
> What we might hope, what wonderful Effect
> From such a wish'd Conjuncture might reflect.
> Sure the mysterious Work, where none withstand,
> Would forthwith finish under such a Hand:
> Fore-shortned Time its useless Course would stay,
> And soon precipitate the latest Day.
> But a thick Cloud about that Morning lyes,
> And intercepts the Beams of Mortal eyes,
> That 'tis the most which we determine can,
> If these the Times, then this must be the Man.

[32] Suggested in another context by Patrick Cruttwell, *The Shakespearean Moment* (New York, 1955), p. 190.

And well he therefore does, and well has guest,
Who in his Age has always forward prest:
And knowing not where Heavens choice may light,
Girds yet his Sword, and ready stands to fight; (131–148)

If the poem is panegyric, then this passage can be read only as Professor Carens reads it: "if the vision of the reign of the saints, ushered in by Cromwell, is suggested as a possibility, it is withdrawn in the very act of offering it to our imaginations." [33] God, then, permitted Cromwell as a second-best leader, but would later send an even greater man who combined grace with power. But this is absurd. Cromwell is clearly intended as the figure of "highest Pow'r"—the whole poem so far has demonstrated that—and his eager service of the Lord must class him also among "th'Elected" (156); he is *par excellence* the man God has elected. If grace, therefore, has been denied him, it must be either because the time of the millennial kingdom has not yet come, and God thus withholds His especial blessing, or because mankind "all unconcern'd, or unprepar'd" is frustrating God's wish to endow Cromwell with the grace necessary to finish His work. No one can know if the first alternative offers the correct explanation, but Marvell *is* certain that "If these the Times [of the millenium], then this must be the Man" whom God has chosen to complete "the mysterious Work." The meaning depends on the interpretation of "High Grace," and on the knowledge of how "Heaven's choice" would visibly "light" on a man.

The conjuncture of High Grace with one already possessed of highest power would occur (if we read literally) "in some happy Hour," and nothing fits the demands of this formula so well as the conferring of grace in the hour of coronation. The significance of this grace had been one of the principal controversies of the civil war, with the royalists claiming that grace confirmed for ever an already hereditary sovereignty, and endued the king's person with special sanctity and healing powers. For the Puritans, the balm was more nominal, and hence dispensable if the king's spirituality proved deficient. The Archbishop at Charles's coronation prayed the king might "joyfully receive the seat of supreme Government by the gift of thy supernatural grace," and Robert Brown in one of the lamentations when the reign had ended declared "the holy Oyl thus employed [in the coronation] is no longer bare and common Oyl, but . . . the *gift of Grace;* which (however vilified by Enthusias-

---

[33] James F. Carens, "Andrew Marvell's Cromwell Poems," *Bucknell Review*, VII (1957), 64.

tiques and Solifidians) betokeneth the Grace of *Christ* and *Kings*." [34] The lesson of the civil war had been, however, that high grace when not allied with highest power was of no avail.

The Protectorate had been called into being by the Instrument of Government, namely, by an Act of Parliament, and no religious ceremony of anointment distinguished the Protector with divine grace. Lacking this unction, Cromwell insisted in his speech dissolving parliament on 22 January 1655 that the terms of the Instrument must be followed if the balance between the extremes of monarchy and democracy were to be maintained:

> The Government called you hither, the constitution whereof being so limited, *a single person and a Parliament*, and this was thought most agreeable to the general sense of the nation, having had experience enough by trial of other conclusions, judging this most likely to avoid the extremes of monarchy on the one hand, and democracy on the other, and yet not to found *dominium in gratia*. [35]

The essence of the Protectorate was its retention of the typical structure of the English constitution, but dispensing with the inalienable privilege inherent in *dominium in gratia*. The time had now come, Marvell believed, to return to the old form in its entirety, and to anoint Cromwell with oil. It was inconceivable Cromwell should anoint himself, and God was therefore powerless to bestow His grace until the people awakened from their apathy. The accepted commonplace that God no longer directly instituted kings as He had occasionally done in Jewish history left the disposal of government to human acts. Of the possible ways in which monarchies could be instituted, succession was of course ruled out for Cromwell, and conquest was no longer a plausible argument as it had been for two or three years after 1649. Election remained the only route to the throne, as Cromwell recognized. "Heavens choice" could not be finally known until the people had consented. The views of the Puritan audience to whom "The First Anniversary" is addressed were admirably expressed in 1654 by the Smectymnuuan William Spurstowe. One call to kingship, he explained, was immediately of God,

[34] *The Manner of the Coronation of King Charles the First at Westminster, 2 Feb., 1626*, edited for the Henry Bradshaw Liturgical Text Society by Christopher Wordsworth (London, 1892), p. 27; [Robert Brown], *The Subjects Sorrow: or Lamentations upon the Death of Britains Josiah King Charls* (London, 1649), p. 10. See also Percy Ernst Schramm, *A History of the English Coronation*, trans. L. G. Wickham Legg (Oxford, 1937), pp. 125, 128–129.
[35] Abbott, III, 587.

The other is mediate; which is by the designation and appointment of man. Thus *Moses* did by the advise of *Jethro*, select and chuse out of the people such persons as were endued with qualifications for Magistracy. . . . And this is the Call which is usuall and constant, which being after a regular and due manner performed, becomes the Call of God. But a Call there must be, to give a title to Magistracy: or else it is not an Authority, but an usurpation; not a mission, by Gods ordinance, but a permission by his providence.[36]

"Is Magistracy Gods Ordinance?" enquired Thomas Hall, "*then none may usurp it, or enter upon it* without a Call from him. As in the Ministry no man may take that honour to himself but he that is called; so in Magistracy none may assume this office to himself, but he that is called of God, either mediately or immediately." [37] In the Puritan mind the call to the magistracy was exactly analogous with that to the ministry, and the process of authorizing a minister included the selection of the candidate, his examination for fitness, his actual election by the people and his solemn installation.[38] Cromwell himself had always represented his authority as a call from the people, or the army officers, and his second speech to his parliament, invoking a great cloud of witnesses in the three nations, is the best illustration of the Puritan doctrine of election I know of.[39]

These were the beliefs to which Marvell appealed, and the first hundred and thirty lines of the poem should therefore be read as the statement of Cromwell's fitness for his vocation, of his election by God. They lend force to an important word in line 133: "And then a seasonable People *still* / Should bend to his, as he to Heavens will." Not until the people had proved once that they could act seasonably (a favorite Puritan word) by electing Cromwell king, could they be seasonable "still." And if they continued to recognize Cromwell's leadership the latter days would surely be hastened, when (as Colonel Lane picturesquely described them) "not a dog shall dare to bark or wag his tail against any servant of the Lord." [40]

[36] *The Magistrates Dignity and Duty* (London, 1654), pp. 27–28.
[37] *The Beauty of Magistracy, in an Exposition of the 82 Psalm* (London, 1660), p. 32.
[38] James L. Ainslie, *The Doctrines of Ministerial Order in the Reformed Churches of the 16th and 17th Centuries* (Edinburgh, 1940), p. 143. The Call was supposed to hinder ambitious men. See the list of quotations from works of the reformers, pp. 140–142. Also [Anon.], *Stereoma, The Establishment* (London, 1654), pp. 89 ff. Election was generally held to be more important than ordination (Geoffrey Nuttall, *Visible Saints* [Oxford, 1957], pp. 88 ff.). Marvell's point is that ordination is also required.
[39] Abbott, III, 451–462.
[40] *An Image of our Reforming Times: or, Jehu in his Proper Colours* (London, 1654), p. 30.

The same Colonel, writing against Cromwell in 1654, used satirically the very arguments which Marvell offered in good faith: "Let us consider *the Policie of the man:* view his Intellectuals a little, and we shall see, that (according to the received opinion of our times, that *grace is but a secondary qualification in Rulers and Magistrates; natural gifts and accomplishments to be sought after in the first place*) he was fit for the Magistracie as any man (of that Judgment) would fix upon." [41] Marvell and Lane concurred in finding Cromwell disgraced, in different senses.

Marvell's disquisition for kingship, spoken like no other section of the poem in the first person singular, never strays beyond the confines of orthodox and millennial belief. Cromwell's works are unquestionable, his election by God secure; he himself "ready stands to fight," but waits patiently for a call; millennarians could understand the need for a captain-general, and all moderate men would rest satisfied with the poet's humility. The creation of a monarchy by popular consent was the natural apotheosis of Cromwell's glorious works. In subsequent parts of the poem, the utilitarian reasons for kingship are enforced by the description of the anarchy which would follow Cromwell's death, and further evidence is offered of Cromwell's suitability for the task.

IV

The coaching accident preceded by only two weeks the debate in parliament on the succession, which was influenced, Abbott records, "in some degree" by Cromwell's narrow escape.[42] Wither was certainly careful to dissociate himself in his poem on the event from those who wished to style the Protector "Emperor." [43] One effect immediately intended by Marvell's lines was to counter the ribald sarcasms for which the fall afforded the occasion. The French ambassador regretted Cromwell did not manage his coach as well as the rest of his business, but for others the horses had shown themselves less pliable than parliament, and the ruder sort commented that Cromwell and Thurloe in the coach were Mephistopheles and Dr. Faustus "careering it in the Air, to try how he could govern Horses, since Rational Creatures were so unruly and diffi-

[41] *Ibid.,* p. 5.
[42] III, 482.
[43] *Vaticinium Causuale,* in *Miscellaneous Works, First Collection* (n.p.: Spenser Society, 1872), p. 9.

cult to be reined." [44] The passage, however, is less transiently polemical
than this, and yet more simple than Carens' suggestion that "the accident,
of course, symbolizes the impulse to anarchy loose in the land," or
Mazzeo's, which links the fall not only (quite properly) with the Fall, but
with a pattern of rising and falling in other places.[45] It is, briefly, an
obituary discourse in which Marvell describes what *would* have happened, had Cromwell been killed: "So with more Modesty we may be
True, / And speak as of the Dead the Praises due" (187–88); and it was a
fine touch to close this section with references to the ascent of Elijah,
one of the favorite texts for funeral sermons in the seventeenth century.[46] The horses, those "poor Beasts" (191) who had endangered Cromwell's life, become metaphors for the people of England left without
their driver:

> Thee proof beyond all other Force or Skill,
> Our Sins endanger, and shall one day kill.
> How near they fail'd, and in thy sudden Fall
> At once assay'd to overturn us all.
> Our brutish fury strugling to be Free,
> Hurry'd thy Horses while they hurry'd thee. (173–78)

No less than his ancient and saintly mother (Cromwell derived from
a stock Puritans could appreciate), no less than his countrymen, Cromwell is subject to the effects of the Fall, and when, for the second time,
Cromwell is compared with "Nature" (204), a reader does well to remember the grace which the Protector still lacks; in fact the overthrow
of nature at Cromwell's death points back to the irony of Cromwell's
position which has been gradually emerging during the course of the
poem. Cromwell's power over the unyielding "Matter" of "the Minds of

---

[44] Thurloe, *State Papers*, II, 656; [James Heath], *A Chronicle of the Late Intestine War*, 2nd ed. (London, 1676), p. 363. For an anonymous "Elogy" see Historical Manu-scripts Commission, Thirteenth Report, Portland MSS (London, 1892), p. 678; also "A Jolt on Michaelmas Day" reprinted in *Political Ballads of the Seventeenth and Eighteenth Centuries*, ed. W. Walter Wilkins (London, 1860), I, 121–124. C. H. Firth points out that the contrast between horses and parliament was heightened by Crom-well's having extracted an engagement to recognize his authority only a fortnight earlier ("Cromwell's Views on Sport," *Macmillan's Magazine*, LXX [1894], 404).

[45] Carens, p. 65; Mazzeo, p. 48.

[46] See Patrick's funeral sermon on John Smith printed in *Select Discourses* (London, 1660); also M. Sylvester's sermon on Baxter, *Elisha's Cry after Elijah's God* (1676), and the anonymous *A Call from Heaven to Gods Elisha's, to Mourn and Lament, When God Takes Away His Elijah's, either by a Natural, or by a Civil Death* (London, 1667) which begins "I know many excellent Funeral Sermons upon this Text are in Print" and cites marginally T. Hooker, O. Sedgwick, J. Collins, J. Gauden, S. Patrick.

stubborn Men" (77–78) is similar to the power of grace; he is also "Angelique" and has learned "a Musique in the Region clear," and yet he is confined to the world of "things," which he manipulates superbly. On the other hand, ordinary monarchs "nor more contribute to the State of Things, / Then wooden Heads unto the Viols strings" (43–44), yet they may reign malignantly for all Platonic years. Nominally they possess the grace and the longevity which Cromwell deserves, although in their own persons they are both ungraced and as mortal as other men. The reasons of state which prevent them from acknowledging Cromwell as their natural leader are abetted by the apathy of his people, but Marvell foresees the day, if "gracious Heaven" permits *him* sufficient life, when a host of kings will "chase the Beast." Until that time he can only commend Cromwell who pursues the Monster "alone," and the implication remains (disguised though it is) that Cromwell may in the future lead the hunt as a king.[47] The international pursuit of Anti-Christ will not begin until Cromwell's anomalous status has been rectified, until grace has been added to nature, and the effects of the Fall become in part recoverable. The "Panique groan" (203) which greets Cromwell / Nature's fall is the more pointed an allusion in that no Christ-like successor was born at the instant of Cromwell's death; justice, reason, courage, religion —the virtues Christ came at that moment to restore—lie obstructed and disheartened. Cromwell's work is lost in a second, and the ship of state founders unsalvageably.

The indisputable proof of the poet's concern with the succession in these lines lies in the reference to Elijah with which the section concludes: "We only mourn'd our selves, in thine Ascent, / Whom thou hadst left beneath with Mantle rent" (219–20). Marvell followed conventional exegesis in ascribing Elisha's anguish to his sorrow, not for Elijah, but for Israel, but neither scripture nor commentary records that the mantle which Elisha wrapped round his shoulders was a "Mantle rent." Elisha tore his clothes, and Elijah's were consumed, but the cloak which symbolized the succession and the double portion of his father's spirit vouchsafed to Elisha was whole and inalienably his. If England were not to be left shivering with dissension, the succession ought to be assured at once.

Elijah was the poet's trouvée, because yet another aspect of the prophet's figura was available to serve as an apt transition to another

---

[47] I would point also to the force of "*Hence* oft I think . . ." after Marvell has discussed, first, the unhappy princes, then angelique Cromwell. It looks like a syllogism.

section. In calling Elijah "the headstrong Peoples Charioteer" (224), Marvell followed the Vulgate text of 2 Kings ii.12, "Pater mi, pater mi, currus Israel et auriga eius," rather than the English version which translated "auriga" as "horsemen." The standard reading of the verse stated that Elijah had assisted Israel more by his prayers than an army of horses and riders could have done;[48] his unwillingness to take part in political affairs was also well known; he had been married to contemplation and solitude, and had been virtually an author of monastic life.[49] Thus he was ideally suited to be a type of Cromwell's reluctance, and hence fitness, to rule, and Lyra had even offered a political interpretation of the text which was identical with Marvell's use of it in the poem: Elijah was both chariot and charioteer because one is led while the other leads, demonstrating "that he rules well who first is led in obedience." [50] The origin of this *sententia* in Aristotle underlines the similarity of this entire section with the *refutatio* in the Horatian Ode.[51] The first half of Marvell's proof consists in the argument from Cromwell's death; the second, with which I am concerned here, refutes those enemies who have always accused Cromwell of tyranny, but also covertly argues for a monarchy as the solution to those arbitrary tendencies which Cromwell's deeds, though fully justifiable, have contained. The innuendo of "For to be *Cromwell* was a greater thing, / Then ought below, or yet above a King" (225–26) is later sustained, for to be Protector is at once to be both inferior to, and yet "above," i.e. to command more arbitrary power than, a king.

In the simile of the "lusty Mate" who wrenched the tiller from the hand of careless helmsman, thereby saving the ship of state, Marvell paraphrased the most famous political metaphor of his day. Originally invented by the author of the *Vindiciae contra tyrannos* to exemplify

[48] Vatablus, in *Critici Sacri* (Amsterdam, 1698), Vol. II, on 2 Kings ii.12; Estius, *Annotationes in Praecipua ac Difficiliora S. Scripturae Loca* (Moguntiae, 1667), on 2 Kings xiii.14; Matthew Poole, *Synopsis Criticorum* (London, 1669), I, 595; Grotius, *Opera Omnia Theologica* (Amsterdam, 1679), I, 158. Annotated editions of the Vulgate also give this interpretation.

[49] Cornelius Lapide, *Commentarius in Iosue, Iudicum, Ruth, IV Libros Regum* [etc] (Antwerp, 1653), 2nd pagination, p. 225 (on 1 Kings xvii.1).

[50] Nicholas Lyra, commentary "moraliter" on 1 Samuel ix in *Bibliorum Sacrorum Tomus Secundus* (Lugduni, 1545), fol. 72ᵛ. Quoted in Lapide, *loc. cit.* See also Martin Del Rio, *Adagialia Sacra Veteris et Novi Testamenti* (Lugduni, 1614), p. 258.

[51] See my "Marvell's Horatian Ode," *PMLA*, LXXXVII (March, 1962), p. 41. To the evidence given there of the ubiquity of the *sententia* may be added Dryden, *Threnodia Augustalis*, lines 233–234 (ed. Kinsley, I, 448), Baldwin's dedication to *The Mirrour for Magistrates*, ed. L. B. Campbell (New York, 1960), p. 63, and [Hawke], *The Right of Dominion*, p. 15.

Calvin's dictum that lesser magistrates had the right to resist the greater in cases of necessity, it had been modified by Independents, Levellers, and later by supporters of the new commonwealth in 1649–51, so that any person whatsoever, not solely a lesser magistrate, could assume command in emergencies; in the early uses of the metaphor the drunken pilot had been asked politely to step aside for the duration, whereas after 1649 he had been cast unceremoniously into the waves.[52] Except for its application to a new event, Marvell's rendering appears completely conventional, but the lines on Noah which follow ("Thou, and thine House, like *Noah's* Eight did rest, / Left by the Wars Flood on the Mountains crest" etc.) contrast so sharply with the image of arbitrary but necessary power in the mate that it is easy to recall while reflecting on this passage the angry and often lengthy objections of the royalists to the Puritan metaphor. At least they established the wholly temporary nature of the usurping helmsman's authority, and they enquired pertinently whether he should not be court-martialled for mutiny as soon as the ship reached port. The simile proved extraordinarily useful and adaptable so long as parliament was seeking to justify its unconstitutional measures, and it was revived in a highly elaborate form at the Exclusion crisis,[53] but it could not serve as a good example of constitutional action in normal times. Marvell says as much:

> 'Tis not a Freedome, that where All command;
> Nor Tyranny, where One does them withstand:
> But who of both the Bounders knows to lay
> Him as their Father must the State obey. (279–82)

The first couplet glosses the preceding incident of the mate; the second introduces the ideal figure of Noah / Cromwell with which the *refutatio* concludes.

By invoking the idea of a *Pater patriae* Marvell went beyond the concept of the Protector as envisaged in the Instrument, and harked back to royalist paternalism and the theory of the mixed monarchy. Except for Filmer, who had reiterated his notions during the commonwealth period, the patriarchal origin of kingship had operated rather as a powerful analogy than as a literal fact. Practically all royalists had been willing to concede a contract or limitation somewhere along the

---

[52] The evidence for these generalizations is given in my note, "Marvell's 'lusty Mate' and the Ship of the Commonwealth," *MLN*, LXXVI (1961), 106–110.

[53] Charles F. Mullett, "The Popish Plot as a Ship's Mutiny," *N&Q*, CLXXIV (1938), 218–223.

line from Adam's kingship, but, as an analogy, paternalism was of obvious usefulness, rendered more so by the common interpretation of the commandment to honor thy father and mother as an order to obey princes and governors. If the kingship of Adam was the cornerstone of patriarchal theory, the kingship of Noah was no less important, and, after the deluge of the civil war, a good deal more relevant to Marvell's poem. . . . Marvell emphasized his intention of proposing Cromwell as a replica of Noah the king when he continued to denounce the *"Chammish* issue" in the diatribe which forms the penultimate section of the poem. Noah's children who laughed at his nakedness had not infrequently been compared with rebellious subjects,[54] and Cham's descendents had been cursed by Noah as the Fifth Monarchists had been cursed by all and sundry, including Cromwell. This wild segment of the people had done much to hinder both the political and religious settlements of the Protectorate (and were to do so still more), and Cromwell, having fought all his battles in the name of the Lord of Hosts, must have found it particularly galling to be denounced as the Little Horn. When Marvell cursed them as the locusts from the bottomless pit (311–12) he was only turning their own imagery against themselves and applying a text which had long been used to condemn heretics and schismatics.[55] The purpose of the philippic is not to relieve feelings, however, or even to please Cromwell, but to expose the Fifth Monarchists as a real danger. The sons of Cham (of whom the chief was Nimrod) are waiting to seize control of the state, and only Cromwell stands between them and the fulfillment of their designs; they are overtly contrasted with the noble family of Cromwell. If the crown is not to devolve on the Chammish issue, as it did in the Bible, it must descend to the worthy offspring.

V

From Noah presiding over the survivors of the deluge, the final scene moves back to Adam watching the first sunset of the world and wonder-

---

[54] Griffith Williams, *Vindiciae Regum; or the Grand Rebellion* (Oxford, 1643), p. 34; Hall, *Of Government and Obedience*, sig. A2ʳ; L'Estrange, *An Account of the Growth of Knavery* (London, 1678), p. 15.

[55] E.g. Andrew Willett, *Sacrorum Emblematum Centuria Una* (Cambridge, n.d.), sig. 14ᵛ; Samuel Richardson, *An Answer to the London Ministers Letter* (London, 1649) begins his tract with a page of the smoke/false-learning analogy. Also John Holland, *Smoke of the Bottomlesse Pit* (London, 1651), and John Tickell, *The Bottomles Pit Smoaking in Familisme* (London, 1651). The Simpson Marvell cites as especially noxious must be John, not Sydrach, as Grosart and Margoliouth annotate.

ing in despair if there would ever be another dawn.[56] At first glance, Marvell appears to be returning to Cromwell's coaching accident, and the relief which had followed its momentary terror. But duplication of that kind would be redundant, and the surprised kings could not have referred to the erasure and rebuilding of the state (352) had they been concerned with the aftermath of the fall in Hyde Park. As an account, however, of the utter blackness into which England had been thrown in 1649 and her subsequent recovery under Cromwell, the extensive simile is significant; it was with this identical sunset image that the royalists had most frequently lamented Charles' execution and had foreseen the rising sun of Charles II.[57] Like the harmonious building, the sun image is inescapably royalist, as John Ailmer knew when he wrote the poem which concluded with an offer of the crown to Cromwell:

> *Benighted* was our *spheare* with all its *Glories,*
> Darke as black *Melancholies* territories,
> As th'*Hermits* vault th'inheritance of *Night*:
> *Confus'd* as *Chaos* lay ere th'*infant light*
> *Usher* to all the *Beauties* were to come
> Had issued from the *Masses* pregnant *Wombe*:
> Till our *Great Oliver* from a budding *Star*
> Full blown a *Sun,* and fixt in's golden *Sphear,*
> Beauty and warmth displaies, and with a *ray*
> Of his *own light* creates us a *new* Day.[58]

Finally Cromwell is the "Soul" of the new England—another conventional image of a king—and "seems a King by long Succession born" (387). The praise of the foreign monarch ends in a riddling couplet which can be read only ironically, as a gloating allusion to the probable collapse of Cromwell's work at his death: "O could I once him with our Title see, / So should I hope yet he might Dye as we" (391–92). When Marvell speaks again in his own person, as he immediately does, he

---

[56] On this image, see E. Duncan-Jones, "Marvell, Johnson, and the First Sunset," *TLS,* 3 April 1959, p. 193, who quotes Lucretius, Statius, and Manilius.

[57] E.g. [Thomas Bayly], *The Royal Charter Granted unto Kings* (London, 1649), sig. A2ᵛ; John Quarles, *Regale Lectum Miseriae,* 2nd ed. (n.p., 1649), p. 49; [George Wither], *Vaticinium Votivum* (n.p., 1649), p. 79; [John Cleveland], *Monumentum Regale* (n.p., 1649), p. 2; and esp. a cavalier ballad, "The Royal Health to the Rising Sun," in *Cavalier and Puritan,* ed. Hyder E. Rollins (New York, 1923), pp. 247–250, and John Sadler, *Rights of the Kingdom* (London, 1649), sig. 3ʳ. Simon Ford, *Primitiae Regiminis Davidici* (London, 1654), pp. 1–2, has an implied comparison of Cromwell the Protector with the middling condition of "Morning-Twilight" between a king and no king.

[58] *Musarum Oxoniensium,* p. 96.

addresses Cromwell for the first time as "Prince"; he cannot resist a final reminder that the Protector is now "venerable" (both aged and regal) and his "End" is in sight. The "End," however, is also the monarchy for which Cromwell is destined and the "Prize" for which the poet has competed. Marvell's purpose may fail if he "contends" further, but even in the last simile of Cromwell as the angel of the commonweal troubling the pool and healing it, Marvell returns his audience full circle to his initial image. The elegiac overtones implicit in the poem's title rise once more, like ripples, to the surface, and Cromwell, if he had caught the allusion to *respice finem*, no doubt put down the poem feeling very old.

The "Poetic Picture, Painted Poetry" of
The Last Instructions to a Painter

by Earl Miner

Of all the "painter poems," *The Last Instructions to a Painter* is generally thought the best and the most likely to be by Marvell. Although the convention flourished for little more than a decade, it became with the dream, the vision, and the biblical analogy one of the most popular devices for political and especially satiric poetry. It began with Waller's *Instructions to a Painter* (1665), itself modeled upon Giovanni Francesco Busenello's *Prospective of the Naval Triumph of the Venetians,* the title given in the translation of 1658 to the celebration of Venetian defeat of the Turkish navy off Crete in 1655.[1] Since the English were engaged in their own naval wars with the Dutch, it was natural for a poet of the Court party to imitate Busenello. And it was equally to be expected that the Country party (to use the distinctions in *The Last Instructions*) would parody Waller's panegyric into satire by the techniques of burlesque introduced by Butler's *Hudibras* (1663–64). The technique of satire by the convention of asking a supposed painter to depict the evils of the time could call upon a long tradition usually identified with Plutarch and typified in the phrase, *ut pictura poesis.*[2] Since, moreover, much of the satire in the painter poems is directed *ad hominem* the convention fitted well with the device of the satiric character of individuals. The major problem facing a poet using the conven-

"The 'Poetic Picture, Painted Poetry' of *The Last Instructions to a Painter*" by Earl Miner. From *Modern Philology,* LXIII (May, 1966), 288–94. Copyright © 1966 by The University of Chicago. Reprinted by permission of The University of Chicago Press.

[1] See George deForest Lord, *Poems on Affairs of State* (New Haven, Conn., 1963), I, 20–21 for a summary of the background; and for Waller's poem, other poems, and discussion of opinions of authorship, see pp. 21 ff.

[2] See, e.g., Ben Jonson, *Poesis et Pictura* in Timber, in J. E. Spingarn, *Critical Essays of the Seventeenth Century* (3 vols.; Bloomington, Ind., 1963), I, 29. For the history of the idea, see W. Rensselaer Lee, "Ut pictura poesis: The Humanistic Theory of Painting," *Art Bulletin,* XXII (1940), 197–269.

tion was that of giving unity to a poem made up of a series of portraits, or of events inchoate and often incomplete. The problem was seldom solved and, for all its excellences, *The Last Instructions* seems to most readers a poem highly various in tone and episodic in action. Without claiming for it a unity comparable to that of *Absalom and Achitophel*, it is possible to show how the painter convention has been made, in this instance, to shape the poem into something like a unified whole.

The variety is obvious. Some of the most memorable passages in the poem are the scurrilous portrait of Anne Hyde, Duchess of York (ll. 49–78); the lovely, almost pastoral scene of the humiliating voyage by the Dutch Admiral De Ruyter up the Thames (ll. 523–60); the heroic idyll of young Douglas (ll. 649–96); and the ironic picture of Charles II trying to lead to bed the nude vision of "England or the Peace" (ll. 885–942). It is not enough to say that such different tones as those in even these few episodes are unified by the painter convention with its but sporadic charges to the painter to "Paint then again," a device used only in the first and last of the examples just given. That charge is, in any event, no more than a device. If unity is to be found, it must be discovered in matters more basic to the poem.

The poetry "painted" in the poem is political, and no little of the unity that the poem does possess comes from its consistent attitude. The poem is anti-royalist, anti-Court, pro-Parliament, and pro-Country throughout. The informing attitude is the undoubted patriotism of a party protesting its loyalty to the throne, but in fact sparing neither the king nor his family nor his government. The poet could call upon the aggrieved patriotism of those humiliated by the impunity with which Dutch ships sailed up the Thames, but yet needed the fiction of loyalty not to antagonize those who rallied to the government during the crisis. Some means was needed to translate the attitude into poetry, however, by shaping the historical narrative of part of the naval war. As Dryden had faced in *Annus Mirabilis* the problem in unifying the English successes of 1665 and early 1666 with other matters, so the Country poet needed to solve it in relating the English defeats and political events that followed. His structural approach to a solution took the form of three central narrative sections representing various confrontations, with preceding and closing sections of portraits of members of the Court. He begins with an attack on prominent members of the Court, who are pictured as debauched and politically corrupt (ll. 1–104). He closes with the satiric picture of the king attempting to force the favors of his naked vision (ll. 885–948). (To this is added a coda, "To the King" [ll. 949–90], in which the painter device is not employed.) In between he presents the three narratives, or representations of action and confrontation: that of the tumultuous sitting of Parliament in the autumn of 1666 (ll. 105–396); that of the Court's seeking frantically to obtain peace (ll. 397–522); and that of the Dutch invasion of the Thames and the Medway in the summer of 1667 (ll. 523–884). The proportioning of the poem provides, then, a well-shaped general disposition of the diverse elements in the poem. The satiric attack is pressed heavily home, relieved as it is only by occasional praise of members of the Country party, or of Douglas, or by that surprisingly lyric tableau of De Ruyter's progress up the Thames. To defend the total integrity of a poem with such diverse passages, it is necessary to consider some of the literary assumptions underlying the theory and handling of the painter convention.

The convention is explicit in varying degrees. It is most explicit in the satiric characters of members of the Court party and least in the lengthy, quasi-narrative sections. It is obvious enough in the portrait of St. Albans, the English ambassador to France: "Paint him with drayman's shoulders, butcher's mien, / Member'd like mules, with elephantine chine" (ll. 33–34). The lines set off with the charge to the painter and continue with vivid detail. It is easy, however, to exaggerate the visual character of such lines. Closely inspected, they will show that what has the most force are words (*butcher's, elephantine*) which direct our emotions rather than our senses. Very nearly the opposite is true of those long passages that often do not make an explicit pretense to be analogous to painting. On inspection, they often prove to have a scenic character which helps the painter convention hold even when not being invoked, as in the description of Parliament as a game of backgammon (ll. 105–16).

Such a scene shows that the painter convention has a greater implicit or assumed function than is at once apparent. The function can best be explained in terms of the chief graphic genres familiar in the late seventeenth century. Probably the best known then were the portraits collected by the Stuarts and their supporters. The relevance of the portrait to the satiric character needs no stress. Another genre, which with the portrait may be considered the main form of Stuart and royalist iconography, is the heroic scene of large-scale events. Sometimes the canvas covers so great a space or includes so much detail that the effect is analogous to narrative poetry.[3] Engravings took on many qualities of

[3] The plates in Lord, Vol. I, are of great iconographical interest and show the ways in which the background of a portrait, legends to pictures, inset scenes, and of course

the portrait and the heroic scene, and commonly went yet further toward
literary devices. Legends are far more numerous and lengthy in engravings than in paintings. Emblematic mottoes or devices abound. Moreover, engravings did not normally seek the tidy formal unity of a painting and, therefore, might often have inset scenes showing the stages in
time of an action whose results or character are summarized by the main
heroic scene. Lord's reproduction (facing p. 124) of an anonymous Dutch
engraving which celebrates Holland's victory at Chatham on June 9,
1667, is an especially useful example, since it shows the great De Ruyter
borne in triumph over the sea in an emblematic tableau, while eight
inset pictures represent, in numbered stages and explanation, the course
of the battle. It is almost as though the *Last Instructions* had followed
this sequence, even to such details as creating an emblematic idyll about
the person of De Ruyter.

Engravings and cuts produced yet another genre even closer to literature in method, if not quality. Throughout the century political and
social satirists often used a rather crude cartoon art to pillory their
enemies. Such cartoons often employ "balloons" containing the words
represented as spoken and labels on the figures insuring that no one
will mistake who is meant. Earlier in the century, the cartoon is apt
to be emblematic—the details are both significant and equitemporal.
The symbolic character of the detail lasts on in the century, but as in
the beast fable and in other genres, the growing narrative and historical
interest assist the cartoon in taking on an element of sequence, if not
precisely of narrative. The result can be seen in the pictures of such
events as "pope-burnings." [4] The cartoons were as much a form of
political inconography for the anti-royalist party as the portraits by Van
Dyck or Lely and Kneller were for the Stuarts. The element of burlesque
and low detail in the cartoon is also significant for the painter poems.
After one has seen cartoons of popes vomiting and worse, one is not
surprised at details in the *Last Instructions*. And one is also prepared to
accept the presence of the painter convention even where it is not consistently employed, as in the passage satirizing the then Speaker of The
Commons, Turnor:

---

symbolic gestures and details gave pictures then a quality more closely allied to literature than today. It was still the habit in the century to "read" emblematic frontis-
pieces, stained glass windows, and pictures.

[4] Sir Walter Scott reproduced in *The Works of John Dryden* (18 vols.; London,
1808), VI, 222, a "Solemn Mock Procession of the Pope." If his engraver omitted to
include the words in the "balloons" issuing from the mouths of figures, the balloons
themselves and the elements of sequence remain.

> Paint him in golden gown, with mace's brain,
> Bright hair, fair face, obscure and dull of head,
> Like knife with iv'ry haft and edge of lead.
> At pray'rs his eyes turn up the pious white,
> But all the while his private bill's in sight.
> In chair he smoking sits like master cook,
> And a poll-bill does like his apron look.
> Well was he skill'd to season any question
> And make sauce fit for Whitehall's digestion,
> Whence ev'ry day, the palate more to tickle,
> Court-mushrumps ready are sent in in pickle,
> When grievance urg'd, he swells like squatted toad,
> Frisks like a frog to croak a tax's load;
> His patient piss he could hold longer than
> An urinal and sit like any hen;
> At table jolly as a country host
> And soaks his sack with Norfolk like a toast;
> At night than Chanticleer more brisk and hot,
> And Sergeant's wife serves him for Pertelotte
> [ll. 866–84].

It can be seen from this passage of what might be called satiric paint-ing how far politics and poetic painting are involved. By contrast, the most graphic section of Dryden's *Annus Mirabilis,* the description of London rising newborn after the fire, employs the wholly different palette and genre of heroic painting:

> Before, she like some Shepherdess did show,
>   Who sate to bathe her by a River's side:
> Not answering to her fame, but rude and low,
>   Nor taught the beauteous Arts of Modern pride.
>
> Now, like a Maiden Queen, she will behold,
>   From her high Turrets, hourly Sutors come:
> The East with Incense, and the West with Gold,
>   Will stand, like Suppliants, to receive her doom.
>
> The silver *Thames,* her own domestick Floud,
>   Shall bear her Vessels, like a sweeping Train;
> And often wind (as of his Mistress proud)
>   With longing eyes to meet her face again
>   [ll. 1181–92].

The pastoral, the regal, the ritualistic, the valuable, and the social con-ception create a myth of England led by royalty that is unrecognizable in the *Last Instructions,* although the poems seem to have been in circulation within a year of each other.[5] The two styles of description are as different as the art of Sir Peter Lely and that of anonymous political cartoonists, although it must be said that in some few passages the *Last Instructions* essays a manner something like that in *Annus Mirabilis.* There were, then, political implications to different styles of art or poetry, for although neither side held monopoly over the grand or the abusive, the enthroned royalists by tradition and position more often used a style that may most readily be called heroic and panegyric, and their anti-Court attackers a style of burlesque and lampoon.

Such a division was wholly natural. Each side had its own traditions and political iconography, and royalism naturally produces a grander style than anti-royalism. As much can be seen in the differences between Waller's *Instructions to a Painter* on the one side, and the satiric imitations that follow. If Marvell is in fact the author of some of the painter poems and of other attacks on the Court, it is wholly decorous that his style should have changed from the delicately controlled amplifications of the Horatian ode on Cromwell and *Upon Appleton House.* Such involvement of styles and politics is the less to be wondered at, since politics had become as much a concomitant and metaphor of painting as the reverse in the painter poems. The erection of statues to Charles II led to amused political attack upon the king in a number of poems, some of which are attributed to Marvell. In these, sculpture inspires political reaction as much as politics takes on the painter convention in other poems, as two stanzas from "The Statue in Stocks-Market" show very clearly.[6]

> But now it appears from the first to the last
> To be all a revenge and a malice forecast,
> Upon the King's birthday to set up a thing
> That shews him a monster more like than a king. . . .
>
> This statue is surely more scandalous far
> Than all the Dutch pictures that caused the war,

[5] *Annus Mirabilis* was published early in 1667—see Hugh Macdonald, *John Dryden: A Bibliography* (Oxford, 1939), No. 9; the *Last Instructions* is dated "September 4th, 1667" in at least one manuscript—see Lord, I, 99.

[6] H. M. Margoliouth (ed.), *The Poems and Letters of Andrew Marvell* (2 vols.; Oxford, 1952), I, 179. Margoliouth assigns the poem without much evidence to Marvell. Lord (I, 266–83) includes three other poems on the statues, attributing them to Marvell with varying weights of evidence.

And what the exchequer for that took on trust
May be henceforth confiscate for reasons more just
[ll. 9–12; 25–28].

The second stanza explicitly if facetiously takes painting and emblems as a *casus belli* and the basis of political comment. The royalists held similar assumptions. In his ode on Anne Killigrew, Dryden has two stanzas on her painting. One (st. VI) compares her turning to painting of classical landscapes to the depredations of Louis XIV upon neighboring countries. The next (st. VII) compares her portrait art to the warlike but reverend English monarchy. So natural was it to think in terms of correspondences between art and action that the two are repeatedly said to inspire and accompany each other.[7]

Such assumptions show that the *Last Instructions* possesses a consistency of conception. It does not prove that the diverse tones are harmonized. To demonstrate this, insofar as it can be demonstrated, it is necessary to consider the rhetorical conceptions of imitation in the Restoration. In brief it may be said that as art imitated nature, it amplified that which it imitated, sometimes by arousing admiration, sometimes by evoking laughter or contempt. It is a question of the kind of "likeness" taken by the painter, sculptor, or poet. As Dryden observed in his "Parallel of Poetry and Painting": "In the character of an hero, as well as in the inferior figure, there is a better or worse likeness to be taken: the better is a panegyric, if it be not false, and the worse is a libel."[8] Although there is more "libel," or satire, in the *Last Instructions* than panegyric, both extremes represent rhetorical amplifications to either side of a

---

[7] "Arts" in the first line of *Annus Mirabilis* comes to signify both the arts of representation and of action: "In thriving Arts long time had *Holland* grown." Thomas Rymer repeats a commonplace when he writes in his preface to Rapin's *Reflections*: "Wit and Valor have always gone together, and *Poetry* been the companion of Camps. The *Heroe* and *Poet* were inspired with the same Enthusiasm, acted with the same heat, and both were crown'd with the same *laurel*" (Spingarn, II, 173).

[8] George Watson (ed.), *John Dryden: Of Dramatic Poesy and Other Critical Essays* (2 vols.; London and New York, 1962), II, 202. In his monograph, "On the Essay of Dramatic Poesy," *University of Michigan Publications in Modern Philology*, XVI (1951), F. L. Huntley discusses Dryden's rhetorical "treatment" of literature—i.e., the habit of thinking in terms of "the aims of the artist," of "the ends and rules (for plot, style, etc.) of the work," and of the character of "the particular audience" addressed (p. 12; see also pp. 14–17). If anything need be added to Huntley's excellent discussion it is that Dryden's conceptions of imitation are clearer in the "Defence of *An Essay*" (Watson, I, 110–30) than in the *Essay* itself. The "Defence" reveals the extent of his debt to, and modifications of, Renaissance imitative theory as it was defined chiefly out of Horace by means of Aristotle and Quintilian.

neutral norm, the reality or "nature" of that whose "likeness" is being taken. The best sustained panegyric is that of the heroic young Douglas, but the passage on De Ruyter is so influenced by the pastoral and symbolic landscapes of the day that it too is a "better . . . likeness." The characters of Clarendon, of his daughter Anne, of Lady Castelmaine, and of others take a "worse likeness." The scene of Charles II pursuing the favors of "England or the Peace" takes a similarly low likeness, but with a fineness of raillery that elevates it, though satirically, in a fashion like the passage on De Ruyter.

The question really becomes one of identifying the neutral norm of "nature" wrom which these amplifications vary. The norm is history, for the *Last Instructions* and *Annus Mirabilis* alike. It is perfectly evident that the authors of the two poems had different conceptions of the actual nature of contemporary events, and that their conceptions are reflected by the kinds of amplification they characteristically employ. But the seventeenth was not the last century in which the record of what actually happened was read differently by intelligent people. Once again Dryden gives the best theoretical explanation and, as might be expected, in terms of imitation and the poetry-painting parallel.

> Such descriptions or images . . . are, as I have said, the adequate delight of heroic poesy; for they beget admiration, which is its proper object; as the images of the burlesque, which is contrary to this, by the same reason beget laughter: for the one shows nature beautified, as in the picture of a fair woman, which we all admire; the other shows her deformed, as in that of a lazar, or of a fool with distorted face and antic gestures, at which we cannot forbear to laugh, because it is a deviation from nature. But though the same images serve equally for the epic poesy, and for the historic and panegyric, which are branches of it, yet a several sort of sculpture is to be used in them.[9]

Omitting the epic as a genre not directly involved, the historical and the panegyric remain in their association, with the satiric but inverted panegyric, as Dryden remarks in effect in his "Parallel of Poetry and Painting." Seventeenth-century assumptions and practices of history strengthened the connection with artistic imitation. The "character" was as much a genre of narrative history as it was of panegyric and satire, as Clarendon's famous portrait of Cromwell shows.[10] Moreover, biography

---

[9] Watson, I, 101.

[10] W. Dunn Macray (ed.), *The History of the Rebellion and Civil Wars in England* (6 vols.; Oxford, 1888, 1958), VI, 91–97.

was thought to be one of the genres of history.[11] History admitted narrations and characters, both of which had their poetic equivalents of various kinds, and it provided the norm from which poets of differing political convictions might not only give their personal readings of the course of events but also, given the existing theories of rhetorical imitation, vary their tones consistently.

Considered as a historical poem in Dryden's sense of a genre allied to panegyric and its obverse, satire, and alternating in careful ways sections of characters and narrative, the *Last Instructions* holds a good claim to being thought a unified poem. If we still have some reservations about its total unity, it is probably due in part to our lack of familiarity with assumptions about artistic imitation in the seventeenth century. In part it is no doubt also due to our lack of familiarity with the painter poems and other of the louder political verse of the time, as well as to our sense that by virtue of their superiority as poetry, *Absalom and Achitophel* or *The Medal* must be taken as norms for unified poems. Yet there can be no doubt that the author of the *Last Instructions*, whether Marvell or another, was a highly conscious user of the painter convention or that he understood its implications in imitative theory. References of varying kinds to the convention appear intermittently in the poem. They may be wryly ironic: "To paint or write / Is longer work and harder than to fight" (ll. 303–304). Or they may show the rhetorical method and ethical purpose assigned to the mimetic function of art.

> So thou and I, dear Painter, represent
> In quick effigie, other's faults and feign,
> By making them ridiculous to restrain
> [ll. 390–92].

The task of art is to imitate or "feign" nature, in this case men's "faults." There is the usual acknowledgment of the special provinces of the two arts: "Where pencil cannot, there my pen shall do't: / That may his body, this his mind explain" (ll. 864–65). There is even a humorous gesture at the convention: "But let some other painter draw the sound" (l. 910). Finally, in bidding the conventional painter farewell, the poet reveals his sense that as both painting and poetry are arts, so nature, or reality, remains the object of their imitation, even while nature herself may turn imitator and artist.

[11] Watson, II, 5–9. In this passage from the "Life of Plutarch," Dryden is apparently the first to use "biography" in English.

Painter, adieu! How well our arts agree,
Poetic picture, painted poetry;
But this great work is for our Monarch fit,
And henceforth Charles only to Charles shall sit.
His master-hand the ancients shall outdo,
Himself the painter and the poet too

[ll. 943–48].

As such passages show, the very considerable variety of tones in the poem has a consistent theoretical center giving it unity. The unity of its conception and its conventions is no doubt more certain than the unity of its effect. Taking account of both conception and effect, however, we must concede at the least a careful artistry and planning to the poem. If Marvell was not its author, some other writer must have been who possessed comparable powers, knowledge of Parliament and the affairs of his day, and who had the gift of a similarly ironic mind. In assurance, in conception, and in literary merit, *The Last Instructions to a Painter* is excelled in its day as a work of political history fashioned into poetry only by the poems of Dryden and Butler. Although the convention of the painter poem flourished for so brief a period, in this instance it produced a work which may justly be regarded as an inheritor of Renaissance theories of artistic imitation, as the satiric obverse of *Annus Mirabilis,* and as a worthy forerunner of Dryden's satires.

Chronology of Important Dates

1621	Born at Winestead-in-Holderness, Yorkshire, March 31, to the Rev. Andrew Marvell and his wife, Anne.
1624	Marvells move to Hull, where Rev. Andrew Marvell becomes lecturer in Holy Trinity Church.
1633	Marvell matriculates at Trinity College, Cambridge.
1637	Greek and Latin poems on Charles I and Queen Henrietta Maria published.
1638	Marvell becomes a scholar of Trinity.
1640	Father dies. Marvell leaves Cambridge.
1640–42	Possible clerkship in trading-house of brother-in-law, Edmund Popple.
1642–46?	Travel abroad as tutor. (Dates uncertain.)
1648–49	Poems on Villiers (authorship questionable), Lovelace, Hastings.
1650	"An Horatian Ode upon Cromwell's Return from Ireland."
1650–53	Tutors Mary, daughter of the Lord General Fairfax, at Appleton House, Yorkshire.
1653	Milton's letter to Bradshaw, recommending Marvell for a government position, February 21. No appointment forthcoming, Marvell becomes tutor to Cromwell's ward, William Dutton. Lives at Eton. "The Character of Holland."
1653–54	Latin poems on Queen Christina of Sweden, Dr. Ingelo.
1655	"The First Anniversary of the Government under his Highness the Lord Protector."
1656	Marvell and Dutton at Saumur, France.

1657   Marvell becomes Latin Secretary under Secretary of State Thurloe.

1658   "A Poem upon the Death of his Late Highness, the Lord Protector."

1659–78   Marvell serves as M.P. for Hull.

1660   Intervenes in Commons to save Milton.

1663–65   Accompanies Earl of Carlisle as secretary on embassy to Russia, Sweden, and Denmark.

1665   England provokes war with Holland. "The Second Advice to a Painter."

1666   "The Third Advice to a Painter."
            "Clarendon's Housewarming."

1667   "The Last Instructions to a Painter." Downfall of Clarendon. War ends.

1670   "On Blood's Stealing the Crown."

1672   The Declaration of Indulgence. *The Rehearsal Transpros'd.*

1672–74   War with France as ally against Holland. Marvell as "Mr. Thomas" active in Dutch-based anti-French, anti-Catholic fifth column.

1674   Second edition of *Paradise Lost,* prefaced by Marvell's poem.

1676   *Mr. Smirke: or the Divine in Mode.*

1677   *The Growth of Popery and Arbitrary Government.*

1678   Marvell elected younger warden of Trinity House, London. Dies August 18.

1681   *Miscellaneous Poems* published by "Mary Marvell."

Notes on the Editor and Contributors

GEORGE DEF. LORD, the editor of this volume, is Professor of English at Yale. His books include *Homeric Renaissance: The "Odyssey" of George Chapman*; the first volume of the seven-volume edition of *Poems on Affairs of State: Augustan Satirical Verse, 1660–1714*, of which he is general editor; and *Andrew Marvell: Complete Poetry*.

JOHN S. COOLIDGE, a member of the Department of Comparative Literature at the University of California, Berkeley, has written extensively on seventeenth-century English poets and the classics.

The late T. S. ELIOT's essay on Marvell is one of his many reassessments of poets ancient and modern which have had an enormous influence on twentieth-century poetic practice and criticism.

GEOFFREY HARTMAN, Professor of English at Yale, has done extensive work in the field of comparative literature as well. His books include *André Malraux* (1960); a collection (in this series) of essays on Hopkins; *The Unmediated Vision: An Interpretation of Wordsworth, Hopkins, Rilke, and Valéry* (1954); and *Wordsworth's Poetry, 1787–1814*.

JOHN HOLLANDER, the well-known poet, is Professor of English at Hunter College. He is the author of *A Crackling of Thorns* (1958), *Movie-going and Other Poems* (1962), and *Visions from the Ramble* (1965).

EARL MINER, Professor of English at UCLA, is an editor of the monumental California *Dryden*, the author of a book on Dryden and of several studies on Japanese poetry.

M. J. K. O'LOUGHLIN teaches English at Yale and is preparing a book on the theme of civic and retired leisure from Homer to Pope.

JOSEPH H. SUMMERS is Professor of English at Michigan State University. He has written mainly on seventeenth-century English poets and is the author of the definitive book on *George Herbert* (1954).

HAROLD E. TOLIVER teaches English at UCLA and is the author of *Marvell's Ironic Vision* (1965).

JOHN M. WALLACE, Professor of English at the University of Chicago, is the author of a book on Marvell's political poems entitled *Destiny his Choice*.

177

Selected Bibliography

Articles or chapters of books reprinted in this collection or cited in the introduction are not listed here.

Editions

The Poems and Letters of Andrew Marvell, ed. H. M. Margoliouth. Oxford: Clarendon Press, 1927; 2nd ed., 1952.

The Complete Works of Andrew Marvell, ed. Rev. Alexander B. Grosart. London: Robson & Sons, 1872–1875. The only available collection of Marvell's prose pamphlets.

The Poems of Andrew Marvell, ed. Hugh MacDonald. Cambridge, Mass.: Harvard University Press, 1952. A compact edition with excellent introduction and notes. Does not include satires of the reign of Charles II.

Andrew Marvell: Complete Poetry, ed. George deF. Lord. New York: Random House, Inc. and Modern Library, 1968. Based on the authoritative manuscript recently acquired by the Bodleian Library, with introduction and notes.

Selected Poetry, ed. Frank Kermode. New York: New American Library, 1967. A generous selection with good notes.

Selected Poems, with an introduction by Joseph H. Summers. New York: Dell, 1966. A fine selection with an excellent introduction.

Selected Poetry and Prose, ed. Dennis Davison. London: Harrap, 1952. Useful introduction and notes.

Poems on Affairs of State: Augustan Satirical Verse, 1660–1714. Vol. I: 1660–1678, ed. George deF. Lord. New Haven: Yale University Press, 1963. Contains satirical verse of the Restoration period by Marvell and his contemporaries. Extensively annotated.

Studies

M. C. Bradbrook and M. G. Lloyd Thomas, *Andrew Marvell.* Cambridge: Cambridge University Press, 1940; 2nd ed., 1961.

Pierre Legouis, *Andrew Marvell: Poet, Puritan, Patriot.* Oxford: Clarendon Press, 1965. An indispensable account of Marvell's career.

J. B. Leishman, *The Art of Marvell's Poetry.* London: Hutchinson & Co., Ltd., 1966.

John Press, *Andrew Marvell.* London and New York: Longmans, Green & Company, Ltd., 1958.

Ruth C. Wallerstein, *Studies in Seventeenth-Century Poetic.* Madison, Wis.: University of Wisconsin Press, 1950.

Articles

D. C. Allen, *Image and Meaning: Metaphoric Traditions in Renaissance Poetry.* Baltimore: Johns Hopkins University Press, 1960. Pp. 93–153.

————, "Marvell's 'Nymph,' " *ELH,* XXIII (1956), 93–111.

Harry Berger, Jr., "Marvell's 'Upon Appleton House': An Interpretation," *Southern Review* (Australia), I (1965), 7–32.

F. W. Bradbrook, "The Poetry of Andrew Marvell," *From Donne to Marvell,* ed. Boris Ford. London: Penguin Books, Ltd., 1956. Pp. 193–204.

John S. Coolidge, "Martin Marprelate, Marvell, and *Decorum Personae* as a Satirical Theme," *PMLA,* LXXXIV (1959), 526–32.

David V. Erdman and Ephim G. Fogel, eds., *Evidence for Authorship: Essays on Problems of Attribution.* Ithaca: Cornell University Press, 1966. Contains discussions of the Marvell canon.

Christopher Hill, *Puritanism and Revolution.* London: Martin Secker & Warburg, Ltd., 1958. Pp. 337–366. Discusses Marvell's political ideas.

Frank Kermode, "The Argument of Marvell's 'Garden,' " *Essays in Criticism,* II (1952), 225–41. Reprinted in *Seventeenth-Century English Poetry,* ed. W. R. Keast. New York: Oxford University Press, 1962.

Pierre Legouis, "Marvell and the New Critics," *Review of English Studies,* VIII (1957), 382–89.

Joseph A. Mazzeo, "Cromwell as Machiavellian Prince in Marvell's 'An Horatian Ode,' " *Journal of the History of Ideas,* XXI (1960), 1–17.

Renato Poggioli, "The Pastoral of the Self," *Daedalus,* LXXXVIII (1959), 686–99.

Maren-Sophie Røstvig, *The Happy Man: Studies in the Metamorphoses of a Classical Ideal,* 2 vols. Oxford: Basil Blackwell & Mott, Ltd., 1954–1958. I, 152–191. A major contribution to the understanding of Marvell's poetry on rural themes.

TWENTIETH CENTURY VIEWS

British Authors